GOD IS NOT
A CHRISTIAN,
NOR A JEW,
MUSLIM, HINDU . . .

OTHER WORKS BY BISHOP CARLTON PEARSON

The Gospel of Inclusion:
Reaching Beyond Religious Fundamentalism
to the True Love of God and Self

GOD IS NOT A CHRISTIAN, NOR A JEW, MUSLIM, HINDU...

God Dwells with Us,
in Us, Around Us, as Us

BISHOP
CARLTON PEARSON

ATRIA BOOKS

New York   London   Toronto   Sydney

ATRIA BOOKS

A Division of Simon & Schuster, Inc.
1230 Avenue of the Americas
New York, NY 10020

Copyright © 2010 by Bishop Carlton Pearson

First Atria Books hardcover edition March 2010

ATRIA BOOKS and colophon are trademarks of Simon & Schuster, Inc.

Scripture quotations marked NIV are taken from *The Holy Bible, New International Version.*® Copyright © 1973, 1978, 1984 by International Bible Society. Used by permission of Zondervan Publishing House. All rights reserved.

Scripture quotations marked KJV are taken from *The Holy Bible, King James Version, Reference Bible.* Copyright © 1994 by The Zondervan Corporation. Used by permission. All rights reserved.

For information about special discounts for bulk purchases, please contact Simon & Schuster Special Sales at 1-866-506-1949 or business@simonandschuster.com.

The Simon & Schuster Speakers Bureau can bring authors to your live event. For more information or to book an event, contact the Simon & Schuster Speakers Bureau at 1-866-248-3049 or visit our website at www.simonspeakers.com.

Manufactured in the United States of America.

10   9   8   7   6   5   4   3   2   1

Library of Congress Cataloging-in-Publication Data

Pearson, Carlton.
God is not a Christian, nor a Jew, Muslim, Hindu : God dwells with us, in us, around us, as us / by Carlton D. Pearson.
    p.   cm.
    1. God.   2. Christianity and other religions.   3. Religions—Relations.   I. Title.
BL473.P43 2009
231—dc22   2008045780
ISBN: 978-1-4165-8443-8
ISBN: 978-1-4165-8504-6 (ebook)

CONTENTS

PREFACE

... No matter what God's power may be, the first aspect of God is never that of the absolute Master, the Almighty. It is that of the God who puts himself on our human level and limits himself.

—Jacques Ellul, *Anarchy and Christianity*

It was the spring of 1983, and I was about fifteen days into a thirty-day fast honoring my thirtieth birthday: March 19. I had dozed off to sleep while lying across my bed in what was supposed to have been a time of meditation. It was a sunny afternoon sometime between two and three o'clock, when I was awakened by what I thought was someone whispering to me, *Pssst, Carley Moses,* the nickname only my grandmother used to call me. I looked in the direction of the voice, and I saw an image of her over in the corner of the room, standing behind the soft blue recliner I liked to sit in while watching television. My mother is her only child, and we affectionately called her "Big Mama." She was a slightly built, fair-complected woman with beautiful mostly black wavy hair. She had passed on nearly twenty years earlier in January 1964, when I was just ten years old. She was only fifty-three, two years younger than I am at the writing of this book. We were close; in fact, I was told I was her favorite of the six grands. Not sure why. During the last two years of her life, I spent every weekend I could with her. We spent literally hours just talking, driving in her big blue Cadillac with electric windows that I loved to play with. I actually got to sleep in bed with her until she was in too much pain for my sometimes thrashing and active sleeping habits.

At first, I thought I was just hallucinating, since I hadn't eaten in nearly three weeks, and strange things were already happening to my body. Having fasted as many as twenty-one days before, I knew how the body and mind could play some fairly strange games when they perceived that you were trying to starve them.

Fasting was common in our family and was an esteemed practice in our particular Pentecostal discipline. I was fasting for special faith, spiritual strength, wisdom, and a more powerful anointing with which to carry out my ministry and fulfill my life's destiny. Jesus had started His ministry at thirty, and the Apostle Paul had encountered Christ in Consciousness at around that same age, as did my mentor, Oral Roberts.

I had founded my church, Higher Dimensions Evangelistic Center, a year and a half earlier in a small storefront building in Jenks, Oklahoma, a sparsely populated suburb just south of Tulsa and only about a ten-minute drive from Oral Roberts University, my alma mater.

What was so strange about this experience, daydream, vision, or whatever you want to call it was that when I located the sound as coming from my beloved grandmother, she wasn't looking at me, but at the foot of the bed. She had this warm and excited smile on her face. She seemed thrilled about what she was seeing. I followed her eyes, and as I did, there appeared at the foot of my bed several other people who had also passed on to what I assumed was heaven, paradise, or somewhere in some wonderful eternal abode.

Needless to say, I was captivated by a scene that seemed to fill the entire room with warm, effervescent light and a peaceful ambiance I hadn't experienced before. This was an unusual encounter, but not an unbelievable one. After all, I'd been taught about the resurrection all my life, and my family—particularly the women—were given to dreams, visions, and premonitions.

We'd been taught about a great cloud of witnesses who had gone on before us and were in the grandstands of eternity, cheering us on—as recorded in the New Testament writings of an unknown author (Hebrews 21:1).

To us, both death and life were states of illusionary limitation. Even God had somehow found a significant place for death, and, according to our Christian doctrine, used it to purchase our redemption and salvation.

I had accepted the presumption that God used life's number one limitation, which was death and dying, to accomplish a divine purpose. In other words, the Christian dynamic articulated itself through the common limitation of life, which was its opposite: death.

Christianity is the only religion that is built around the death of God and His subsequent resurrection as its primary premise for the redemption of humankind.

Apparently, God needed to die in order to conquer death. God, in effect, had to succumb to man's number one fear and flaw in order to be triumphant and omnipotent. It has always been a conundrum to me that death should play such a prominent and seemingly important role in life or our concept of it, and that death and dying somehow dominated our theology and its proceeding doctrines and dogmas.

This book is not necessarily about believing in God, just a discussion of *what* you believe about God and why you believe it.

I won't name all the people who were assembled at the foot of my bed, as the names would be insignificant to most readers. I will simply say that they were all people and ministers who had impacted my life in deep, abiding, spiritual, and sentimental ways. They were spiritual heroes and heroines whom I'd observed and admired when they were alive and whom I wanted to in some way emulate. I felt they had come to urge and encourage me to move forward with my thirty-day fast and with pursuing my life's calling and destiny, just as they had done when they were alive.

I had known these people well enough and long enough to see their human limitations, and yet I deemed them to be some of the most godly people I knew. They were all known to be persons of great faith and were associated with healing, miracles, and what is known in Pentecostal circles as special ministries of deliverance.

One person that some of you may recognize was Kathryn Kuhlman, a renowned televangelist with a worldwide ministry. Ms. Kuhlman had transitioned some seven years earlier in 1976, only four months after my first and only appearance on her program, which happened during her last series of tapings of her popular Sunday morning show. She was diagnosed with an enlarged and congested heart, and passed away in the same hospital where the son I never thought I'd have would be born in 1994.

Kathryn was the most spiritually gifted and phenomenal person I'd ever encountered. She was known for great healings in her "Miracle services," as they were called. I'd attended several of them from as far back as 1965, when my parents took us to see her in the great Shrine Auditorium in Los Angeles, California. The Shrine was always packed, with all 6,700 seats filled. We had seen incredible manifestations of what we called the supernatural presence and power of God for miracles.

Because of my upbringing, I've always believed in God and in many ways felt I've known God, but mostly through those who claimed to represent Him, or "It." All of whom were human and imperfect. Even those with great faith died of sicknesses that their great faith didn't or couldn't heal. They were all Christians with profound faith in God, but they were also obviously limited as such. They all were "cracked vessels" but used nonetheless by God. I fought hard to not allow their imperfections to in any way indict God or impede my concepts of "Him."

And yet the entire Christian image of God does exactly that. It makes God more like us fickle and ego-driven humans than the pure and holy Spirit that the Ultimate Reality and Intelligence we call God is more likely to be.

When I say God is not a Christian, I am saying that God is not limited as Christians have made Him (It) to be. I need to say right from the outset that I no longer view God as a god or *the* God, but just God. Not a He or She, but more of an "It"—an infinite or Ultimate Creative Intelligence, Reality, or Existence. I use capital letters to emphasize a superiority I tend to presume upon God. Guess it's a habit with which I'm comfortable.

Even Jesus, presumed by most Christians to be God in the flesh, is an expression of divinity infleshed in human limitations, but no more or less than any other human created, according to the Bible, in God's image and likeness.

The question remains, are we made in God's image and likeness, or is God made in ours? The answer is probably both. We are created in God's image and likeness, but we have also created a god in our image and likeness, even our religion, whether Christian, Jewish, Islamic, or some other faith tradition or discipline.

I considered all the persons I saw at the foot of my bed as men and women of God. I also assumed subconsciously the God of those men and women to be a Christian; indeed, a Pentecostal, evangelical, fundamentalist Jewish Christian. This was not a contrived perception; it was an assumed one. It came naturally and automatically with my conceptual "Christian faith."

I am drawn to the quote used at the beginning of this chapter—"the God who puts himself on our human level and limits himself"—in a way I never would have admitted only a few short years ago, because it hews close to the heart of what I have come to believe about God. I say "come to believe" because contrary to what the more totalitarian aspects of modern faith would have you believe (and I will use words like *totalitarian* to describe the controlling corners of the religious world not because they are provocative but because I believe them to be true), faith does and should evolve with time and understanding. I used to view faith as a supernatural grace, and I suppose in some ways I still do, but I also view faith as an admission of limited knowledge and perhaps a sophisticated form of doubt. Religious faith is belief in a God limited by and limited *to* whatever influence one has or is accustomed to. That in itself is a limitation. Faith is basically the belief in a finite description or impression, often illusory, of an infinite reality, presumably "God." My faith has evolved to the point where I can ask myself a profound and intimidating question that I never would have considered asking a few years ago: *Does the God I've heard about and preached all my life exist?*

Religion is a faith journey into the mystery of God and things considered both divine and worldly or experienced in this world. Institutional or organized religion is a system of doctrines, dogmas, and human-constructed disciplines that has become idolatrous and has begun to die and perhaps lie. Theism is not God, just a belief about God. God is not a religion. Religion is a human construct and involves a definition of God that assumes that God is a being or a person that can be *known,* rather than simply or even profoundly experienced. Most have assumed this God to be a "Supreme Being": supernatural in power, dwelling outside the world, and occasionally invading it to answer prayers or to effectuate Divine will. I was raised to believe in that God and believe that about God.

I have believed and preached this definition of God most of my life and have done so under what I would consider *His* blessing. However, this image of God has been mortally wounded by the evolving consciousness and experiences of millions of people of all religions who seem to have awakened to a broader awareness of self, soul, and inner divinity. There is a new perception of the concept of God emerging as a global shift in religious sensibilities. This shift is causing many to rethink God and Divinity. Religion is being shoved to the backseat, and "New Thought" is emerging on the largest scale in recent history. People are coming to the realization that, as Gary R. Renard wrote in *The Disappearance of the Universe,* "If you always do what you've always done, then you will always get what you've always gotten. It's time to get off the unmerry-go-round."

Whether or not God exists is as much a personal choice as anything else. After all, billions of people believe in God in some form, and all have their own separate and highly personal beliefs concerning divinity and the Deity from which the Divinity emanates. Belief in the Divine manifests in many guises. There are those who believe in a personal Deity who created the universe in six days, intervenes in daily life and answers prayers, and is a constant presence for good or ill in their days. There are those who believe in a "clockspring" God who created the basic mechanical underpinning of the cosmos and then turned it loose to run according to natural laws.

Some people believe in a divine energy and consciousness that pervades reality but does not take the form of an actual godlike being—God not as person but as presence or universal mind. Still others believe that God resides within us as part of our own divine nature. And, of course, there are many who reverence the sacred in nature without believing in anything supernatural or transcendent, along with those many often-angry atheists who seem to think that anyone who believes in any of these forms of God must be a simpleton.

These are all valid ways of coming to terms with the nature and mystery of existence; the great questions that humans have grappled with for millennia. Faith evolves as we do; it is not static. Mother Teresa, one of the great religious figures of our age, confessed in writings published after her death that she went through years of her own "dark night of the soul" during which she could not feel God's presence and had doubts about His existence. As terrifying as that must have been for her, she continued to labor on God's behalf.

Believing in God or having faith seems to be in our DNA. It is as much a part of human consciousness and experience as thinking, breathing, eating, and drinking. Interestingly, your thoughts, as well as what you eat and drink, can be and often is influenced by what you believe about God and about yourself. That's just how much God, belief, and culture seem inseparable and intrinsically consequential.

I believe God is real and that we are in the process of defining our "God experience" in a new way that will replace the dying theistic definition and tradition of the past.

Part of my God experience and expression encompasses a belief in life after this one. I guess this is because a belief in an eternal reality called "God" suggests and in many ways emphasizes such a belief. After all, God is supposed to be eternity past, present, and future, right? Then we, supposedly made in such an image, would have to have an eternal past, present, and future. The people I referred to earlier were conjured up and informed by my particular brand of belief or faith in God. Even though mine has been a Christian faith, many other faith traditions and disciplines believe in life after and perhaps before this one as well. Tomorrow always seems illusory, but we tend to believe in it anyway, because we somehow remember being here yesterday.

ON THE EDGE OF FOREVER

> We do not find our own center, it finds us. Our own mind will not be able to figure it out.
>
> —Richard Rohr, *Everything Belongs:*
> *The Gift of Contemplative Prayer*

On our fifteenth wedding anniversary, my wife, Gina, gave me a card that said, "We will become what we are willing to evolve to." Finding our center both as individuals, couples, or as a collective is an evolving process. Personal evolution is an act of your will and awareness.

Most people live, think, and worship on the edges of spirituality. They view their religious presuppositions as spirituality, but what they are really doing is avoiding and/or substituting the more sublime realities of self and soul realization. They live on the edge of ultimate reality, out of touch with their whole selves and accustomed to the façade of religion, comfortable in a spiritual compromise that sometimes provides them with wealth, status, and a sense of social connectedness in exchange for truth. Sometimes they are rewarded with poverty and lack, yet they remain committed to an ideology that doesn't necessarily make sense but feels comfortable to them. They know only what they know and have learned to make the irrelevant relevant nonetheless. They no longer realize religion's blatant superficiality. I lived there for decades, but when I began to feel empty and hollow, I sought change and found it.

CENTER YOURSELF

We all came from the center and will all return there. The edge is an unstable place, full of artificial assumptions, all of them artifacts of a contrived religious past that no longer fits or feels relevant. Sadly, many refuse to acknowledge this and insist on living in denial. They seem afraid of the spiritual center. In fact, most people are completely unaware of that place, except in the deepest recesses of their spiritual memory. Frightened by concepts of *pantheism* (God in all things) and *panpsychism* (universal mind), they condemn enlightenment practices ranging from yoga to Reiki therapy as either dangerous and/or sinful. They (and we) tend to look for

God somewhere in the sky or in a remote place in the ether, unattainable and inaccessible except through some type of man-made religious construct that is usually overbearing, cumbersome, obnoxious, and obligatory.

In his book *Everything Belongs,* Richard Rohr calls us a "circumference people with little access to the center." I say little awareness *of* the center, rather than access *to* it. We all have access to it; we've just forgotten the path. Rohr says that we "live on the edges or boundaries of our own lives, confusing edges with essence; too quickly claiming the superficial as substance."

Christianity, like most other institutional religions, tends to do as Rohr suggests: claim the superficial as substance. Christianity has gotten so far from the accurate realities of the Christ Principle that even Jesus would probably distance Himself from it. Jesus was a mystic operating in the Christ Presence and Principle, who was in touch with His divine nature and taught us to be in touch with our spiritual center, our pre-incarnate self. This is Christ Consciousness, something much more potent, plausible, and viable than the religion bearing the name. The same is true of all religions.

You may ask, "How do we get there from here? How do we set aside thousands of years of religious conditioning and false, comforting self-delusion to come into awareness of this reality?" Religion won't get us there; it can only teach us things like praying, fasting, meditating, reading sacred Scripture, and so forth. Helpful disciplines all, but not for true transcendent discovery—or perhaps I should say *recovery.* The truth of who we are does not lie in or live in what we are taught or what we learn as much as in what we remember. We already know these things; we've simply forgotten them.

We all originated in the womb of the universe—the mind and movements of God or of some Divine Reality. This womb is the center of our existence even if we fail to recognize this reality. We came from the place that I like to call the "opulent ovum," and we will all return to it. Why we go and return is not yet completely known, but the fact or supposition that we do adds great spiritual substance and stability to our life's journey.

THE HUNGER FOR ONENESS

Our enduring and endearing relationship with the God idea is probably the result of our desire for oneness with the self or soul. Because we miss ourselves and are, in fact, lonesome for reconnection with our inner priests and peace, we keep seeking something or someone outside ourselves to satisfy our longings—and in some ways to blunt the loathing of the self. These appetites are sometimes confusing but seem necessary.

In their book *Why God Won't Go Away: Brain Science and the Biology of Belief,* authors Andrew Newberg, Eugene D'Aquili, and Vince Rause put forth the hypothesis that "spiritual experience at its root is intimately interwoven with human biology. That biology, in some way, compels the spiritual urge." I would say that the urgency—and to many, the emergency—of religious or spiritual inclination is innate to human biology and psychology in ways we've never fully understood. Yet we have added an admixture of the mythical to the mystical realities of the self and have thus diluted our spirituality—even contaminating it to the point where it must remain violently opposed to the rational side of our humanity that is equally vital for our existence as conscious beings. Yet we remain not only spirits but Spirit at our essence.

Christian, Jewish, and Islamic theologies teach that we were all created in the image and likeness of God. If this is even close to the truth, then to believe in God is to believe in yourself—in your own soul. This may be as close to God as we ever get in this realm of human consciousness. Interrogating and excavating my own soul has helped me recover a lost, languishing part of myself. I don't feel this is so much a discovery as a *recovery.* It's as if I am remembering some birthright that I forgot during my years spent neck-deep in fundamentalist Pentecostal dogma. It's a kind of spiritual, mystical déjà vu. I have begun to remember the essential nature that was submerged deeply beneath the waters of self-imposed ignorance. Others seem to be awakening to this same awareness. I might add here that my deep Pentecostal roots in transcendent consciousness pointed me in the direction I am now headed and helped inform my renewed theology and evolving mystical and expanded aware-nesses.

THE CHOSEN ONE

I used to think I *had* to believe in God. In my faith tradition, this was never a question. God simply was accepted, woven into the warp and woof of all things, all times, and all states of mind— custodian of all of which we were merely tenants. To treat belief in the "God of my fathers" as a choice would have been like treating breathing as a choice—and would have gotten me all but kicked out of my parents' house to boot. But I now get to think and to choose which God I want to believe in. There is a smorgasbord of them out there. I also get to believe in a God I don't know and re-main as fascinated and curious as ever about the nature of divinity and myself. The fascination and curiosity doesn't ever have to end. I can always know, learn, experience, or simply remember more about God.

I was once interviewed for an article in *Psychology Today* titled "Atheists in the Pulpit." I wasn't aware that would be the name of the article when I consented to the interview, but I found it curious that I was the only interviewee who still not only had faith but faith in God. I was quoted as saying that I didn't necessarily believe in *a* God or *the* God, but that I simply believed in God, whoever and whatever God is. There's a fine delineation there. I believe in God not just because I was raised to do so or by the formula my parents and the preceding generations worshipped, but because I enjoy believing in a God I can't define. I find this to be the most satisfactory view of God, as a force and/or source that is beyond human understanding. In fact, I see clearly now that all of the world's religions are exercises in the same impulse: to give form and substance to something that is utterly above and outside our brains' ability to comprehend.

For the first time in my life, I don't feel an obligation to literally know God. In a sense, I'm getting in touch with the God I perceive to be with me, for me, in me, and perhaps as me. Mind you, I've always encouraged people to know God for themselves personally. I also felt for many years that the only way you could know God was through Jesus Christ as your professed Lord and Savior. As difficult as it is for me to confess it, I no longer believe such religious nonsense, though I love and believe in God and feel as close as ever to Christ as a person and a principle. I also love Jesus as much as I ever have and consider myself an honest and earnest follower of him, at least in principle. However, I am, for the first time in my life, willing to admit that the most certain thing I can say about God is that I don't know much about Him, Her, or It, at all. (Note: I use the gender reference *Him* when talking about God out of habit and because it's widely recognized, but I don't believe that God can be bound up in gender terms. God is beyond such concepts.)

Ignorance can be a wonderful state if it is paired with humility. I'm starting to see a certain energy and openness in it that is both liberating and empowering.

THE OBSOLESCENCE OF THE CHURCH

For someone who was raised in a fourth-generation Pentecostal family, going to church was my life. It was all but impossible to separate the church from God. In a way, church *was* our God, or at least our human identification with God. Not only was the church a kind of idol, but all things associated with church, including and especially the pastor, were idolized as well. This idolization has given rise to the near deification, in certain fundamentalist circles, of people like Billy Graham and Oral Roberts and granted massive cultural and political influence to people like Pat Robertson, the late Jerry Falwell, and organizations like Trinity Broadcasting Network and Focus on the Family. Even the Dalai Lama, Muhammad, the Buddha, and those who seem less obtuse also wield huge and often larger-than-life influence as spiritual leaders in our world and on the various cultures.

We are taught that we are created in the image and likeness of God. We are also taught in Scripture that God seeks to be worshipped. If this is true, then would it not seem likely that all of us would desire to be worshipped as well, even if we never speak of it directly? I think we inadvertently display such desires regularly. Why else would we as preachers stand before swaying, writhing, praying gatherings of thousands and preach "God's Word" as if we know what the Divine really has to say, as though God's intent can be worn like an off-the-rack suit by each individual who claims to be His minister? Why else would we create a culture of celebrity in which people who sometimes can barely string three words together become idolized by millions, or lionize our political leaders and celebrities just before we start savaging them like lions let loose on Roman-era Christians? Clearly, we subconsciously perceive the God within and mistake our need for worship to be His need for worship.

In a very real way, God is the mirror of the culture that lends Him a face and a name and so is usually given a male gender and more than a bit of chauvinism. Science-fiction author Robert Heinlein once wrote, "Men [*humans*] rarely [if ever] manage to dream up a god superior to themselves. Most gods have the manners and morals of a spoiled child." In many ancient cultures, God was plural (the pantheon included numerous gods, one for each force in nature) and regularly in a bad mood; hence the statement

"The gods are angry." I agree with the statement, but only since we contain God within us, the anger stems from mankind—from our religion-fueled intolerance and hatred for those whose beliefs do not exactly reflect our own. We have met the angry gods, and they are us. We adopted this habitual, ritual anger from the misperception that God is angry, profoundly temperamental, and can be easily provoked, while at the same time preaching the Scripture that says God is "slow to anger, abounding in love" (Psalm 103:8) and that "His mercy endures forever" (Psalm 136). Belief in and worship of this image of God has produced the deep-seated anger and paranoia that persist within the cult(ure)s of most global religious communities and animosities.

Now, there is a charged word for you: *Cult.* My use of it in the context of the world's monotheistic faiths has fired tempers and sparked furious outcries, because we all know what the word implies. Cult members are considered to be brainwashed, unthinking adherents to blatantly manipulative codes of belief and conduct which to those outside the palace walls appear not only insane but patently for the benefit and authority of those handing down the holy edicts. Think David Koresh and the Branch Davidians, and you get the picture.

My family knew at least two people who belonged to the Reverend Jim Jones's People's Temple and died in the 1978 Jonestown massacre. They, along with hundreds of other misguided and faith-filled followers, drank the cocktail laced with toxic and lethal cyanide. They first believed the lie then imbibed it literally. Millions superficially continue to operate in the same clonish, clownish error to their own detriment.

Now, I ask you, how is that picture any different from mainstream Christianity, Islam, Judaism, or the other great faiths? Would not their doctrines look utterly alien and delusional to someone not steeped in a lifetime of their traditions? A bitingly satirical and borderline-offensive poster I once saw read:

> Christianity: The belief that a cosmic Jewish zombie who was his own father can make you live forever if you symbolically eat his flesh and telepathically tell him you accept him as your master, so he can remove an evil force from your soul that is present in humanity because a rib-woman was convinced by a talking snake to eat from a magical tree . . . yeah, makes perfect sense.

When you look at it from that perspective, doesn't much of Christian doctrine break down to the ridiculous, just a little? Come to think of it, all religious doctrine tends to go down the same path toward the absurd. I'm not talking about the teachings of Christ, or necessarily those of other great mystical teachers; those remain sublime and mighty and astonishing in their humane and transcendent wisdom. But it seems to be that the layers of ritual, dogma, politically motivated preaching, and control have infected the world's faith cultures and have in fact turned them into cults and covens of religious incest. In a colossal irony, I submit that Christianity and the other world faiths, which in theory were created in order to serve as conduits between the human and the Divine, have devolved to the point where they now serve only as *barriers between humanity and the divine reality of God within us.* Consequently, religion as we practice it today is fast becoming irrelevant and obsolete. As a result, religion as we know it today could dissipate and perhaps disappear altogether over the next hundred years or so. Faith in God or the transcendent will never go away, but the varying brands of religion are becoming increasingly irrelevant in these modern, mystical, spiritual, and more scientific times.

THE NEW THEOLOGY

Most of my past friends of the faith would protest that what I'm saying is not an accurate interpretation of Scripture, faith, or religion—at least not the Christian faith. I say to them that this is what makes my position that much more authentic, at least for me. For the first time in over a half century of living, my experience of God is not jaded, hindered, or hampered by Scriptures, though I know and love the Scriptures and teach and live by many of them in principle. They are valuable sources of wisdom and have inspired and enhanced my faith. But I no longer believe that they are inerrant sources of truth, as I once did. Truth resides within each of us. I've come to believe that authentic truth is not so much learned or taught as remembered in the deepest recesses of the soul (self), the ultimate essence of the Spirit of which we all partake.

Millions of people believe in the value and virtue of Scripture but don't necessarily define God by them or confine God *to* them. I am one of those persons. This transition was at first painful and halting for me but over time has become fun and gratifying. Our world would be different if millions of us entertained new thinking and broader perspectives—if we treated holy writ as a source of inspiration and learning to fuel our own growth and self-discovery, rather than as an owner's manual for how everyone else should live their lives; an attitude that, sadly, is all too common and, I might add, insultingly narrow-minded.

For years, I didn't know that such personal and spiritual freedom was possible. My emotions are a bit scrambled when I say that I believe in a God I don't have to know or seek to know. I think it's easier to be God than to know Him. Being comes naturally; knowing involves effort, work, and self-manipulation. Some would say they know God by faith. I think it takes more faith to *be* than to know God.

This is a wonderfully liberating but stunningly different and disconcerting mind-set for people who were raised as I was, in an intensely Christian tradition built around one principle: one must accept Jesus Christ as one's personal Lord and Savior or spend eternity in God's personally customized torture chamber. New Thought is for me a consciousness wonderfully liberated and liberating from that kind of bone-deep fear, a consciousness I am eager to see millions enjoy.

I don't view Jesus as saving us from God but perhaps *for* God and from ourselves, not so much by His death but by His life and the light of His expanded consciousness and transcendent teachings.

I am, for the first time in my life, enjoying *knowing*/being the God (and good) that I am. It is wonderfully renewing to feel and perceive the creative and intuitive gifts of God within myself and others. It's fun being God. Does that sound egotistical? Perhaps you would feel more comfortable if I just said that it's fun just being. After all, that's probably the closest to Divinity any of us will ever get absent a hard-earned enlightenment experience of the order described by veteran mystics, meditators, and monks. Being is the "is-ness" of the other and "ether" reality that we call God. It is where our pure consciousness resides, the part of us that lies beyond the reach of that incredible neocortex that houses our titanic powers of reason and is so vital to our survival. Being is timeless and without effort or thought. It just *is*. That is why we are called human *beings*, not human *doings*. We are walking dualities, simultaneously very earthly creatures of thought, emotion, and action and beings of pure consciousness. However, in our childlike ignorance, we call and mistake God for something outside of ourselves. Each one of us partakes of a divine whole and inner code of consciousness that belies and defies man-made religious constructs. If this sounds like pantheism and panpsychism, it well should, and I'll address it further later on.

I have preached about the old God, studied Him, read everything I could about Him, and sought to know Him all my life. In doing so, I realized that I knew and worshipped the wrong guy or god. What I was taught was the so-called true and living God was something far less than that; He was a sort of Big Daddy in the sky, a vastly less awesome principle than a pure and sublime consciousness residing within all living entities, even things that seem inanimate. The old God was not at all what I was experiencing personally, even though I was preaching him publicly. My experience and my theology were in conflict. My heart and my head were in a tremendous battle for both dominance and clarity. My heart won, as you have discovered if you read my previous book, *The Gospel of Inclusion.*

The image of God that has been handed down to us over the centuries and millennia, with which humanity as a whole has grappled awkwardly since we first attempted to define such a concept, is inaccurate. It is indeed, for the most part, a superstitious deception. We are taught that God is angry, hostile, judgmental, and vain. The rules, rites, regulations, and rituals necessary to appease this monster continue to increase as we, in a kind of panic, try to dodge His wrath, which we have been taught will punish us for violating any of the rules. And if God doesn't redeem us, then His devil gets a crack at our souls, which is where the weeping, wailing, and gnashing of teeth comes into play.

Again, for the first time in my life, I no longer, as a preacher, feel that I must find and protect millions of people from some villainous being we have all perceived to have been an angry, wrathful God terrorizing humanity from its beginning and who will intensify such terror as we get closer to the end.

I am completely resistant to the lies and power plays, the fear and abuse, the distortions and justifications in the name of these false idols. I am resistant at heart and soul and resistant in my own God Consciousness. Enough! It is time more of us woke up and began to think for ourselves without the filtering or rituals of religions blocking us from our own individual paths to enlightenment and the discovery of God within us. God is not a Christian. Nor is She a Jew, Muslim, Hindu, Jain, Sikh, Mormon, or any other label that we wish to plaster on our perception of the transcendent. God is. Divinity (God) dwells within us and without us at the same time, and defies any rules imposed from other sources. God is you and yours. At the risk of sounding blatantly presumptuous, this book is the first step toward sharing and spreading this "new Gospel" to the world.

Now that I've slaughtered my share of sacred cows, shall we begin our journey together? I am honored to have you by my side, even if not on it.

Carlton D. Pearson
October 2009

GOD IS NOT
A CHRISTIAN,
NOR A JEW,
MUSLIM, HINDU . . .

BUSTING GRANDMA AND GRANDPA OUT OF HELL

By the time my dad, the eldest of seven children, got to his mother's bedside in the hospital emergency room, she had expired. The doctors had done their best, repeatedly resuscitating her, while my dad stood outside, anxiously awaiting his chance to see her and praying that she would survive. He could hear her screams—sometimes loud, sometimes muffled—as she came in and out of consciousness; a convincing argument for Do Not Resuscitate directives if ever there was one.

When my grandmother finally passed, the room became silent and still. The medical team slowly filed out, and a nurse escorted my dad behind the curtain, where he saw his mother lying on the gurney, arms hanging off the sides, breast still exposed, mouth gaping, her eyes in a glazed, lifeless stare. With tubes, gauze, used needles, and other medical paraphernalia still lying around, Dad moved slowly to his mother's body and quickly covered her breast, closed her mouth, and pushed her eyes shut. He didn't want his sisters to see their mother this way. It was disrespectful and stunning to the memory of the deceased, who was still his mother.

By the time he relayed this story to me, my father had carried this horrifying scene around in his head and heart for nearly thirty years. He was almost eighty years old when we talked about it, but it became clear to me that the worst of it was not the undignified posture the hospital personnel had left my grandmother in upon her death. It was that all of this time, he had assumed his mother was in hell. As she herself had taught him, that was where people like her, who had walked away from God or who had sinned without being washed clean by the blood of Jesus, would spend eternity, weeping, wailing, and gnashing their teeth. The idea that the woman who had birthed him, raised him, nursed him at her breast, and given him and his siblings life was writhing in agony in eternal hellfire haunted my father for decades.

I suspect this was the beginning of it all for me, or at least the grain of sand around which the pearl of my restless and unspeakable thought would begin to form years later, launching me on a journey that has cost me so much but given me more.

GRANDMA

Grand Mama Pearson was what we called my father's mother. She was, at one time, a fine and upstanding missionary (female preacher) in the local Church of God in Christ (COGIC, for short). Four generations of our family had grown up in this church. Her husband, my grandfather Elder Elector Pearson, had founded, built, and pastored the second physical COGIC church in San Diego, the St. Luke Church of God in Christ. My dad and his brothers had built the pews in the Boys Club across the street from where the church building still stands to this day, though it has a different name. I walked past it hundreds of times en route to the service station that my father and maternal grandfather owned and operated, where I worked each afternoon when I was in junior high school.

The Pearson name was known and respected in our religious community, and it was a tight-knit community indeed. My dad's uncle and aunt had founded and built the third COGIC church in the San Diego area just south of town, about five miles north of the

Mexican border. They began by conducting Sunday school classes in a converted chicken coop on their small pig ranch. They had migrated west from Oklahoma in a covered wagon before the Depression, during which time Dad's father (Grand Daddy) sold fertilizer. In fact, there are those who would say that selling manure might be the perfect training for a future preacher.

Now Grand Mama was dead, and Daddy assumed her to be in hell. Several years prior, she and her sister, my aunt Carrie, had both "fallen from grace" and gone back out into the world and begun drinking, smoking, and fraternizing with sinful and worldly people. After her death, we learned that my grandmother had played the dogs in Tijuana the day before she passed away of a massive heart attack. There was no way she could have made it to heaven with that sort of offense on her soul, even though she and Aunt Carrie had reportedly "come back to the Lord," as we termed it, after over twenty years of being "backslidden."

My grandfather was no angel, and some of the blame for this has to be laid at his feet for his womanizing. He was a good-looking, part-African and part–Native American man, with beautiful skin, wavy hair, and light green/hazel eyes. Though always sincere, he never seemed quite as serious as my grandmother about the things of the Lord and the strict demands of our holiness traditions. In fact, this was a struggle for many of the so-called holiness people, especially the preachers, all of whom were held to a higher standard. Men were perceived to have a greater struggle with sexual fidelity than women, though it takes two to tango. As a kid, this mystified me. It seemed always to be the men and never the women who were considered adulterers and fornicators.

Few of the African-American holiness preachers of that era had much formal education. Many, my grandparents included, could barely read; some not at all. They were simple, humble people still wrestling with Jim Crow laws and racial discrimination. The civil rights movement and Martin Luther King would not hit their stride until the mid-1960s, and my family had been struggling to live holy and preach holiness for at least twenty years before Rosa Parks refused to give up her seat on the bus.

HELL 24/7

In those days, all the so-called sanctified people (we called ourselves the saints) had was home, work, and church. We avoided involvement with worldly things, people, or practices as though we were trying to prevent contamination by an infectious agent, which we presumed everything outside our sacred circles and world to be. We were taught to do as the Bible commanded: "Come ye out from among them and be ye separate" (2 Corinthians 6:17, KJV). The reference was to avoid being "unequally yoked" with unbelievers. The alternative was hell. In fact, we prided ourselves in and repeated the slogan "It's holiness or hell." We all believed this and sought desperately to live up to it, looking down on any who didn't, especially those who claimed to be saved, sanctified, and filled with the Holy Ghost but didn't live up to the standard. Twenty-four hours of every day, we were engaged in a struggle for our immortal souls.

My family believed strongly in fasting and praying to keep the devil from influencing or infecting our lives, causing us to lose our fragile souls and therefore our salvation. Some of my friends were children of holiness preachers, and we used to discuss the secret lives lived behind the closed doors of their homes. Severe beatings and verbal, psychological—and sometimes even sexual—abuse were rampant in far too many homes. Living right was a struggle that at times became violent. We were taught that to even look upon a woman lustfully (desiringly, even admiringly) was to have committed the sin of adultery. This is what Jesus is quoted to have said in Matthew 5:28. We strove to have what we called "sanctified and pure minds." We used to sing a song: "I woke up this morning with my mind stayed on Jesus, Hallelu, Hallelu, Hallelujah!" The song was based on the Scripture that says: "I will keep him in perfect peace whose mind is stayed on the Lord" (Isaiah 26:3).

We were like martial artists practicing an intensive discipline to suppress our natural human impulses and keep ourselves walking the straight and narrow path. I always wondered how I could keep my mind absolutely stayed on the Lord 24/7. We quoted the Scriptures, like, "I can do all things through Christ who strengthens me" (paraphrasing Philippians 4:13) and "Greater is he that is in you, than he that is in the world" (1 John 4:4, KJV), but it wasn't easy for any of us, and, in fact, it exerted a baleful kind of stress and fear over our lives lest we fail and wind up bound for hell—or, almost equally dangerous and menacing, causing someone else to go there.

We weren't supposed to watch television, listen to secular radio or music, or go to movie theaters. Playing sports was evil to the most severe holiness people. We were taught to literally "love not the world, neither the things that are in the world" (1 John 2:15, KJV).

My dad had all this in his mind as he stood over his mother's body, both there in the hospital emergency ward and later at her funeral. I imagine that the rest of his six siblings wrestled with this sad and somber issue as well, not to mention everyone else in the church that day, all of whom were aware of Grand Mama's presumed spiritual condition. Three of my dad's brothers were alcoholics—one of them a preacher—and all of them, including my dad and his two sisters, struggled with fear, guilt, and shame. They were all representative of the religious culture in which we were raised and had become acquiescent to. The psychological wear and tear has been obvious to me for my entire adult life. In our constant struggle to avoid the momentary, unforgivable lapse that would cause God to fling us into hellfire, we had created a kind of personal, emotional hell for ourselves. I don't agree with all of the points that "new atheist" writers like Richard Dawkins and Christopher Hitchens make in their books, but about this they are correct: holding this kind of existential fear over the head of a child from the time he or she is old enough to comprehend it is a kind of abuse.

THE BEGINNING OF THE END OF THE BEGINNING

I have always wrestled with the concepts of hell and eternal damnation that most Christians embrace. They don't make sense; it is clear to me that the concept of hell is a human creation used to terrify the masses into behaving as their religious institutional guardians desire. This is why I have come to the conclusion that God is not a Christian, even though I remain one—though not in the way that many Christians define themselves. Yes, due to my own awakening, I have truly left the reservation (or plantation), to the sadness, chagrin, and anger of many precious and beautiful people whom I love dearly. In expressing my insights, revelations, visions, and envisioning, I know that I am sure to shock, appall, offend, and perhaps enrage some of those people whose only offense is that their eyes remain closed and they remain enslaved to the fear-based theology they call faith. I say this only because I see this theology as destructive, damaging, and counterproductive. In tracing my own journey, I hope to blaze a trail for others who dare to wonder and ask, "Does what I've been told really sound like a God I would want to worship and devote myself to?"

I suppose that the beginning of the end for me came around the time I got the letter from the Jewish Federation of Tulsa after they'd learned about my theological shift into Inclusion Consciousness. They wanted me to meet with them for a breakfast meeting at one of the popular restaurants in Utica Square, arguably the most exclusive shopping center in Tulsa. This was a strange and unexpected invitation. What did the Jewish Federation want with me? I was profoundly curious, intrigued, and a bit intimidated. I had never even heard of the Jewish Federation of Tulsa. I loved Jews but had not considered interacting with them, even though I considered my Judeo-Christian ethics and theology very important and precious.

Jews and Christians have always tried to have a mutually courteous relationship, though it's been problematic over the years. We've always tried to be friendly, if not exactly friends. As a Christian, I was always eager to see them come to Christ, confessing Him as their Lord and Savior as billions of Gentiles had—a stance that, with my new eyes, I regard as deeply offensive to their ancient and beautiful spiritual tradition. I have been to Israel nearly a dozen times since 1975 and led hundreds on Holy Land tours there. After all, Jesus was a Jew, and our Bible came from and indeed *was* a Jewish spiritual inheritance. The Apostle Paul, a profound and almost Pharisaic Jew himself, had written to the Christian Church in Rome that "all of Israel would be saved." I would have thought my invitation from them would be a huge step toward this end, but I no longer believed that Jews or anyone else needed to accept Jesus to be saved. To my new way of thinking and believing at that time, God accepted them and all humanity through Christ, and thus were already saved. So this invitation was a doorway to a wider world that my Christian brethren seemed to fear: a world where not everyone believed in lockstep with Pentecostal fundamentalist doctrine.

I remember later proudly relating to Oral Roberts that I had received an invitation to speak at one of the local Orthodox synagogues. His response was, "What on earth would you preach in a synagogue?" I was surprised at his question, since he had earlier insisted that I was not a Hebrew scholar (something I'd never claimed to be anyway) and that some of his rabbi friends had told him I was misinterpreting the Hebrew language and Scriptures in some of my sermons. He also boasted that he had Jewish friends with whom he frequently discussed Scriptures and Abrahamic history and had done so for years. Clearly, he was comfortable in the Hebraic milieu; why should he assume I would not be?

This was my first conversation with Chancellor Roberts since my Gospel of Inclusion had become a source of controversy in the Christian charismatic world. Everyone knew I was an Oral Roberts protégé and his so-called black son, so his opinion of me and my new "erroneous" doctrine was important to many, me included. His son Richard, then president of Oral Roberts University, had already publicly denounced me with the consent and approval of the Board of Regents, from which I had resigned after fifteen years of service. It was a dramatic and the most professionally traumatic episode of my life as a Christian and minister. I was coming to grips with the deepest assumptions, presumptions, and realities of my life as a Christian. I was confronted with whether or not God was what I was, as opposed to me being what God is.

My friend Dr. Robin Meyers, professor and senior minister of the Mayflower Congregational Church in Oklahoma City, says, "It's more important what Jesus says about God than what the Christian Church says about Jesus."

GOD IS NOT A CHRISTIAN, BUT I AM

As a fourth-generation fundamentalist evangelical Pentecostal preacher, I had always assumed God to be not only the God of Christianity but essentially Christian. I have now come to the realization that the God of Christianity is one thing, while the idea of God *being* a Christian is another altogether. One is a matter of doctrine, a human invention. The other is an assumption about the nature of the Almighty that I simply cannot embrace.

I first heard myself saying "God is not a Christian" as I was defending the philosophical and theological position I detailed in my book *The Gospel of Inclusion*. In speaking to groups and congregations, I would often say, "God is not a Christian, but I am." I wanted to make the distinction between what I was religiously and what I perceived God to be—or perhaps not to be—spiritually. I've always taken great pride in being a Christian, and for the first fifty years of my life, I assumed Christianity to be the only authentic, God-approved religion. I considered all others false, cultish, and dangerous. Yet until I opened my eyes and stepped back to consider the true face of this faith that I clung to for so many years, I didn't perceive its incredible power to influence—and, in some cases, infect or warp—the lives of those who believe in it.

Christianity is arguably the most powerful religion in the world and in human history. Born out of Judaism, Christianity has grown in size to dwarf its mother religion, with more than two billion adherents. The Yahweh of Judaism is also the Jehovah of Christianity and the Allah of Islam, yet, of course, where the three great monotheistic faiths part company is in the role of the Christ. Christians insist that Jesus, who is called Christ (*Mashiyach*), a Jewish ideology, is God in the flesh, something that neither Jews nor Muslims accept. Muslims consider Christ a prophet only, not unlike Muhammad or Abraham. Many Jews are still awaiting the appearance of the Christ of their faith and expectation, their predicted messiah, or sent One.

Here's where things get sticky: because most Christians believe that Jesus is God in the flesh, we also believe God is Jesus (savior) in Spirit—which would basically make him both Christ *and* a Jew. If this seems convoluted, that is my point. The entire concept of Christianity, as opposed to Christ the Person or Christ the Principle, leads to all sorts of disagreements and nonsensical pronouncements. Christ was not a Christian; the religion built on His name and sacrifice was begun after His death and is an abstract form of Judaism. Jesus was a Jew by birth and a mystic-prophet in consciousness and actions, with a mission not to found a religion but to transform the thinking of the time by making people aware of the Christ Principle in and of God.

At this juncture in my life, I tend to emphasize the Christ Principle more than the Person, because it takes as much faith to believe in the Principle as it does the Person. I do believe in Christ the Person but no longer because I feel I must in order to be saved. *Belief compelled through fear is not belief,* it is blind and forced obedience. I believe in Christ the Person because I *want* to. It is a choice I've made, not an obligation. What I believe most about Christ is that He believes in me. He represents the "God thought" that waits to be rediscovered within every human being; a concept I tend to personalize. For God to be a savior God, He must believe in what He saves and consider it worthy of preservation, rescue, or redemption. Nothing else makes sense. God either loves us all, or He doesn't. If He doesn't, then He's not the God of Scripture that billions have put their trust in. The is-ness of God is love and "knowing." That has nothing to do with any gender or religious reference to "It."

These questions, which most Christians never ask, at least not openly, raise the specter of the fundamental split personality of most Christian creeds. Most Christians prefer Jesus as God—the New Testament God of love, grace, and salvation—as the one to whom they pray and whom they (we) serve, at least in principle. After all, Jesus seems to have come to protect us from God by rescuing us from His wrath-inspired hell and conquering death. Jesus is presumably better at being God than God, like the eldest son who takes over the family business and immediately proves he can run it ten times better than the old man. Christ, who is Jesus to some, is a preferable deity simply because He is a kinder, gentler God than the one of the Old Testament. Amid the tension, most Christians lead a fearful, anxiety-ridden existence and consciousness. We fear one version of God and follow the other. It's like having a loving mother and a terrifying, abusive father. We follow the kind, gentle, and nurturing mother while fearing the mean, intimidating father—and we're supposed to love and be committed to both! That's an untenable situation; the epitome of a sick duality.

A Call to Conscience

When my administrative assistant told me that Michael J. Fox had called requesting an interview with me, I wondered what it could possibly be about. I'd always loved him as an actor and was actually using the phrase "back to our future" as a reference to where I expected all of humanity to go one day. But I didn't know what to expect. Of course, I said yes.

While at dinner, I asked Michael what had interested him so much that he and his assistant, Asher, would fly to Tulsa to personally meet with me. His response was that he would not have chosen to be stricken with Parkinson's disease—certainly not in the prime of his life and career, which was when he learned that he had it. He emphasized that the disease had chosen him, not the other way around. He went on to say that he was interested in me because he admired the courage I had to walk away from all I had achieved and that I had done so in the prime of my own life and ministry.

I listened humbly to his flattering remarks but then begged his pardon as I corrected his assessment that I had willingly walked away. I told him that I was *called* away in my prime and that I could no more resist that call than Rosa Parks could fight the call to refuse rising from her seat on that bus in Montgomery, Alabama, in 1955. I insisted to Michael that destiny had called him, me, and many others to where we were in life, and that we had somehow agreed to come here in our pre-incarnate consciousness. I told him that in my view, the universe has aligned itself and us with irresistible change and challenge, and us with it.

As painful as his illness has been for him and his lovely wife, Tracy Pollan, Michael has also raised more money for medical research into the cause and treatment of Parkinson's than anyone in history. To think that both he and Billy Graham, one of my favorite people, suffer from this debilitating disease is interesting and touching to me. It seems that many people from all backgrounds are being called to bring about change in our world.

I have always resisted the idea of a "post-Christian" era. At first I was unable to conceive of such a thing, since all my life I thought it was my calling to Christianize and thus save this world. Today it tends to be difficult for me to conceive of a world without Christianity because I still think there is a powerful role for Christianity to play—one it has never really played to its fullest positive potential. This is possible only if it comes from the proper perspective and sheds many of its most cherished but destructive myths. The difference between the Christian and the non-Christian is not salvation. In proper Christian theology, salvation is given, not just offered, by grace to everyone. Christians are simply those charged by God with a special mission, to bring light, wisdom, and self-awareness to the world. Not necessarily to convert the world, just to convince it of the innate beauty and love it has mislaid or forgotten.

For all of my life, saving the world meant converting it to Christianity while proclaiming Jesus as Lord or winner of the great cosmic conflict. That was our mission as Christians. We call it the Great Commission. Even if we were *getting others saved*, we worried about not doing it well enough, not getting or winning enough to Christ. This was and is an unending anxiety for all Christian evangelists. It has been indoctrinated into us that we must preach the Good News that the world is saved only and exclusively through Christ and to compel others to accept Christ as their personal Lord and Savior. We expect people to believe this Gospel, but Christians as a whole don't believe what we expect others to. We offer up a kind, loving Savior with one hand, while remaining convinced that most of the world is doomed to condemnation by the wrathful Father with our other hand. Yet we continue to try to save the world from its sin, our God and His devil. No wonder there is so much paranoia and dysfunction within our ranks.

While it has been my culture to try to save souls, it is no longer my conscience. Deep down in my heart, I've always known that something was wrong with my dogmatic constuct. I've finally accepted that my perception of the Great Commission was really the Great Delusion: another means of control that had as an unfortunate side effect the alienation of millions who were understandably offended at being told by strangers (whose own lives may not have withstood much scrutiny) that they were damned. However, my ministry was at a level of success and notoriety that it would have been suicide to change emphasis when I was nearly a half century old. Losing everything to start over again didn't make much sense. The same is true for many other well-meaning and well-intentioned Christian leaders. I hear often from retired ministers from many different denominations, ranging from United Methodists to Pentecostal bishops, who say they have pondered or even believed as I do for years but couldn't afford to acknowledge it publicly without losing their ministries, credentials, homes, salaries, and retirement. I had to consider the risks of losing everything, and indeed did.

However, I came to a place where I could no longer hide my theological crisis in the success of my ministry. Since then, I have made the leap into the broader hope of my calling. I've had to rethink what I believed and why I believed it. I feel somewhat as the Apostle Paul in Scripture may have felt when he spoke to the ruling religious court of his day.

In Acts 23:1–4, Luke writes:

> Paul looked straight at the Sanhedrin [the "Supreme Court," or ruling council, of the Jewish religion] and said, "My brothers, I have fulfilled my duty to God in all good conscience to this day." At this the high priest Ananias ordered those standing near Paul to strike him on the mouth. Then Paul said to him, "God will strike you, you whitewashed wall! You sit there to judge me according to the law, yet you yourself violate the law by commanding that I be struck!"

Those who were standing near Paul said, "You dare to insult God's high priest?"

How dare I confront the system? Where do I come off insulting the powers that be, the traditional leading influences of the day? Where do I get the audacity to speak up and demand change? I do it, as Paul, Martin Luther, Martin Luther King Jr., Mahatma Gandhi, and others did, because of conscience. Conscience is literally calling me out to proclaim a higher reality. Conscience has attacked my moral amnesia and caused me to remember that we were all created in the image and likeness of God and that anything else is an impersonation, an illusion, and an outright deception. Truth demands expression, and its call is irresistible. In Scripture, the word *conscience* is the Greek word *suneidesis,* which means "co-perception"—that is, "accompanying moral consciousness and awareness." Conscience is, in effect, to have uncommon knowledge or awareness. It is the consciousness and awareness of the soul. It is not only what you know but what you undeniably are.

THE PRICE OF VISION

People like the Apostle Paul, Dr. King, Rosa Parks, and Gandhi had this uncommon awareness. They saw what others either didn't see or refused to acknowledge. The mystical or metaphorical meaning of the word *conscience* is to see as God perceives, to see things as they can become. Or perhaps as they are in another reality, rather than as they appear.

Mind you, I do not flatter myself with comparisons to these giants. I humbly submit that I can only hope to capture some small shadow of the light of their greatness and courage. I bring them up only to illustrate that to perceive things outside the box and to try to bring about both spiritual and practical evolution and revolution inevitably comes with a great price. Visionary minds are always met with violent opposition born of fear. Higher knowledge is costly. It cost Galileo, Dr. King, Gandhi, Paul the Apostle, Jesus, and scores of lesser knowns their lives or livelihoods. People who hear the call to conscience follow what they know inwardly— what they know in consciousness or at higher levels of awareness. I call this *irresistible knowing*. It is a form of divinely transcendent memory.

Deuteronomy 8:18 reads, "Remember the Lord your God, for it is he who gives you the ability to produce wealth [*or be wealthy*] and so confirms his covenant, which he swore to your forefathers, as it is today." According to this passage of Scripture, we all have the ability to get wealth, but I am not talking just about money. I am referring to progress and improvement of soul and mind, the overall progress and improvement of human life. As inferred earlier, I am not so much attempting in this book to teach you the truth as to remind you of it, to help you recall that which you already know but may have forgotten.

Dr. King *remembered* his vision of a world "where my four little children . . . will not be judged by the color of their skin but by the content of their character" from another consciousness. He recalled the innate knowledge we all share as our birthright: *that we are all safe with God and that we all participate in the fullness of the Divine and the continuing creation and evolution of this world.* Somehow, in our very human failure, we forgot this truth. Perhaps we buried it beneath strata of dogma, politics, legalism, and lust for power. But Dr. King reminded the world that indeed all people were and are created equal. This is the message of Jesus and all His true disciples, both Christian and non-Christian. The call of my conscience is to hear and herald this same powerful truth to my generation.

Original truth is not something we learn. It is part of our spiritual DNA. We are all living and loving monuments to the higher consciousness and divinity in us all. That is the Christ Principle: that we are divine, each of us an aspect of God, already saved and/

or safe, and prepared for the great work of the Original Mind. This is the higher cause and course of life: to remember who we are in God's original plan. To experience, express, and expose our divinity in this world and do it corporately as well as individually. This message has been forgotten by many who embrace a fear-based theology, taught by dogma and doctrine that man is evil and flawed and sinful and balancing forever on the precipice of damnation. This misguided mentality creates and proliferates the pain and pathos of the destructive behavioral patterns we tend to glorify as sin. Nevertheless, this truth remains eternal, needing only to be noticed and embraced, even if not fully understood.

There is a God-ordained revolutionary in each of us. Dr. King recognized this. Jesus was perhaps the first recognized in Judaism to see it. As referenced earlier in the New Testament book of Acts 23:1, we read:

> Paul looked straight at the Sanhedrin and said, "My brothers, I have fulfilled my duty to God in all good conscience to this day."

Again, the Apostle Paul looked straight ahead, not behind or to the side in fear, reticence, or intimidation. Such resolution can cost you. You can lose things, people, friends, family, reputation, position, and even your life, simply because of what you profess to know and how you see things, especially if it is different from what others see or will admit. My vision initially cost me dearly in terms of finances and possessions, status and relationships, and my self-imposed illusions about how loving and tolerant many of my Christian brethren and friends were. It turns out that many of them were loving and tolerant so long as they believed I thought as they did. Once I did not, I became to them a heretic, rebel, or radical, and, to some, a perceived adversary. I'm sure I reaped some of what I had sown when I lived at the same spiritual or religious address as my detractors.

Heresy is the Greek word *hairesis,* which means "a choice"—that is, the choice to separate or become sectioned off from the norm or tradition. It is a derivative of the Greek *aihreomai,* which means "to take for oneself," or to "prefer or choose personally." Heresy is a choice based on the way you view or envision a thing, particularly religious orthodoxy. How much are you willing to pay for believing that things can and should be different and adjusting your life to make them so? This is what the people in New Dimensions, the church I founded in Tulsa, now merged with the All Souls Unitarian Universalist Church, and others are helping me do. That is our new Great Commission—and yours if you embrace the message of Inclusion. We believe the world of injustice, religious bias, and hatred is wicked and unwarranted. We believe God loves everybody equally and has provided safety in Christ—but not necessarily Christianity! We're not talking about religion; we are talking about a relationship with a Creator God in consciousness who (or which) created us all, equally loved, cherished, and divinely purposed.

I want a different world. So do you, or you would not be considering this audacious *heresy* that I'm spreading. Bravo and blessings to you for it. I am cocreating that world even now in my consciousness, and I invite you to do the same. We are charged with releasing our loved ones—and ourselves—from a self-created and imposed hell. In slaying the dragons of illusion, legalism, and power-based dogma that underlie much of today's religious culture, we will do just that.

PART ONE

IT AIN'T NECESSARILY SO

It is the eye of other people that ruin us. If I were
blind I would want, neither fine clothes, fine houses
or fine furniture.

—Benjamin Franklin

What I admire in Columbus is not his having
discovered a world but his having gone to search
for it on the faith of an opinion.

—A. Robert-Jacques Turgot,
French economist (1727–1781)

CHAPTER ONE

A CHURCH IN CRISIS

In Christianity, neither morality nor religion come into
contact with reality at any point.

—Friedrich Nietzsche

Just who and what is God?

In many circles, that is not even a permissible question, and
therein lies the crisis referred to in the title of this chapter. It seems
to me that what I will call (with only the slightest irony) the
"spiritual-industrial complex" has asked us to abdicate our minds
in order to develop our souls. According to that way of thinking,
intellect and spirit cannot coexist. They annihilate each other in
the same way that water and metallic sodium, when combined,
combust instantly and violently. Yet this same spiritual Mason-
Dixon Line is also responsible for the bitter divide between science
and the world of subjectivity, enlightenment, and consciousness. It
is as if we are divided into two armed camps, each defending what
it sees as the more important aspect of being human. And as Jesus
said and Abraham Lincoln quoted, "a house divided against itself
cannot stand."

Why are we on the spiritual side of this debate so opposed to
questioning? Why do we demonize intellectual curiosity, scrutiny,
scientific knowledge, and rational thinking? Is it because we fear
exposure of our faith as unsupportable by fact in an age when fact

occupies the pedestal where God once stood? That should not matter; faith is belief in the unseen, that which cannot be proved. Yet rather than deal with a changing world and the terrible consequences of the rift between faith and reason, many religious communities sequester themselves in an alternate reality where there are no questions, and all media, art, and culture reflect these simple ideas: Fundamentalists teach that God is good, God is everywhere, Jesus died for us, to avoid hell you must accept Him as your personal Lord and Savior, and so on. Many embrace conservative political views because such views stand for turning back the clock; a refusal to embrace unsettling changes in our social fabric, our sexual mores, and our environment. What some call faith is little less than a religion of denial and delusion.

In his Gospel, John is said to have written: "Light has come into the world, but men loved darkness rather than light, because their deeds were evil." I define light as "higher consciousness." Light has not only come, light has always been, but people refuse to acknowledge it, because their deeds or functioning ideologies are not only evil but also awkward and disingenuous.

This withdrawal from the world or reality achieves nothing except to make such faith communities at best irrelevant and at worst corrosive to the idea of bringing the worlds of faith and intellect together for the common good. How did we get here? How did a religion inspired by a man whose very purpose was to question the nature of the political and religious milieu into which He was born turn into something like a parent who doesn't want to tell his child whether or not there is a Santa Claus? I think such things begin as all movements do: with one question left unanswered and its asker discouraged from asking again. Suppression of inquiry is like a disease. So as I examine the reasons why God is not a Christian, I'm going to ask some heretical questions.

Again, Who and What Is God?

> God is like a mirror. The mirror never changes, but
> everybody who looks at it sees something different.
> —Rabbi Harold Kushner

The God question is a complex one. The question of and the quest for God have existed as long as humankind has had the ability to look at the stars or the lightning and ask, "What does that light mean, and where does it come from?" The concepts of God, divinity, cosmic consciousness as the great mystery make more sense than the increasingly monstrous entity that our imaginations have concocted over the millennia. In fact, the God billions worship is a human creation that, we are taught, gave Its life in order to answer our endless quest for life's meaning. We have created this child's God, the white-bearded father living in the sky, in our own image rather than the other way around.

The God to whom I was introduced as a child was basically a Jewish one: male, fatherly, Anglo-European, bearded, angrily loving, judgmental, righteously indignant, and frighteningly powerful, not to mention present everywhere and all-knowing. In trying to make sense of this God, man has continued to manufacture and manipulate images of this perceived deity. The images have changed over the centuries, based on the mood of the times. During kind times when harvests were abundant and peace reigned (admittedly rare in the ancient world), God was benevolent. When plague and famine killed millions, God was portrayed as enraged and vengeful.

To this day, this emotionally infantile God remains in power, a fear-based aberration produced by fevered imaginations, promoted by those who understand how such a deity can be used to gain and consolidate power over believers, and protected by flocks of billions who refuse to question their damning God for fear of their own damnation—or out of an even greater immediate terror of social and cultural isolation. But I argue that it is precisely this image of God—an infantile, simplistic, ridiculous notion of the sublime power that underlies the world—that is destroying civil religion, fueling the rage of the "angry atheist" movement, and pitting science against the spiritual at a time when we should be using every tool within reach to discover what it means to be human—and divinely human at that.

TO SAVE GOD

Interestingly, the Greek word for God, *theo*, is where we get our English words *the, thee, this, thou*, and so forth. It is also the source of the word *theory*. A theory is a speculative idea suggested to explain an observation. Theories must be proven before they can be considered scientific. However, it's always been my opinion that since we can't prove scientifically that God exists, then neither can we prove scientifically that He or it doesn't. That means the question of God doesn't meet philosopher Karl Popper's famous requirement that scientific inquiry means an idea can be proven false, so the issue of faith is beyond science. It is a matter of subjective experience and personal revelation, perhaps more than observation. However, science itself is a kind of God and may indeed be proof of divinity, depending how one defines or divines it. It seems to at the very least suggest supreme intelligence or order.

Lately, I'm not sure that proving or disproving God is even important. What seems important to me is that most people—billions of them—believe in a God and that superficial differences in the nature and pronouncements of that God (the content of the "owner's manual," as it were) are the spark and gasoline for much of the global conflict that has consumed the planet for thousands of years, before the Crusades and the Hundred Years War to the modern jihadi movement. In his book *Conversations with God*, Neale Donald Walsch says that all behaviors are based on belief systems and that we can never hope to change behaviors until we understand the beliefs that underlie them. That is my goal with this book.

What you believe or are convinced of, you are convicted by. Both the words *convince* and *convict* are derivatives of the Latin word *convincere. Vincere* means "to conquer" in Latin. In other words, whatever you believe has victory over you. You are conquered by what you are convinced is true. We are all victims of and convicted by what we believe and, in often awkward ways, of what others believe. I say this because our lives are shaped in great part by the core religious beliefs of others; they have much to say about our politics, our morals, our societal institutions, and, of course, whether and why we go to war. Those who say that faith and religion are irrelevant to modern life are mistaken; like it or not, they are extremely relevant, and it is worth spending some time and thought examining the reasons why narrow differences in how religious creeds interpret the reality or edicts of their deities fuel differences that in turn power the wheels of war, terrorism, oppression, and hatred. If we allow them to, they could also spark love, compassion, tolerance, and global brotherhood. Most religions have, somewhere in them, a capacity to inspire human grace and greatness in ways they rarely fully allow.

I take issue with the position of the neoatheist crowd that says faith is an obsolete remnant of mankind's past that needs to be jettisoned as we would lop off a vestigial tail. However, I agree that the largely unquestioned concepts that underlie most of the world's faith traditions must be questioned and the fundamental assumptions of our spiritual lives revised if we are to survive this new session of turmoil and global change. Faith must evolve. God must evolve. Man must be the means of its reinterpretation. As God saved us, it's now up to us—as if it were possible—to save God. If you ask, save God from what and for what, my answer is, from superstitious mischaracterization and superficial misrepresentations.

God is too important to too many for us to make It out to be
something so vengeful, derogatory, and paranoid as many perceive
Him to be. We'll deal with this more throughout the book.

WE HAVE MET THE ENEMY

Albert Einstein once remarked, "No problem can be solved by the
same consciousness that created it." I think he meant that it takes
different people to solve a problem created by others, but I believe
that once we transform our own consciousnesses, we can indeed
gain the perspective so vital to healing the wounds in the body of
Christianity and perhaps its sibling faiths, Islam and Judaism, as
well as others when and where needed. What is needed is a mutual
"stepping back" and a brutal reexamination of the so-called truths
of Christianity from the perspective not of a traditional believer
but someone encountering faith for the first time. From that clari-
fying, terrifying, dizzying perch, Christianity, the religion of my
birth that I have loved all my life, has some deep, staggering dys-
functions—and in the eyes of millions of Christians themselves,
has itself become the problem.

When I say God is not a Christian, I am also implying that
Christianity in its present form and function is less godly or virtu-
ous. It has, over the centuries, become increasingly gaudy and
ghastly. Racism, bigotry, sexism, elitism, arrogance, and ignorance
have become its hallmarks, whether you're looking at the horrific
child abuse scandals of the Roman Catholic Church or the attack
politics of the religious right and its obnoxious hypocrisy. As I have
moved freely among non-Christians as well as many of the opposing factions within Christianity, I have been confronted with the
reality of the statement "We have met the enemy and he is us."

This is not a new problem. It goes back centuries, yet at the
same time has shaped our modern age. The originators of Communism (Karl Marx, Friedrich Engels, and Moses Hess) were Jews

and were no doubt influenced at least somewhat by their religious and cultural mores. Adolf Hitler was recorded as saying to one of his generals, "I am now as before a Catholic and will always remain so," and "My feeling as a Christian leads me to be a fighter for my Lord and Savior. It leads me to the man who, at one time lonely and with only a few followers, recognized the Jews for what they were and called on men to fight against them . . . As a Christian, I owe something to my own people." Der Führer also used the famous temple scene of Jesus driving out the "brood of vipers" as a motivation for his evil—never mind that his statement was a venomous twisting of Jesus' words and intentions. Jesus' opponents were the Romans and the Pharisees, not the devout Jewish laity of the time.

In her book *The Christ Conspiracy: The Greatest Story Ever Sold,* Acharya S writes, "Whether or not Hitler was a 'true' Christian is debatable, as he also reputedly considered Christianity a Jewish invention and part of the conspiracy for world domination. Additionally, his paternal grandmother was allegedly Jewish. But Hitler himself was raised Catholic, and was very much impressed with the power of the church hierarchy. He pandered to it and used it and religion as a weapon. All during his regime, Hitler worked closely with the Catholic Church, quashing thousands of lawsuits against it and exchanging large sums of money with it."

No, it's not fair to condemn Christianity on the basis of brutal and inhuman acts committed by a man who, had he not had religion to excuse his crimes, would have found some other justification. However, it is a hallmark of the "faith motivated" that many religious zealots use the "will of God" or the "inerrant" proclamations of a sacred book to justify thoughts and acts that range from the embarrassing to the horrifying. Is this a fault inherent in faith or in the faithful? I submit that it is both. On one hand, human beings appear to have a need, at this point in our evolution, to exert power over others using whatever justification they can find that will sway others to their cause. As Hitler did, those who would bend the plowshare of religion into a sword would doubtless do the same with skin color, language differences, ethnic origins, or sexual orientation. The need for power and allies always finds a way. The use of religion always comes in handy in facilitating such viciousness.

But going deeper, religious belief itself, in its current form, breeds separation. We see God as outside of ourselves, and by engaging in different threads of belief, we endorse differing "brands" of God. There's the God of Christianity, the Allah of Islam, the Yahweh of Judaism, the polytheistic Godhead of Hinduism, and many more. This naturally creates an us-versus-them mentality in what becomes armed religious camps—made worse by what we have already spoken of, that the claims of religion cannot be disproven. If you insist that your God told you to blow yourself up in a Jerusalem marketplace, no one can plausibly gainsay you. How would I know, especially if I believe in the kind of God who does kill, maim, and murder those He doesn't like or approve of?

Changing human nature is perhaps the only more daunting task than changing the nature of organized religion, and it's one I will not take on in these pages. However, as we realize that "church in crisis" equals "world in crisis," we see that we must take action in another essential arena: transforming the global perception of God and faith so that the Divine cannot exist as a context for intolerance, violence, and hatred. Our mission, my friends, is to make it so apparent that God would never condone the evils done today in His name that when a pastor suggests that God wants the congregation to support legislation that denies basic rights to women, homosexuals, or so-called undocumented aliens, even a child would be able to stand up in church and confidently say, "No, He doesn't want that at all!"

But it's hard to get there from here. To reach that point, we must radically transform our entire culture's perception of God, perhaps beginning with gender. Since God is beyond the concept of gender, despite the traditions that insist God is male, I think I will point out the ridiculousness of attaching gender bias to a cosmic being by referring to God as *She* for a while. If you find that repulsive or unacceptable, then all the more reason for you to labor through it. The problem would be you, not the reference.

THE KINGDOM OF HUMANS

Many Americans and other Westerners equate Christianity with love, compassion, integrity, and generosity, and, in fact, it's amazing how ecumenical we claim to be regarding other faiths. A *Newsweek* piece by Steven Waldman presented the evidence for this:

> One of the central tenets of evangelical Christianity is that to be saved—to earn admission into heaven—you must accept Jesus Christ as your savior. Yet 68% of "born again" or "evangelical" Christians say that a "good person who isn't of your religious faith" can gain salvation, according to a new Newsweek/Beliefnet poll.
>
> This is pretty amazing. Evangelicals are among the most churchgoing and religiously attentive people in the United States, and one of the ideas they're most likely to hear from the minister at church on a given Sunday is that the path to salvation is through Jesus. Apparently, rank-and-file evangelicals have a different view.
>
> Nationally, 79% of those surveyed said the same thing, and the figure is 73% for non-Christians and an astounding 91% among Catholics. The Catholics surveyed seemed more inclined to listen to the catechism's precept that those who "seek the truth" may gain salvation—rather than, say, St. Augustine's view that being "separated from the Church" will damn you to hell "no matter how estimable a life he may imagine he is living."

The question might come to mind: How and why could or would so many Americans who call themselves Christians so easily lay aside such a fundamental element of evangelical doctrine? I submit that the *Newsweek* story suggests that many Americans are seeking a more uniquely personal concept of spirituality, creating a more focused, unmediated relationship with God that supplants dogma and same-sect exclusionary arrogance. As the old Negro spiritual says, *we ain't gonna study war no more.* People the world over are beginning to demand and openly prefer peace and respectful coexistence on the planet.

It seems that both adults and an entire youthful generation are forging a personal relationship with God as opposed to depending on an institution or organization to dictate to them a particular form or formula for worship and piety.

I find the basic premise of the article very exciting, even though I must boast slightly that genuine Pentecostals may respond differently to the questionnaire with regard to the worship experience in particular. However, the survey suggests that Americans are at least beginning to allow themselves to experience the transcendent without the mediation of a church or religious dogma. That is the kind of evolution I think many of the "spiritual but not religious" crowd could and would support. But where is that open-mindedness in practice? Do we claim one brand of belief in public in order to make ourselves feel better while playing up the divisiveness and politics of religion in private?

Christians talk about the kingdom of heaven, but they are often referring to the kingdom of humans. There is a difference. In the kingdom of humans, the rulers control their subjects through manipulation—fear disguised as faith. Christianity Inc. is big business, as are most other institutional religions. Many see these fallacies and ignore them, others protect them, and still others remain oblivious. Some see their religion from an "If it ain't broke, don't fix it" perspective. For them, their religion works, regardless of how painful or pitiful it may be. They've grown accustomed and desensitized to it. The New Testament calls this having your conscience seared with a hot iron, suggesting a kind of cauterizing of the conscience (1 Timothy 4:2).

Many Christian doctrinal requirements or prescriptions for salvation, like confessing Christ and being baptized, are all related exclusively to being a Christian and joining one of the most exclusive religious clubs, with its doctrinal disciplines. These rites have nothing to do with saving you, except perhaps from the wrath of those Christians who believe you are damned by God if you don't do these things. The absurdity of such presumption is something I was guilty of for the first half of my life. I believed it and preached it along with the rest of evangelical fundamentalism. Scripture describes Jesus as being despised and rejected by men, and evangelical Christianity today states that those who are not Christians are despised and rejected by God. Irony is alive in the church I once called my own. I still love its virtue. It is its vice to which I object.

I denounce religious arrogance because its smug discrimination creates the kinds of tensions that support the proliferation of hatred, wars, and horrendous brutalization in the name of the various brands of God. Who is to say that the collective consciousness of such negativity doesn't somehow contribute to the creation or occurrence of the cataclysmic reactions on the planet that we call "natural disasters"?

MYTHS OF TERROR

Christianity (though not exclusively) has become a kind of survival-of-the-fittest ideology. Charles Darwin's theory of evolution, particularly the hypothesis about the adaptation to environment, in many ways reflects the dynamics of most religions. It is one thing to adapt to a hostile environment by developing webbed feet, as the Galápagos Islands lizards did; and another thing to resist the environment by attempting to change, confront, or retaliate against it. Religion does both. It attempts to adjust to the hostility it encounters (in this case, the perceived attacks of science or the refusal of more enlightened people to tolerate its sanctioning destructive acts) by changing its story (creationism becomes intelligent design, for example), and at the same time, it promotes a virulent theology in which we must placate not only an angry, violent God but also Her equally vicious and sinister devil. The result is predictable: intelligent, open-minded people of a spiritual disposition are driven away by blind extremism, and what remains are the cowed and the clueless, more terrorized and enslaved than ever.

The angry, vindictive, and all-powerful God was not a central concept to ancient Christianity, but it has certainly become so today. It is a doctrine that is psychologically destructive to those who submit to it in a way that those who do not dwell within an immersive, impassioned community of faith cannot understand. That is the world in which I was raised: an alternate reality where every aspect of daily life, the fall of every sparrow, is enmeshed with the spirit and intent of God. God was in and of everything we did, felt, touched, ate, and said, and She could not have been more real, especially to someone raised in that world. For people enveloped by an overpowering evangelical theology, God is behind every door and in every thought. The devil is, too. Imagine the soul-deep terror of being told that this deity was poised like a jungle cat to pounce on you at any time in your life for the slightest infraction and send your soul into the eternal depths of a fiery hell where you would suffer without solace forever. I had nightmares about it. Anyone brought up in that tradition who says he didn't is probably lying.

Getting past this man-made caricature of God can bring about an element of peace on the planet that all of us desire but are afraid to accept conceptually. It's as if we are stuck in a pathetic rut of fear, shame, and guilt brought on by the image of a God who sees us as pathetic as well. Many so-called believers don't believe or know the

Gospel, they just believe and know the gossip! They don't preach Christ, they preach crisis!

In 1 Timothy 4:7, Scripture reads, "Have nothing to do with godless myths and old wives' tales; rather, train yourself to be godly." Notice it said "train yourself." One of my next books will follow up on this, as a training manual for those who desire to train themselves to be godly. Doing so has nothing to do with being a Christian or any other religious affiliation. It has to do with recovering and then *being* your authentic self.

The King James Version uses the word *fables,* which translates to the Greek word for myths, which is *muthos.* (As in my previous book, I will use the etymology of the Bible in order to reveal its true meaning.) It comes from the Greek word *mueo,* meaning "to initiate," and is the base of the word *musterion,* the source of our word *mystery.* This is where we get the idea of rites of initiation, secret oaths, and mysterious vows. This is actually one of the definitions of occultism.

Much of Christianity today has deteriorated into a kind of cult of myths and secret rites of initiation rather than a free and open spiritual consciousness of the Christ Principle and Person. Christ has gotten lost in the mix of doctrinal elitism and exclusionary dogma. This is why a great man of God like Gandhi said, "I may have become Christian, were it not for Christians." Yet have you ever wondered where some of our traditions and orthodoxy come from? *Orthos* is Greek for "straight" (orthodontists straighten teeth, orthopedic surgeons straighten joints, and so on). *Orthodoxy* means "to correct [straighten] doctrine or teaching"—presumably truth, not teeth. But correct according to whom? In the days that our Christian doctrines were written, Roman spirituality prevailed. Christianity was not even a half century old when most of the New Testament letters were written and the doctrines were being developed. Some of the *alleged* writers actually knew the man who was the Rock for the new faith—knew His teachings, knew the touch of His hands, and the compassion of His heart. He was not some abstraction upon which the avarice of our time can be projected. Jesus of Nazareth, called Christ, was physically and forcefully real for these authors.

How then can we pervert what they had to say about Christ's intent and assume our interpretations are more valid? How can we ignore the simple beauty and truth of Christ Consciousness? I would suggest that we can afford to do so no longer.

GOD OF THE CLOUDS

In the Bible, clouds are always associated with heavenly things or with God. Clouds are also metaphors for sorrows, sufferings, or providential circumstances. Yet it is through these very clouds that the Spirit of God teaches us how to walk by faith. If there were never any clouds in our lives, we would have no need for faith. God cannot be recognized sometimes except by the imprint She makes on the clouds of our lives. She does not always come in clear, shining brightness. She is often foggy and murky and difficult to perceive.

However, it is not presumed true that God only wants to *teach* us something via our life's trials. Perhaps God uses clouds to assist us in *un*learning things. Her purpose is to simplify our beliefs until our relationship with our own divinity is exactly like that of a child—a relationship simply between God and our own souls, and where other people and things are but shadows. Until other people's opinions, dogmas, and versions of faith become as shadows to us, clouds and darkness will block our vision, not clarify it. Ask yourself, Is your relationship with God becoming more simple or more complicated?

There is a connection between the strange providential circumstances allowed by God and what we know of Her or of the Divine, and we have to learn to interpret the mysteries of life in the light of both our knowledge of God—and our ignorance of Her. Contrary to what some religious leaders would have you believe, we do not know God. We do not comprehend Her thought or know Her mind: "For my thoughts are not your thoughts neither are your ways my ways," declares the Lord. (Are you hanging in there with the "Her" references?) Scripture supports this premise in Isaiah 55:8. There are numerous interpretations of this presence that we call God:

- an anthropomorphic, unitary being who intervenes in each person's life and judges souls as bound for heaven or hell (the traditional interpretation);
- a dispassionate watchmaker who set the universe in motion and now sits back and observes;
- a universal Consciousness that underlies all creation but does not have an individual identity, a view known as panpsychism;
- a Consciousness that dwells within each conscious being, making each human a sort of "Mini-Me" version of God, also known as pantheism, Greek for "God in or of everything";
- the earth and nature, a pagan view personified as Gaia (a female deity) that comes from Greek mythology.

All of these views may be valid, none of them may be valid, or the answer may lie somewhere in between. The point is that we do not know God, so to assume that She conforms to any mold based on human ignorance, observation, speculation, fear, and self-delusion is to commit an arrogant fiction. Until we can come face-to-face with the deepest, darkest facts of life without viewing God in the evil ways in which we regard Her now, we do not yet know Her, or have not encountered her accurately.

Our view of God and Christ is so clouded by politics, deception, time, and delegated authority that the whole concept of faith becomes a blank canvas upon which anyone can project any version of God that justifies his or her desires or actions. In Mark 9:7–8, we read, "Then a cloud appeared and enveloped them, and a voice came from the cloud: 'This is my Son, whom I love. Listen to him!' Suddenly, when they looked around, they no longer saw anyone with them except Jesus." This was on the Mountain of Transfiguration, where Moses, representing the Law, and Elijah, representing the Prophets (sounds like a boxing match or a court battle, doesn't it?), had appeared along with Jesus. All this happened in a cloud that brought fear and confusion, and after the cloud disappeared, all the disciples were left with was Jesus, the Christ Principle. Jesus is the fulfillment and infusion of both the Law and the Prophecies, and yet most of those claiming to be followers of Christ still hold to the confusion of the Law and Prophecies, neither of which most people have ever fully understood. Perhaps we don't expect to.

JESUS CHRIST, SUPER . . . HERO?

Now I'll go back to referring to God as Him for convenience. How much did it jar your perception to have God referred to as She for a while? What does that say about how hardened your idea of God is? Even I still struggle somewhat with referring to God in the feminine, due to my own preconceived conditioning (and perhaps a little chauvinism to boot).

The purpose of this section is to break through two millennia of confusion about God and Christ—to set you and all of us on the path of understanding and investigation of a presumed more accurate nature of God and man. This is not an easy task, for self-deception about Christ in particular began not long after His death. Jesus is the man; Christ is the mind. We can read in 1 Thessalonians 4:9–13:

> Now about brotherly love we do not need to write to you, for
> you yourselves have been taught by God to love each other. And
> in fact, you do love all the brothers throughout Macedonia. Yet
> we urge you, brothers, to do so more and more.

Make it your ambition to lead a quiet life, to mind your own business and to work with your hands, just as we told you, so that your daily life may win the respect of outsiders and so that you will not be dependent on anybody.

Brothers, we do not want you to be ignorant about those who fall asleep, or to grieve like the rest of men, who have no hope. We believe that Jesus died and rose again and so we believe that God will bring with Jesus those who have fallen asleep in him. According to the Lord's own word, we tell you that we who are still alive, who are left till the coming of the Lord, will certainly not precede those who have fallen asleep. For the Lord himself will come down from heaven, with a loud command, with the voice of the archangel and with the trumpet call of God, and the dead in Christ will rise first. After that, we who are still alive and are left will be caught up together with them in the clouds to meet the Lord in the air. And so we will be with the Lord forever. Therefore encourage each other with these words.

This kind of language was used in the first-century church to encourage people who were floundering in their faith and trying to understand why such horrible things were being allowed to happen to followers of Christ. The people were frightened, confused, and losing courage daily. Nothing was making any sense. There was no great emphasis on miracles or preaching or soul-winning crusades. The church leaders were all now in or approaching their seventies and eighties. Jesus had been gone for nearly forty years, and all hell was breaking loose on Christians and Christianity—not so much by resistant Jews but by an entire imperial structure with sword-bearing armies and coliseums full of Roman citizens eager to see the Christians fed to wild beasts and otherwise tortured in a paid public forum. It was the equivalent, in spirit, of today's "torture porn" movies or cage fighting.

In this insane time, people were looking for Jesus to return and rescue them like some sort of bearded Superman. In my more wicked moments, I can see him swooping in like Mighty Mouse, or Batman, perhaps coming from the Christ Cave with his faithful sidekick Messiah Boy, singing, "Here I come to save the day!"

Blasphemous? Perhaps. But that is how infantile our perceptions of God have become, supported by such pandering spiritual ineptness as the Left Behind series of novels. In the early days of the church, such tales had a purpose: in the face of these unexplainable horrors, all the Apostles could do was emphasize (and perhaps fantasize) the second coming of Christ, when all of this horror would supposedly end and the church would be transported into the glorious, blissful presence of God. Well, it didn't happen then and it won't happen now, at least not in the elementary and superstitious, fairy-tale way we have been taught it would. Millions of Christians were reportedly tortured and martyred during those awful years. What grew from that time was an angry and bitter religion, the leaders of which later implemented these same hateful schemes against any who violated or even challenged church dogmas. We became what our tormentors were and remain so, though we dignify our tactics now as patriotism or "defending the faith and preserving Christian morals and values."

TIME TO GROW UP

We are losing this so-called war because we have fallen into blind dogma and the perpetuation of religious hierarchies rather than the teaching of the fundamental principles of Christ Consciousness. Christ is a principle, a consciousness, a purpose, and finally a person. Christology is an ideology. Jesus was a person, Christ was the principle. Jesus was a man, but He is not a superhero coming to rescue us. That and many of the other simplistic tales underlying today's deeply divisive Christian culture are nothing more than fabrications that have gained the patina of truth by virtue of being repeated for centuries.

And why should it be different? Why should we want a super-hero Christ to come back to earth on a fiery chariot and deliver us from Satan? What is the difference between being subject to the rule of an eternal being versus an infernal being? Either way, we are relegated to eternity as lesser creatures subject to the whims of our betters. We stop evolving and growing. That couldn't be God's or creation's intention for us. Jesus, also called Christ, did not come to mankind to lay the foundation for His rule over us; He came to inspire us to become like Him in spirit and consciousness. That is Christ Consciousness, a grown-up version of belief in which God is a true parent, teaching His children what they need and turning them loose to make mistakes, perhaps suffer injury, but in the end to mature and transform. Jesus didn't necessarily die to save us from our sins; He was instead killed because we in our religious misinformation are sinful. From Zeus to Jez*eus,* humankind has forever sought to appease a perceived hostile deity. Jesus' death was a wake-up call, not a gateway to some mystical dimension. As with Dr. King, sometimes it takes a sacrifice to open the eyes of the world. The Old Testament requirements for blood as atonement are supposed to be replaced by grace and gracious love. Because this was not understood, Jesus was executed. Jews saw it as justifiable retribution, Christians see it as justifiable restitution. Either way, it is at worst senseless and barbaric, and at best, violent and excessive misinterpretation.

It is time to grow up as Christians and as a world community of faithful in whatever brand of God we support. It is time to understand that "God" is simply a concept we use to allow our limited human minds to grasp the oneness and eternity of the presence that dwells in everything—and within us. We cannot continue along our path of religious and cultural elitism. The Christian

Church, as well as other ambitious religions, cannot coexist with a vile viciousness of spirit. We must wake up and see what we are becoming and where we are going as a world, a nation, a church, and a people. Albert Einstein defined insanity as doing the same thing over and over again and expecting different results. I know this seems abrupt, and even abrasive, but let's see if our world can be different by trying some different tactics, even if they seem a bit radical.

Biologist and complex systems expert Stuart Kauffman writes in his book *Reinventing the Sacred: A New View of Science, Reason, and Religion,* "Shall we use the 'God' word? We do not have to, yet it is still our most powerful invented symbol. Our sense of God has evolved from Yahweh in the desert some 4,500 years ago, a jealous, law-giving warrior God, to the God of love that Jesus taught. How many versions have people worshipped in the past 100,000 years? Yet what is more awesome: to believe that God created everything in six days, or to believe that the biosphere came into being on its own, with no creator, and partially lawlessly? I find the latter proposition so stunning, so worthy of awe and respect, that I am happy to accept this natural creativity in the universe as a reinvention of 'God.' From it, we can build a sense of the sacred that encompasses all life and the planet itself."

Whether you accept or reject the idea of God, the sacredness of all life is a goal devoutly to be wished.

CHAPTER TWO

GET THE HELL OUT OF MY BIBLE!

Since God is just, I believe there is a hell; since God is
merciful, I believe there is no one in it.

—Bishop Fulton J. Sheen

I can still see the tears streaming down my father's cheeks when I convinced him that his so-called backslidden parents, both of them Pentecostal preachers, were not being eternally tortured in the fires of hell. He, like millions who are so entrenched in the hell-bent theology, continues to struggle with his new freedom and occasionally regresses into its mental horror, but for the most part, he, now well into his eighties, lives above such obscene thinking.

Devotion to hell, demons, and a chief evil entity called the devil is one of the most pronounced insanities in the human religious construct. It has been such a part of my life and consciousness that even today it is difficult to think outside that mental perspective.

In the Old Testament book of Jeremiah, chapter 19, 4–6, we find some of the most indicting scriptural passages ever written: "They [the Israelites] built high places for Baal in the Valley of Ben Hinnom [Gehenna] to sacrifice their sons and daughters to Molech [chief deity of the Ammonites], though I never commanded, nor did it enter my mind, that they should do such a detestable thing and so make Judah sin." As verse 6 declares this entire concept of a literal "Hell" is that "Valley of Slaughter"!

Gehenna is commonly used by misperceiving Christians to mean hell, when in reality it was a garbage dump. I now believe that the entire concept of hell in traditional evangelical Christianity is erroneously based on both superstition and the influence of ancient pre-Christian pagan mythologies. Yet the idea of hell remains the most pernicious myth of Christianity and one particularly unique to Christianity. Judaism does not have a place called hell; Islam has one, but it is not a central feature of doctrine. What about Christian theology—and what about us as people—compels us to perpetuate the idea of a cosmic torture chamber where billions of our brothers and sisters will be tormented in brutal agony forever? What does this say about the kind of people we have become? Just as important, what does this fervent evangelical belief say about where conservative Christians stand in relation to most Americans, who, according to that previously quoted study, think people can save their souls not by adhering to some outdated doctrine but simply by being good people? As I see it, the evidence is incontestable: Christians risk becoming utterly irrelevant in their own culture if they continue to separate people into "We, the Saved" and "They, the Damned." Again, I ask, do we need Jesus to protect us from God? Is that what Christianity as we've known it is about? Are we saved from God by God?

MY OWN HELL

Most people have such a commitment to the concept of God's customized torture chamber, hell, that the hatred inherent in such a concept manifests itself in a thousand proclamations, speeches, news stories, and sermons. Those who believe in hell's invention create it for themselves and everyone else. As you may know from my first book, *The Gospel of Inclusion,* I have experienced this hell of rejection and rage due to my own perceived heretical, clear, and self-transforming views on the subject of God and hell (and so, mercifully, I won't rehash the entire story, dear reader).

Because of my appearances on the TV show *Dateline NBC* and the other media appearances, the buzz is that Bishop Pearson doesn't believe in hell anymore. This is both true and false. I do not believe in hell the way most Christians have been taught for the last several hundred years, a concept completely different from the hell taught by first-century Christianity. More importantly, I feel certain that the psychotic serial killer God who could create such a place does not exist. I do believe in hell as a state of being or consciousness, and believe that people can dwell in hell and that many do, right now, today, on this earth before rather than after death. I will argue in this chapter that hell is the most erroneous, outdated, misunderstood, and misguided dogma in all of Christianity, and the one that must be discarded if this spiritual tradition is to survive as anything more than a contemptible curiosity.

Hell was never God's intention. It is man's invention. It is a human-manufactured religious icon, no less idolatrous than deifying a statue. Starbucks actually has a quote from me as such on one of its coffee cups.

Both Satan and/or the devil are invented, then invited into our realities. The power of our human imagination is such that we indeed become what we think about most, and we, like the God that most humans project and profess, have the power to create. Look back at the passage on the first page of this chapter: the Old Testament church both created and borrowed Gehenna, its idea of a hell, from its surrounding countries and so-called heathenish cultures. God or Christ had nothing to do with it. Unless you twist it to contain such a message, the Bible does not support the idea of a place where souls go to be punished for eternity for their sins. Let's get empirical for a second and break down exactly how often the idea of hell is mentioned in Scripture, shall we? My universalist friend Gary Amiralt has done the math:

NUMBER OF TIMES *HELL* APPEARS IN THE TEXT
OF ENGLISH BIBLE TRANSLATIONS

Bible Translation	Old Testament	New Testament	Total
"Authorized" King James Version (KJV)	31	23	54
New King James Version (NKJV)	19	13	32
New Living Translation	2	17	19
American Standard Version (ASV)	0	13	13
New American Standard Bible (NASB)	0	13	13
Revised Standard Version (RSV)	0	12	12
New Revised Standard Version (NRSV)	0	12	12
Revised English Bible	0	13	13
Amplified	0	13	13
New International Version (best-selling English Bible)	0	14	14
Darby Translation	0	12	12
New Century Version	0	12	12
Scarlett's New Testament (1798)		0	0
The New Testament in Greek and English (Kneeland, 1823)		0	0
Young's Literal Translation (1891)	0	0	0
Twentieth Century New Testament (1900)		0	0
Rotherham's Emphasized Bible (reprinted, 1902)	0	0	0
Fenton's Holy Bible in Modern English (1903)	0	0	0
Weymouth's New Testament in Modern Speech (1903)		0	0

Bible Translation	Old Testament	New Testament	Total
Jewish Publication Society Bible—Old Testament (1917)	0		0
Panin's Numeric English New Testament (1914)		0	0
Centenary Translation of the New Testament (Montgomery, 1924)		0	0
The People's New Covenant (Overbury, 1925)		0	0
Hanson's New Covenant (1884)		0	0
Western New Testament (1926)		0	0
New Testament of our Lord and Savior Anointed (Tomanek, 1958)		0	0
Concordant Literal New Testament (1983)		0	0
The New Testament, A Translation (Clementson, 1938)		0	0
Emphatic Diaglott, Greek/English Interlinear (Wilson, 1942)		0	0
New American Bible (1970)	0	0	0
Restoration of Original Sacred Name Bible (1976)	0	0	0
Tanakh, The Holy Scriptures, Old Testament (1985)	0		0
The New Testament: A New Translation (Greber, 1980)		0	0
Christian Bible (1991)	0	0	0
World English Bible (in progress)	0	0	0
Orthodox Jewish Brit Chadasha (New Testament only)		0	0

Bible Translation	Old Testament	New Testament	Total
The Original Bible Project (Dr. Tabor, still in translation)	0	0	0
A Critical Paraphrase of the New Testament (Roth, 1960)		0	0
The Holy Bible: A New Translation (Moffatt, 1922)	0	0	0
Williams New Testament (Williams, 1937)		0	0
The Original New Testament (Schonfield, 1985)		0	0
Complete Jewish Bible (Stern, 1998; New Testament and Old Testament)	0	0	0
The Bible (Leeser, 1905, Old Testament)	0		0
New Testament Recovery Version (1991)		0	0
The Power New Testament (Morford, 1998)		0	0
Translation of the New Testament from the Original Greek (Godbey)		0	0
The Scriptures (1998)	0	0	0
Greek/English Interlinears			
Zondervan Parallel New Testament in Greek and English (1975)		0	0
Interlinear NASB-NIV Parallel New Testament in Greek and English (1993)		0	0

The KJV and the NKJV are the only two of the major translations in the list above to use *Hell* in the Old Testament. Even in
these two, the NKJV used the Hebrew word *sheol* twelve times,
while the KJV used *hell* thirty-one times, in the following passages:

2 Samuel 22:6, Job 11:8, Job 26:6, Psalm 16:10, Psalm 18:5, Psalm 26:13, Psalm 116:3, Isaiah 5:14, Isaiah 28:15, Isaiah 57:9, Jonah 2:2. *Sheol* appears to have originated as a reference to a communal burial pit, although, as time went on, it took on meanings more in line with the afterlife. In effect, it simply meant death or referred to a type of annihilation.

It seems that even in the King James tradition, the use of the word *hell* is decreasing. The NKJV, RSV, ASV, NRSV, and NASB are all technically revisions of the original King James Bible. From fifty-four times to thirty-two and then to twelve or thirteen times—who knows?—maybe the next revision will bring it in line with the many Bibles that have eliminated the pagan word *hell* altogether.

Even more revealing, other translations contain footnotes, marginal readings, and appendices pointing out that several key Greek and Hebrew words regarding *hell* have been *mistranslated* in such versions as the King James. These include the Companion Bible (King James Version), the American Standard Version (1901), the Newberry Reference Bible (still published by Kregel Publications), and the Riverside New Testament, by Ballantine (1934).

HELL ON EARTH

Now, one could argue (and many have, in asserting that I am completely wrong in my view of hell) that the reason the references to hell are diminishing with the years is that modern people are becoming less willing to face the hideous though purely speculative reality that hell is out there . . . waiting. So they produce glossy, happy renditions of Scripture that ignore the terror of perdition. I certainly agree that is one explanation, but I do not think it is the right one.

In *sheol* and other references, the Bible does speak of souls crying out from the grave and the dead waiting in a grim afterlife to be judged by God. But remember that these are nothing but references that suggest a place of waiting and punishment for the souls of the wicked, and these writings are influenced by millennia of fear-based theologies about a frightful, hostile God who has a serious anger management problem. Indeed, God is portrayed that way in Scripture, but there is none of the detail of Hades, the Greek underworld, and the tortures awaiting those who do not accept Jesus.

Nowhere does Jesus expressly state that those who do not accept Him as their personal soul-saving superhero will be cast into endless fire. One reference suggests that not believing can result in the illusion of alienation and isolation from God, but the most any hell-loving Christian can say is that the King James Bible *suggests* the existence of hell: human culture has done the heavy lifting, and the terrorizing embellishments are largely (as I wrote about in my last book) due to Dante and John Milton. But here's the question I can't get out of my mind: if you are going to build an entire theological culture that exerts mastery over the lives and minds of millions, shouldn't it be based on an idea with a stronger basis in your key texts and teachings than hell is in the Bible? Shouldn't there be a lot less sizzle and a lot more steak?

At the bottom line, there is little if any scriptural or historically based theological support for the concept of a yawning abyss where the vast majority of humans, including all non-Christians and disobedient or backslidden ones, will be condemned, doomed, and damned for all time. Instead we have built the concept of hell as a profoundly human construct by weaving it into our cultural fabric. Evil is always more interesting than good, just as bad news sells much better than good news. The Satan figure is far and away the most fascinating character in Dante's entire *Divine Comedy*. (And that is exactly what the hell concept is.) This obsession with hell has influenced human culture in ways we are just beginning to comprehend. Where do you think Hitler got the idea that people should be punished or executed en masse by fire? Did he not borrow the concept from a religion that teaches that God torments His enemies by burning them infinitely? And Hitler didn't work alone. Hundreds of thousands assisted him, and millions of others (including his allies, the Roman Catholic Church, as well as some in the American and British leadership) looked the other way.

People ask me all the time about whether Hitler will be in heaven. My response is that, first of all, we're all potential Hitlers (*hurt-lers* and *hate-lers*). Any one of us could have been him and can still become him, unless we change our deeply held belief that some people or peoples are inherently less worthy—and more disposable—than others. Hitler was able to commit his crimes in part because millions tacitly considered his execution of Jews to be an expression of God's vindictive wrath against the people connected directly or indirectly to killing Jesus. The depredations of Joseph Stalin, Pol Pot, and other mass murderers succeeded in part due to the same fundamental belief: that part of what makes "us" is the power to persecute and punish the "other" for whom and what they are or are not. This is the same spirit that says AIDS is God's curse on homosexuals and that spending millions on research is an exercise in futility because AIDS, like natural disasters, is an act of God's judgment. At one time, I actually preached such obscenities. Can we not see the vicious patterns of such vulgar and immoral thoughts? From Auschwitz to Rwanda, such "they must be punished for their sins" thinking divides us into persecutor and victim, predator and prey, and fuels genocide and other human atrocities throughout the world, done in the name of God or the gods.

CREATING HELL ON EARTH

In more than three thousand years, God has not been perceived outside a concept of a devil, and heaven has not been perceived outside a concept of hell. It is as if one is incomplete or unacceptable without the other. We have, over the centuries, adopted all kinds of so-called pagan and superstitious myths into our Christian theology. The Apostle Paul called them "doctrines of devils." In 1 Timothy 4:1–6, he writes that "in later times some will abandon the faith and follow deceiving spirits and things taught by demons. Such teachings come through hypocritical liars, whose consciences have been seared [the Greek word used is *kauteriazo,* which means "cauterized, numbed, or dumbed down spiritually"] as with a hot iron. They forbid people to marry and order them to abstain from certain foods, which God created to be received with thanksgiving by those who believe and who know the truth."

In other words, Paul predicted that Scripture (including letters and writings sometimes forged) would be selectively used as a tool to exert psychological power over others and compel them to conform to a code of conduct at the pleasure of whichever human being determined the rules. The popularization of hell comes about as a natural outgrowth of this, a reflection, perhaps, of the idea expressed by the character O'Brien in George Orwell's *1984,* that the way to assert power over another man is to make him suffer. If you cannot make him suffer physically (since laws prohibit random torture on the streets), then make him suffer psychologically. Torture him with visions of terrifying, brutal, screaming agony that never ends and that he is on the knife edge of being cast into . . . unless he lives according to your rules. Out of this thinking came the bizarre Mormon vision of Joseph Smith, the incriminating speeches of Daniel Webster, the hideous declarations of Leviticus, and the hate speech reverberating from a thousand pulpits.

Hate and fear create hell on earth. The kind of bitter hatred that would burn and torture over six million human beings is truly the gall of bitterness and thus hell. Hitler lived in hell in his twisted and warped consciousness, and thus invented it for others. His inner weeping, wailing, and gnashing of teeth was his hell. He was a miserable wretch of a person, and his misery was acted out historically and was supported by nearly all of Eastern Europe. Will he be saved? In perfect Christian doctrine, the answer is yes, because, according to Scripture, all humans are saved by the sacrifice of Christ, which is to say that all of us have the potential to live forever in Christ Consciousness, and that good and God are the only rational ultimates. But can such a person as Hitler and every potential Hitler ever come to that exalted consciousness? That is the question for every man and woman, from tyrants to saints, from presidents to parents.

I believe it is possible and perhaps reasonable that those who create a hell for themselves and others in this life may experience it once they leave this limited consciousness. But I can see it only as remedial, corrective, or purgative rather than punitive, and never eternal. The word *sin,* among other things, is an acronym for being "separate in nature"—separateness from God and from other divine humans. That separation is an aberration. It is a derisive and destructive illusion. The mind that believes in sin also believes that he or she is separate or separated from God (or can be), and that God does not exist compassionately for them, hates them, and will not be there for them. The false perception of separation from God is hell. Loneliness is hell. Hell is heaven's delay more than its denial. In a cosmos where our destiny and purpose are to come to Christ Consciousness and be as one with God and with each other, the man or woman who harbors such hate, rage, and isolation that he spends all eternity in a state of separation from God and from other human beings is in hell. Hell is not "other people," as the French philosopher Jean-Paul Sartre wrote. It is the complete lack of other people.

WHY DO WE NEED HELL?

I am continually astonished at the willingness of many fundamentalist Christians to believe that their dear departed *sinful* relatives are now in hell and will be there infinitely. I have spoken to parishioners about cherished parents, grandparents, children, and friends and seen them struggle against the idea that because the loved one in question may have committed certain sins or never accepted Jesus, as they'd been taught was necessary, he or she was forever in torment. In the end, few can let go of the idea and rebel against the teachings of the church, and I find myself asking why. Why do we cling so desperately to a doctrine that terrifies and tortures us emotionally, theologically, and psychologically? Again, those who believe in hell create it for themselves and others.

I am not speaking of the power players in religion who wield the threat of hell as a way to exert control over their flocks. That's an obvious motivation and no mystery. In reality, many of them actually *don't* believe in the hell they preach and promise. But why do millions persist in their eager belief that all those who refuse to accept their brand of Christianity will burn in eternal fire? When I was growing up, one notable group that fell into the hell-bound was Catholics. The way we saw it, though they were Christians, Catholics held to their own doctrine that—because it was not "pure" enough compared to our stern, strict codes of living—guaranteed that they would spend the afterlife immersed up to their chins in boiling blood or some other gothic form of torture. I have witnessed fear mixed with genuine glee over the demonic fate of the "unchurched." In some faith traditions, some of what makes paradise blissful is that the saved get to watch the damned writhe in their infinite suffering. Imagine a Friday night in heaven: "Honey, let's go watch the damned get ripped apart by hellhounds for a while before we meet the Johnsons for dinner and heavenly karaoke afterward."

What kind of twisted, sick impulse do we serve with this kind of mentality? I believe that the need to believe in hell, and the pleasure some believers take in their knowledge that some (not *them*, of course) will spend eternity there, is the metaphysical extension of class warfare; it is the ultimate *false* self-esteem booster. If you are a hell-embracing Christian, no matter what your socioeconomic standing, your feelings about yourself personally, or your place in the political spectrum, you can gaze out at the majority of people who your creed tells you will roast in hellfire and feel a false sense of superiority (I'm not sure about security). The need for hell is the spiritual version of parking a brand-new SUV in your suburban driveway: it allows you to feel that you've one-upped the Joneses. No matter how bad your life, how much you owe or how marginalized you feel, there's always hell, the great leveler, and only the privileged few get to miss it. This idea is not only absurd, but obscene and ultimately vulgar.

Yet this entire concept runs counter to the benevolence and mercy of the God that most of these same people profess to believe in, worship, and serve. Those who relish the vengeance of hell are living a religious lie of confusing and self-contradicting duality. In reality, Inclusion (also called the doctrine of Universal Reconciliation) is more consistent with the idea of the God that is expressed throughout the New Testament. According to the early Christian scholar Origen, God will enact *apokatastasis,* the "restoration of all things," in which all souls who have been punished temporarily in some form of hell will be released to God's Kingdom. In the most rigorous, scholarly versions of biblical doctrine, hell is at most a place of temporary punishment, where errant souls are corrected and reeducated in preparation for their eventual transition to heaven, along with all other beings.

The idea of an eternal hell stems largely from the mistranslation of the Greek word *aion,* which actually means "age," as in a defined span of time, such as the Iron Age. If there is any spiritual destination of pain and suffering (and this remains doubtful), it is at most a temporary place of learning and expiation of one's ill deeds, where one may become purified, gain wisdom, and repent (rethink) for the acts of life—overcoming that false perception of separation from God and becoming one with God and man. Eventually everyone is paroled. Why is this idea so unpalatable to many Christians? I believe it is because of the hateful need for superiority and separation that the current faith has cultivated in many of its flock. It also proceeds from an image of God as being angry, hostile, and unforgiving, not to mention prejudicial and bigoted.

Again, as John wrote in his Gospel (and I paraphrase it), light has come into the world, but people preferred the darkness because their deeds and perceptions were warped. In other words, because of our deep-seated sin consciousness, people chose to sleepwalk in fear and spiritual darkness rather than choose the freedom of enlightenment and higher awareness. In a sense, they have been knocked unconscious by the vicious and merciless blow of religious dogma.

And think about this: hell is a state of separation and stagnation. Many of the most radical, angry, and fear-based Christian congregations exist in a parallel sphere where all ideas are based on their entrenched theology; they have no exposure to information or media that does not reflect and support their extreme theology. They exist in a state *separate* from the rest of humanity, a little bubble of exclusionary, ignorant, spiritually elitist hatred. Based on our definition of hell, are these so-called Christians not already dwelling there? These arcane wheels within wheels demand that we examine our beliefs in God, salvation, and damnation as what they must be: reflections of our feelings toward ourselves and one another.

Chapter Three

What Devil Made You Do It?

If the devil does not exist, and man has therefore created him, he has created him in his own image and likeness.

—Fyodor Dostoyevsky

The devil made me do it.

—Flip Wilson

On September 19, 2006, Venezuelan president Hugo Chávez made headlines for referring to U.S. president George W. Bush as the devil. Radio and television talk shows had a field day discussing and debating the effect of an appropriate response to such a reference to the president, a professed born-again Christian who believes that he was ordained by God to preside over our nation at that critical juncture in history.

Here's a commentary I posted on my website in response to the hullabaloo:

President Chávez is not the first and certainly not the only person to call President Bush a devil, or to perceive him as such . . . Many Americans view him as devilish as well; they just don't have the platform to say it in such a public format. President Clinton and all U.S. presidents and politicians face the same tags and titles as well. It is nothing new. Demonizing anyone and anything we don't like or with which we disagree is an American pastime.

Reacting to such childish and inflammatory name-calling only dignifies it and gives Mr. Chávez the attention he craved when he made the statement. It was a stunt for an appreciative audience in the UN, nothing more. But I found it interesting for another reason: our perception of the devil as the personification of evil. People believe so strongly in the pagan superstition of a personal devil that we allow such delusional ideologies to be acted out in human reality. I have followed my thoughts about hell with my insights about hell's putative master, the fallen angel, the son of the morning, perdition, the imp, the deceiver—pick one of many names. My views on the subject of the devil are similar to those about hell.

In our obsession with sin and damnations, Christians have endowed a devil with power rivaling God's. This imposing, powerful, invisible, ubiquitous entity has become the great tempter, the trapper of souls who, despite God's presumed will and all-powerful nature, can lure the unwary into iniquity and thus consign them to everlasting torture. In a way, we are more interested in Satan than in Christ, and we grant him greater influence. He is skulking around every corner, waiting to drag or drop us into the boiling pit.

The devil is also the excuse for every human failing and every scandal that hits the fundamentalist churches, where he's already the main topic of discussion and preoccupation. We spend millions of dollars on churches, temples, cathedrals, and the like to supposedly worship God, but subliminally and indirectly, we worship the devil as well. We not only demonize this devil but we also deify him. We have faith in him. We pray, pay, and display passion, attention, and emotion to combat the devil with all the religious rigor and righteousness we can muster. What you resist persists, and what you fight, you often ignite.

How often have we heard a beleaguered pastor of some evangelical church, hit with accusations of sexual misconduct or embezzlement, claim that the entire affair is "Satan's attack on our church"? It's ironic that the devil is usually depicted with a goat's head; he's our all-purpose scapegoat who allows believers to duck responsibility for their actions. According to the Old Testament narrative, Levitical priests in Israel used goats to carry away their sins and called them scapegoats. This is where the term comes from (Leviticus 16:9–10). Seems strange that on one hand the goat is a symbol of the demonic and on the other a symbol of redemption and atonement.

This thinking hampers our ability to evolve as a just, mature people, contributing positively to our global community and taking responsibility for our actions and reactions. Our insistence on a personal devil condemns us to a kind of earthly hell by imposing on us a congenital paranoia and sense of victimization that is emotionally debilitating.

A DEVIL OF A SURVEY

I do not believe in a personal devil. I do believe in the personification of evil or of destructive thoughts, habits, and behaviors. Believing in a personal devil empowers his or its existence in consciousness and character. Believing in a personal devil or in the person or purpose of the devil causes one to act out what that belief system expects and dictates, just as a belief in hell does. What and when you deem doom and damn in your mind, you deem doom and damn in your actions. Live in fear of the devil, and you live in fear of life itself—you live in fear of God and of yourself. This is a kind of terrorism that even terrorists can't inflict.

In his book *The Devil: A Biography,* British author Peter Stanford writes, "The devil is with us, causing trouble." Quite how he does this, or how it is done in his name, is one of the questions at the heart of this chapter. Does the devil in fact have a physical form, or is he just a popular metaphor for the abstract reality of evil? Is he a myth of our collective psyche passed down through the ages and given a form that reflects the terrors of each passing era?

Stanford's book continues: "The devil has been around for some 2,000 years in the New Testament and maybe for a good deal longer in various other guises and incarnations. Indeed, exact details of the birth, parentage, and education of this doughty time traveler are impossible to come by. Like so much else about him, they can only be guessed at. There are as many estimates as there are people who feel that he has touched their lives."

What are your own attitudes about the devil? You've heard of Ambrose Bierce's *The Devil's Dictionary;* consider Carlton D. Pearson's "Devil's Survey":

THE DEVIL'S SURVEY

- Do you have a testimony of how the devil has touched and changed your life?
- Does he, as the songs says, walk with you and talk with you and tell you that you are his own?
- Who or what is this devil that made or makes you do stuff?
- By what authority and power does he command your life and his supposed legions of demons?
- Is he to blame for your afflictions, failings, and transgressions; a sort of cosmic little brother you can point to and blame when something gets broken during life's rough horseplay?
- What do you imagine him to look like?
- What race, ethnicity, or nationality is he?
- Is he part angel and part animal, as many artists portray him?
- Is he part human?
- Is he omnipotent, omniscient, and omnipresent, like God is purported to be?

- Is he universal, like most people believe salvation and redemption aren't?
- Just who is this world-renowned and infamous character we call the devil?

As you reflect on your personal concept of hell, reflect on your acceptance of the idea of a devil and its effect on your life. For as we shall see, there is even less justification or logic behind the horned and hoofed, pitchfork-wielding personal devil than there is for an eternal hell. It has been my experience that many evangelical Christians insist that you believe in and accept the devil as they do and that you believe in and accept Jesus in order to be saved.

THE DEVIL IN THE DETAILS

Though inferred, a personal devil is not mentioned in the Old Testament, leading us to believe he may not be a Jewish concept. There is mention of a Satan, but that is a reference to any opposition to what Israel is or their national presence and purpose as a people.

The King James Version mentions devils, as in Leviticus 17:7: "And they shall no more offer their sacrifices unto devils, after whom they have gone a whoring. This shall be a statute forever unto them throughout their generations."

According to Strong's exhaustive concordance, the Hebrew word for *devils* is *sa'iyr,* and it translates "shaggy," as in a "he-goat." This is where we get the idea that devil worship involves goats or goat heads. *Sa'iyr* comes from the word *sa'ar,* meaning "to storm, to shiver, to be cold, alone and frightened, to hurl as a storm, to come like a whirlwind." It is a violent idea triggering alarm and intimidation. It was not a concept taught in Scripture by Israel's God. It came from foreign concepts of deity—of "goat gods," goat idols, or demons. This is where the concept of fearing the devil comes from. Devils and storms are primitive subjects of idolatry, and over the years they grew to inspire fear and dread, even terror.

The word *devil* in the Old Testament is always mentioned in the plural, suggesting not *a* devil as a personal entity, but a concept of demons of idolatry, the worship of idols—the false gods or deities of the heathen or pagan peoples that surrounded the Israelites geographically. The second mention of devils in the Bible is Deuteronomy 32:16–17: "They provoked him [God] to jealousy with strange gods, with abominations provoked they him to anger. They sacrificed unto devils, not to God; to gods whom they knew not, to new gods that came newly up, whom your fathers feared." (KJV)

God, like the devil, has always been feared, portrayed as strange, distant, and intimidating. This is an Old Testament concept, one that Jesus attempted to dispel. The church leaders would have nothing of it and rejected this new vision or version of a fatherly God. Why did Israel keep forsaking its God for foreign gods or deities? Was there something intriguing about the other gods that attracted Israel to them? Perhaps there was magic, astrology, or something of the paranormal inherent or manifested through worshipping these goat gods that drew the respect and attention of the Israelites, just as reading their horoscope can be attractive and intriguing for some?

I would suggest that the priests of Israel, not unlike those of Christianity and Islam, were employing the tactic of damnation by association—linking the supposed worship of false gods to an entire population of the faithful in order to claim that the faithful had offended God and thus angered Him, making them more dependent on the authority of the clerical class to placate the enraged Deity.

The God we tend to worship and fear is not the God that Christ preached. The God Jesus preached was devil-less; He didn't need the devil to define Him. Can you imagine God without comparing Him to a devil? To do so is basically inconceivable for most religious people. We are so steeped in the duality of the two loyalties—the tree of the knowledge of good and evil, God and devil—that we are stuck in this strange dichotomy. It seems that the human concept of God needs the human concept of the devil, the yang to God's yin. The history of philosophy tells us that light cannot exist without darkness, and good cannot be without evil. Context defines reality, and in the context of an external, all-benevolent God, the idea of the devil appears to be the price we pay for having that powerful good in our consciousnesses.

But how did the devil gain such stature, to the point where he is equal to and sometimes greater than God?

DEVILS REAL AND IMAGINED

The devil's first mention in the New Testament is in Matthew's Gospel, in reference to an encounter Jesus reportedly had with him. Interestingly, most of the references to the devil in the New Testament are from Jesus, who is said to have conquered him and destroyed his works through the Cross and subsequent resurrection. (I John 3:8) Let's note the first mention of a perceived personal devil by name in Scripture, Matthew 4:1: "Then Jesus was led by the Spirit into the desert to be tempted [scrutinized and enticed] by the devil." Notice that the text says that Jesus was "led by the Spirit into the desert." Why would the Holy Spirit lead Jesus or anyone into the wilderness for the purpose of temptation?

The King James Version uses the Greek word *eremos* for desert, meaning wilderness, or loneliness. Why would the Spirit of God lead Jesus into a lonely place? Have you ever felt led into a time or term of aloneness and separation? I've been in that place now for several years—in the sense of feeling isolated and alienated from what was familiar to me religiously. Have I been tempted or scrutinized in this place? You bet I have, and in ways I never imagined.

I never saw or heard a personal or materialized devil, but I entertained thoughts and ideas that could be perceived as devilish—
thoughts that tempted me to surrender my ideals and take the easy
path of conformity and compromise.

Though demons are not mentioned in the Old Testament, the
New Testament implies that Jewish religious leaders believed in
them and even exorcised them. It is not inconceivable that the
concept was borrowed from ancient Egyptian concepts that pre-
date the Jewish era or that they are at least influenced by Greek
mythology, where demons are called Furies. The Furies lived in the
underworld and ascended to earth to pursue the wicked. They
were one of a group of goddesses of vengeance. They were probably
personified curses but possibly were originally conceived of as
ghosts of the murdered.

This frightening and intimidating concept was gradually
adopted by the known world. It certainly influenced the New Testament writers and perhaps even Christ's references to them in His
teachings. Demons were so accepted that they materialized as they
do today in the parts of the world where they are more strongly
believed in, like Africa, India, and some parts of the Far East. Understand the mind-set of the time: terrible events such as plagues,
floods, and crop failures had no scientifically known explanations.
There was, in fact, no science as we understand it in modern times.
It would have been impossible for the people of the time to accept that their just God could have been responsible for these horrible occurrences, so they had to concoct something (or someone)
to blame. Hence the rising of the concept and idea of devils and
demons.

Let's get back to the aloneness of the wilderness of temptation
in Matthew chapter 4: "After fasting forty days and forty nights, he
[Jesus] was hungry. The tempter came to him and said, 'If you are
the Son of God, tell these stones to become bread.' " We are all

sons (children) of God and have the ability to create what we need. We constantly fight the devilish thoughts that there is something we need that we don't already have, or that we are something we're not. This is how human thoughts amass over generations to pro-duce a false and debilitating image of a devil that convinces us we are naked (uncovered and unsafe) and less than or desperate and in need. This is why in Old Testament Scripture God is said to have asked Adam and Eve, "Who told you, you were naked [vulnerable and unprotected]?"

THE BIBLICAL DEVIL

Let's look at Genesis 3:1–14, with my own notes about the text in brackets:

> Now the serpent was more crafty than any of the wild animals the LORD God had made. He said to the woman [womb of man, place of incubation . . . thought], "Did God really say, 'You must not eat from any tree in the garden'?" [*Did God say you are not free? That you are restrained and constrained from maximized enjoyment of the plane or planet on which you live as persons of dominion?*]
>
> The woman said to the serpent, "We may eat fruit from the trees in the garden, but God did say, 'You must not eat fruit from the tree that is in the middle of the garden, and you must not touch it, or you will die [*die off or die to oneness and unity with God, entering a sense of duality and separation*]."
>
> "You will not surely die," the serpent said to the woman. "For God knows that when you eat of it, your eyes will be opened, and you will be like God, knowing good and evil [*God and Devil*]." When the woman saw that the fruit of the tree was good for food and pleasing to the eye, and also desirable for

gaining wisdom, she took some and ate it. She also gave some to her husband, who was with her, and he ate it. Then the eyes of both of them were opened, and they realized they were naked [they misperceived themselves as human and vulnerable, rather than partakers of the nature of God in wisdom, insight, and confidence], so they sewed fig leaves together and made coverings for themselves. [*They invented religion, concocting their own ceremonial coverings to take the place of the covenant that had formerly covered them.*]

Then the man and his wife heard the sound of the Lord God as he was walking in the garden in the cool of the day, and they hid from the Lord God among the trees of the garden. But the Lord God called to the man, "Where are you?" [*In consciousness; an omniscient God, of course, knew where they were in body. The question was for self-reflection on Adam's part.*]

He answered, "I heard you in the garden, and I was afraid because I was naked [*suddenly human with a false sense of spiritual separation*], so I hid." [*Hid within a disguise of superficiality and artificiality: religion.*] And the Lord said, "Who told you that you were naked? Have you eaten from the tree that I commanded you not to eat from?" [*Duality gives us a sense of alienation leading to the impulse to blame.*]

The man said, "The woman you put here with me—she gave me some fruit from the tree, and I ate it." Then the Lord God said to the woman, "What is this you have done?" The woman said, "The serpent deceived me, and I ate." [*The devil made me do it.*] So the Lord God said to the serpent, "Because you have done this, cursed are you above all the livestock and all the wild animals! You will crawl on your belly [*literally a delusion without a leg to stand on*], and you will eat dust all the days of your life." [*As long as we allow this deception to live in our consciousness, it will gnaw at our humanity, the dust from which we were made.*]

Now note Paul's words in his second letter to the church of Corinth (2 Corinthians 10:2–6):

I beg you that when I come I may not have to be as bold as I expect to be toward some people who think that we live by the standards of this world. For though we live in the world, we do not wage war as the world does. The weapons we fight with are not the weapons of the world. On the contrary, they have divine power to demolish strongholds. [*The Greek word used is* ochuroma, *meaning "fortified and defended places, thoughts, concepts, and ideologies."*]

We demolish arguments and every pretension that sets itself up against the knowledge of God [good], and we take captive every thought to make it obedient to Christ [*the Personification of the Principle*]. And we will be ready to punish every act of disobedience [*the Greek word for disobedience translates as "inattention" or "ignorance"*] once your obedience [*the Greek is* hupakoe, *meaning "hearkening, compliance, or submission to higher truth"*] is complete.

Perhaps this desert or wilderness was a place where Jesus was not so much tempted by a literal devil, as we have imagined, as confronted with His self as it related to His purpose on earth. Think about the kinds of things that you feel and think about when you are alone. What if the devil is the deceptive, confusing thoughts you think when you are alone, when you are confronted with your own hunger, nakedness, and vulnerability? Satan represents the deceiving phase and phrase of mind (i.e., words, thoughts, impressions) in each of us that promotes fixed ideas in opposition to the ultimate truth of our greater consciousness.

SUPERSTITION AIN'T THE WAY

In giving the devil form, we commit the same error (and terror) we commit in making God a bearded, white, angry, and suspicious wizard in the sky, and Jesus a loving but judgmental superhero: we take the transcendent and make it anthropomorphic. We give the immaterial an eternal human form, and then we're surprised when that human form becomes endowed with the sins, weaknesses, fears, and faults of humanity itself, and acts it out on or toward us.

In a sense, all religion is a form of *superstition*. The word is derived from a Latin word that means "to stand or stay over" as a witness or survivor. It is a belief or practice resulting from ignorance: fear of the unknown, trust in magic or chance, or a false conception of causation; an irrational, nonscientific subjective attitude of mind toward the supernatural, nature, or God, resulting from belief in the unknown or unprovable. Most Christians like to call this "faith," while to agnostics or atheists, faith in God is equivalent to a belief in spirits, both good and bad. To them it is little less than legend and fairy tale.

Belief in a physical devil is a form of superstition that diminishes us in every way: it imputes our own potential or propensity for evil or error to something inflicted upon us from the outside instead of an inherent state of human perceptions, and it infantilizes our own fears by turning the curious chaos of existence into a bogeyman under the bed.

Superstition is one of the words used in the Greek translation of the word *religion*. Note Acts 25:19: "Instead, they had some points of dispute with him about their own religion and about a dead man named Jesus who Paul claimed was alive."

The KJV uses the word *superstition* for religion, which is translated from the Greek text as *deisidaimonia*. *Deisidaimonia* is made up of two Greek words: *deilos*, meaning "dread" or "fear," and *daimonia*, meaning "demon" or "entity." I would venture to say that most religious are that in some form or another. Sometimes the very deity that is worshipped is little less than a kind of glorified devil, one we've invented in the mirrors of our own fearful souls.

This distracts us from recognizing the growing perspective that all things related to the Divine are manifestations of ourselves. Notice Jesus' comments in John 14:30–31: "I will not speak with you much longer, for the prince of this world is coming. He has no hold on me, but the world must learn that I love the Father and that I do exactly what my Father has commanded me."

"The prince of this world" has been interpreted for centuries as the devil, but when you look at the context, it was actually about the hostile, dogmatic religious leadership of Palestinian Israel at that time. This event occurs on the Thursday night before what we now call Good Friday, just hours before the religious leaders would apprehend Jesus and turn him over to Roman authorities to be executed via crucifixion. The term *prince of this world* was a reference to the "principles" that influenced the Jewish religious world of thought at that time. It was that world of thought—and its religious legalism, tradition, and dogma—that would insist upon Christ's death. He was executed at nine o'clock the next morning and dead by three in the afternoon.

A physical devil tempting you is an illusion of defeat and paranoia. We all experience it, as did Jesus. However, to presume that a hairy, horned, and hoofed entity with fangs, claws, and a pointed tail is behind any of life's travails is superstitious childishness that makes the myth part of your reality. Jesus, too, wrestled with and wondered about God's will for His life as it related to His will for the world. Remember the plea, "If it be possible, take this cup from me . . . nevertheless, not mine but thy will be done"?

Believing in a personal devil empowers its existence in both consciousness and character. It causes one to act out what that belief system dictates. The same is true of the concept of hell. To believe in an equal rival to God is to become that rival in consciousness. You find yourself resisting God and truth in ways you would not if you did not hold such strong, deviant convictions. Remember, you become what you think about, and you attract what you believe.

CURING THE DEVIL WORSHIP

Faith is believing what you know ain't so.

—Mark Twain

I was brought up with the devil. I believed in him almost before I believed in God, and certainly as much. I had faith in his power and omnipresence. I expected the devil in nearly every aspect of my life. I never had to beg him to be present, as I felt I needed to beg God to be with me. The result was almost constant paranoia. I thought of the devil when asleep and awake. He was with me, and often, I thought and was taught, literally *in* me: in my thoughts, my ways, my friends, and my relatives. He was lurking in everyone; a constant and terrible threat. It was easy to imagine him as more powerful than God, but even that thought could cast us into the devil's realm as blasphemy. It was a hard, dark way to come of age and begin to detach myself from such obscene loyalties.

This brand of devil was a kind of figure of worship himself; a human sickness, a mental and spiritual illness that was always threatening, intimidating, and manipulating our consciousness. How then can we be healed from this pernicious and audacious mental illness suffered by most human beings, especially Christians?

The book *A Course in Miracles,* by Dr. Helen Schucman and Dr. William Thetford, says at one point, "Healing involves an understanding of what the illusion of sickness is for. Healing is not possible without this understanding. Healing is accomplished the very instant the sufferer no longer sees any value in the sickness or the pain caused by the sickness." Religious sickness is a decision. It is a choice to be weak by foisting responsibility for good and evil onto cosmic beings separate from ourselves. It begins with dual consciousness: good and evil, God and devil, heaven and hell, life and death. It presumes that we exist only to be buffeted by forces greater than ourselves; that we have no power to resist. In such thinking, the devil concept or personification grows great and mighty.

When we strip the illusion from our eyes, we see that our so-called good times in this world are good only in comparison to our "bad times." As we grow in the deeper consciousness, we learn that it's all a trick. Both good and evil, as we perceive them, are impostors. They are impermanent illusions. Neither lasts or is infinite, as is God. All things are what our minds make of them.

The trick we all seem to fall for is that our mind is simply lying to us. We wouldn't listen to our unconscious system of thinking if it didn't cloak itself in metaphors and dogmas reflective of our own endemic self-deprecation. This aspect of the self, which reminds us of our fears, frailties, and ill deeds, terrifies us because it demands that we be aware and accountable. How much easier to call it the devil and blame temptation for our fall? I think Jesus somehow learned to live outside this asylum, and He's calling us to come out and join Him in the broader reality of light and true life. For our part, we keep trying to drag Him back into the asylum through dogmas and orthodoxies; at least that appears to be what occurred during His life and times.

But once we awaken to the original idea that spawned our existence, we return to it in consciousness. The "homesickness" that causes our pain ceases. We realize that what we think we want we already have because we *are* it. We are self-fulfilling prophecies. We were created to be so. We can only sabotage ourselves through illusions and doubts that we call the devil, or Satan, or the tempter. We created the devil. Divinity is our reality. It is the substance of who you really are. The only devil is the one in our minds; the one we've imagined into an artificial existence. We've imagined him into being, and we can imagine him out along with illusions like poverty, alienation, and sin.

CHAPTER FOUR

WE'RE ALL LEFT BEHIND

Our brains are no longer conditioned for reverence and awe. We cannot imagine a Second Coming that would not be cut down to size by the televised evening news, or a Last Judgment not subject to pages of holier-than-thou second-guessing in the *New York Review of Books.*

—John Updike

Fear of missing the Second Coming of Christ and being left behind with the Antichrist or accepting the infamous mark of the beast began terrorizing me as far back as I can remember. We called it "Judgment Day," and we were all tormented by both its possibility and inevitability. Terms like "the Second Coming" and "rapture" were rarely used in the simple circles we traveled. I didn't start hearing such terminology until high school, mostly in my senior year. We expected Jesus' return with mixed emotions. We wanted the world to end so that we could go to heaven, but we also feared it, as we never felt we were ready enough for heaven. It would be basically a sin not to anticipate Christ's glorious return, but we also feared we'd be caught with our work undone or in some other compromising place or position: like at a football game, a theater, or some other secular and sinful place, or perhaps in the middle of telling a lie—little white or otherwise.

We also saw the Second Coming or rapture as a way to escape

the "Great Tribulation" and the world dominance of the infamous Antichrist, called also the "man of sin" or "son of perdition"—a term that has actually been applied to me by some.

All these terms were more than frightening to us as children brought up in the strict fear-based traditions of fundamentalism and remain so for millions of innocent—and in most cases, ignorant (uninformed or less enlightened)—people to this very day, both Christian and non-Christian.

On a website called RaptureTransfer.com, you can designate who will receive your earthly property after you have been taken home by Christ during the Rapture. Seriously. It's billed as a way to make sure that your terrestrial assets won't fall into the hands of the government after you're gone and therefore be used in the service of the Antichrist. It's also exhibit A in my evidence of our culture's obsession with the return of Christ and the end of the world—the third myth of Christianity that is bleeding the faith dry of relevance, respect, and any ability to focus on what should be its true mission: uniting all the children of God as a single people for peace, health and hope, and joyful anticipation of good.

Due to my appearance on the 2007 National Geographic Channel TV series *Secrets of Revelation,* people began saying, "Carlton Pearson doesn't believe in the Second Coming of Christ." As with so many other aspects of the Christian faith (and in particular, *my* Christian faith), this is a gross oversimplification.

I think that most people actually misunderstood the first coming of Christ. The way some of us have been taught it, the coming of Jesus to earth was little less than a suicide mission in the first place. We are taught that He came to die and that when He comes back, He will capture or rapture both those already dead and those still here who won't have to, even though Scripture clearly says, there appointed to every person, once to die. (Hebrews 9:27) That's a whole other subject we won't venture any further into.

I *do* believe in a Second Coming of Christ, just not the literalist view traditionally held by evangelical Christians. In light of the long-anticipated literal return of Christ to earth, I believe it is more reasonable to see the Second Coming of Christ as the return of *Christ Consciousness* to the world, not the magical appearance of a physical being descending through the clouds. I have read and preached the New Testament Scripture on which most Christians base this two-millennia-long anticipation and view it metaphysically and metaphorically rather than literally. This makes so much more spiritual sense and is more logical to me.

The Second Coming is an expanded consciousness of Christ realized through self-actualization and recognition of your personal calling and cause.

CHRIST CONSCIOUSNESS

Christ Consciousness refers to a higher awareness or revelation of self and soul. This is the realization that each of us carries Christ—the principle, purpose, and presence—within us, with the same potential and power for healing and creation. As with the other aspects of Christian myth and misconception we've lacerated so far, this is a far more adult and mature version of the faith, replacing the superhero Jesus (arriving in the nick of time to take us away from all of this) with an internal Christ who says, "You're responsible for saving yourself." This is Christianity as grown-up responsibility, breaking away from the childish notions that now inform its popular dogma. The Apostle Paul called this "putting away childish things or ways."

The coming of Christ is an elevated awareness of Christ, not the man and mediator but a mystical and spiritual recognition of the Christ Principle embodied by the Christ Person, which in part is each one of us as we recognize, realize, and actualize our authentic selves and souls. I can hear Jesus asking again, "Who do people say the son of man is? And then who do you or the church in this twenty-first century say the son of man is?" He came once in the flesh and was crucified, but He comes a second time only in spirit and is glorified by His expression in every man, woman, and child on earth. When that occurs, this new awareness will be reflected in our attitudes and actions, bringing about peace and healing in us individually and ultimately throughout the world. I see subliminal aspects of this Christ and this consciousness in all the religions of the earth. It is a principle, not a person. This is the only true Rapture: the rapture of joy and wholeness that comes when all people behave as a family. That is the paradise on earth that will come about, no dragons or bowls of blood required. If you are waiting for the Rapture like a teenager waiting in line for a ride at an amusement park, I beseech you to open your eyes and see the world around you.

It's worth being left behind in.

APOCALYPSE WHEN?

If you want to see a born-again, Second Coming–believing Christian become truly animated, just mention the Rapture and Armageddon to them. I've seen mellow believers get a fire in their eyes when they talk about being spirited away in a twinkling of an eye to leave the rest of humanity behind for the tribulation: the conflict between Christ and Satan and the judgment of the dead. But far from being exciting or transcendent, I think that this enthusiasm represents the true cancer that is eating away at modern Christian tradition, threatening to turn the entire faith into a backwater of superstition and infantilism.

The impulse behind the zeal for Judgment Day is essentially a nihilistic expression of passion for death and destruction and a hatred for the world because the Christian believer *doesn't think it will happen to him.* It's cut of the same cloth as the enthusiasm for hell and the devil: a malefic kind of glee for the burning of the world and the casting of souls into perdition (to which the believer will, of course, remain immune). It's as if the small community of the

"Rapture ready" are the nerds in high school, enduring the wedgies and humiliations of the jocks and popular kids (the rest of the world), while telling themselves the day will come when Jesus comes back and stuffs their persecutors into lockers. It's a narrative that has Christians as victims, nonbelievers as the enemy, and the Second Coming as the settling of scores.

Believers will howl that they didn't create their so-called reality of apocalypse, that it's just the way things are and that it's all in the Bible and confirmed there. But if we are to approach faith and religion honestly and fearlessly, we must file this form of Second Coming alongside hell and the exterior, horned devil as human creations that mirror our own ugliest instincts and needs. Look at some of the passages that started it all, the Revelation of John, the last book of the Bible. This account, almost certainly a dream by an addled recluse in a cave some ninety years after the death of Jesus, has become the sacred text of the Second Coming for many. Revelation 1:7 reads, "Behold, he [Christ] cometh with clouds; and every eye shall see him, and they also which pierced him: and all kindreds of the earth shall wail because of him. Even so, Amen." (KJV)

Why would we not all rejoice upon the return of Jesus? Isn't weeping, wailing, and gnashing of teeth associated with hell? Is Christ's reappearance cause for unimaginable rejoicing and celebration, or for terror and suffering? If the latter, why would anybody be eager for Him to return? Is He making a list, checking it twice, and ready to find out who's naughty and nice? I don't mean to sound cynical, but some impious language is in order to get us to reconsider the image of God we Christians project to the world: a so-called loving God and Savior who may sneak up on us as a thief in the night, catch the world off guard, and kill all but an elect few with merciless wrath and bitter rage. What does the fact that so many people look upon this scenario with eagerness say about Christians? How insecure are we that we look forward to mass murder and torture on a scale that dwarfs Stalin's purges?

THE BLANK CHECK

The way I see it, there are four possibilities:

1. Christ will return as promised in Revelation, with fire and blood and war.
2. Christ will return in body but without the war and suffering parts.
3. Christ will return only as a principle, Christ in man, ushering in a new era of Consciousness.
4. Christ will not return at all, as either man or principle.

I do not accept either number one or number four. The God behind the idea of a corporeal Second Coming that acts out the dreadful predictions in Revelation would have to be a savage psychopath. Were it possible for God to have such human emotion, He'd probably be offended by these fanatical portrayals. In general, the God we're presented with in the Abrahamic faiths suffers from multiple personality disorder. He is good and evil, loving and hateful, forgiving and unforgiving, pardoning and vengeful. He is portrayed as paranoid and schizophrenic in Scripture and thus has become a reflection of the duality of the tree of the knowledge of good and evil, which that same body of Scripture says Adam was forbidden to eat. From this perspective, forbidding man from eating the fruit of that tree makes perfect sense; waking to duality and separation from man's true nature has planted in us a religious schizophrenia. As for Christ returning as a physical being without the tribulations, I don't see the point. He would have to preach His message all over again, likely to the same result. I have wrestled with these images for years and come to my own conclusion that they are man-made superstitions birthed of fear-based theologies that originated long before Jesus or His disciples walked the dusty streets of Palestine.

Believers have been talking about a Second Coming for over two thousand years now, since not long after Jesus' death. Masses of people have waited and continue to wait for this coming. There is a thriving industry in speculation and discussion about the Second Coming, last-day prophecies, Armageddon, cataclysmic catastrophes, and ominous events that supposedly foreshadow the end-time. The ardor for such subjects has fueled countless best-selling books and films and filled the coffers of many churches and Christian organizations. The end of the world, it seems, is big business.

These speculations and the paranoia behind them are not new. They go all the way back to both the Old Testament book of Daniel and other prophetic writings as well as the thoughts and writings of men who were close to Christ, including the Apostle Paul, who claimed to have had a dramatic spiritual encounter with Him, and John the Beloved, a blood relative of Christ who is believed to have written the book of Revelation, and may have been hallucinating on some of the herbs and mushrooms he scavenged for food while exiled on the Isle of Patmos, where he is said to have written the Apocalypse. And yet wars are not new. Natural disasters and plagues have been present in every generation both before and since Christ. Earthquakes and tsunamis have occurred across the planet for millennia, but only recently have we had access to media to report what seems to be their increase. But are they increasing, or do we simply know more about disasters and portents because of instant media access? What makes war, famine, or flood any more religiously significant today than three thousand years ago?

The Second Coming is every generation's religious blank check. It's a risk-free doctrine: charismatic leaders can claim "we are in the end-time" or last days to simultaneously terrify and exhilarate their flocks and find proof in a scan of Google News, but they never have to make predictions or be held accountable for them. It's always "You don't know the hour," but when the hour doesn't come, no one questions the doctrine. They just assume God decided to wait—again. He's been waiting for twenty centuries, while each generation decides that its wars, diseases, and political upheavals are unique, that they *must* be the signs everyone has been waiting for. The Second Coming is the ultimate bait and switch.

A SIGNIFICANCE ADDICTION

I believe that our fascination with a violent Second Coming stems from our desire to have significance in our lives. We create drama and trauma in our worlds to elevate them—and us—above the mundane: Godzilla, Dracula, conspiracy theories about 9/11, invasions of sovereign nations, UFOs, and on and on. Society seems hell-bent on trauma and drama to keep its emotional adrenaline pumping and to keep us feeling like players in a great drama rather than men and women going through the motions and movements of our daily lives.

We seem to be addicted to adrenaline highs and dependent on those who sell the stimulants. Violence and horror in movies, along with national and international news, have become a multibillion-dollar industry that beams misery into our homes, laptops, and theaters. If art imitates life, then some of today's art is an indictment of the church's lack of positive affirmation and influence on the culture. I hold the church responsible for abrogating its duty to enlighten and elevate all people—to remind us all that there is nobility in carrying out the day's routine and bringing light and love to the people around us, and that our higher destiny is to be the proxies of Christ in Consciousness, spreading peace and hope. That's a far more significant outcome than any UFO theory, even if UFOs are someday proven to be real, as many believe them to be.

But with many Christians focused on their own lack and petty natures, no wonder we hope the world will end soon. Even Christians who live abundantly want out. Why, if life with Christ is so fulfilling and peaceful, are we so obsessed with breaking out of this spiritual jail or asylum? Why the overwhelming preoccupation among many Christians with escaping the present world, that is, according to 2 Corinthians 5:19, already reconciled to God through Christ: "that God was reconciling the world to himself in Christ, not counting men's sins against them. And he has committed to us the message of reconciliation"?

Sixty million copies of the Left Behind series have been sold worldwide. Do that many people believe that God will abandon billions, banishing them to His customized torture chamber to writhe in hideous torture and agony forever? How did we ever get to the place where our God is a God of hate and paranoia? This is the true cloud that Christ is coming through: a cloud of ignorance and self-delusion broken by self-awareness. I now see Jesus in those clouds in ways I had not before.

For me, the Second Coming is when all mankind is transformed by the rise of Christ Consciousness, thus rediscovering our power as healers, educators, and makers of peace. This makes more sense, both scripturally and spiritually. I want people to be alert to their own responsibility for transformation, not alarmed at the possibility of every event being a harbinger of damnation. Alertness makes you wary, while alarm makes you weary. I am very much aware of what's happening around me on the earth and how I should relate to it, but I am no longer alarmed by it. Again, some preach Christ, while others preach crisis.

A CULTURE OF LOATHING

There are those who preach that we are now entering the final stages of a civilization that will ultimately be destroyed, ushering in "a new heaven and a new earth" when the "former things are passed away. And I will make all things new" (Revelation 21:1, 4–5, KJV). These voices use Scripture to cite the secularization of life, terrorism, nuclear weapons, the Israeli conflict, other Middle East tensions, the growing emphasis on sex, violence, materialism, and so forth. Apocalyptic predictions hold a mirror up to the specific fears of each age.

However, a careful study of history reveals that civilizations have never been destroyed by divine fiat. Usually, great civilizations are not even brought down by external conflict. Civilizations have risen and fallen based on the rise and fall of the human consciousness that guides them. The fall of Rome, for instance, was an inside job. Its own decadence, corruption, and sloth set the stage for the Visigoths to raze the empire. If humanity is in danger today, it is not because of the wrath of God but because of the darkness in men's minds. That darkness both flows from our poisoned perception of God and shapes how we spread this message (mess-age) to others.

In reality, the fascination with the end-time has always been based on a culture of loathing for one's fellow man. It is built on the duality that is inherent in the division between God and devil, good and evil, Creator and creation. In man's world, there is us and the other. Christians see themselves as an armed camp of the elect few who see the truth and will be taken away from this vale of tears at the appointed time: everyone else is damned and therefore damnable. Since the cloistered belief of the faithful cannot be questioned, any who do not share it are lesser beings. This makes it easy for believers not only to accept that billions will die in fire, but to even look forward to it with a kind of sick and immoral anticipation.

In America, some of this paranoia is fueled by ugly racism. Religious conservatives, goaded by their political allies, love to cry that America is being invaded by foreigners who blow down Twin Towers, or by waves of Hispanics who will soon wield such voting power and numbers that the people who have controlled this country for hundreds of years may one day become the minority, and may soon lose their hold on power. This is more "other" thinking, creating new demons out of modern times, ignoring that America is a country of immigrants, and ignoring that each newcomer is a Christ in essence, no different from the most pious minister, priest, rabbi, or imam. The insistence that the world is about to end becomes an excuse for ignoring immigration, the environment, war, and poverty. People are not necessarily blind, just blindfolded. Religious ignorance and arrogance have blindfolded millions, and books like this one are designed to remove the blinders and expose them to both the light and darkness of a system in stagnation and stultification.

The danger is not in the nuclear bomb, the envelope filled with anthrax, the suicide bomber, or the political movement in an Islamic country. It is man, who is frustrating his inherent potential by ignoring his spiritual essence, his immutable and permanent self and soul. The Kingdom of God is within you and all of humankind; the Christ Mind lives within each of us. We are all Christ's resurrection in consciousness and spiritual culture. Our divine nature is inherent in us. We are intrinsically, originally godlike. Unfortunately, most people have been lulled into spiritual amnesia and are struggling to recall their divinity, while religious systems insist they forget it or replace it with a pious replica. Where we should be celebrating our universal reconciliation to God and our divine nature that makes us all equal children of Divinity, we focus on separation, unworthiness, and conflict between beliefs that differ superficially. Instead of centering our lives around the divine nature that binds us together, we base our thoughts and actions on status and being "right" about dogma, about which brand of God is better. I call this "penance envy." Whose penitence or penance system is best or which religion has the grandest form of dues-paying membership and penance or penalty for sin.

This is where the church has failed the planet. We are here not to convert the world to Christianity but to remind or convince people of their inextricable connection to the God who created us all. This was the message and ministry of Christ on earth through Jesus. The world is a place of infinite possibilities. Every moment contains opportunities to shape or reshape the Kingdom of God outside our religious minds, something already happening but which many refuse to recognize. The division, loathing, and fear that dominate our consciousnesses take shape in our exterior world as we seek more to dominate than understand one another. We have created a kingdom, and it rarely rises to the level of heaven on earth, but in the broader realities and hopes, we can change this and actualize a "heaven on earth" reality.

A GREATER VISION

We tend to look at the temporal things that surround us and find our identity only in them. We find proof of our worthiness in our possessions or lack of same. If a tsunami strikes a nation, it must be because those people were unworthy of God's favor and protection. We focus on the outward to the exclusion of all else, so it's no wonder that we decide this flawed world would be better brought to an end. But this is a false, incomplete identity. It is in this tunnel vision that the illusions of poverty and limitations of the human mind originate and subsist.

The illusions lie to us first and then they lie about us, sending inaccurate messages and signals into the universe that we then ratify in consciousness, causing them to materialize in our lives. This is why the Second Coming of Christ in Consciousness is so important—and it is also why the concept has been reduced to such elementary fear mongering and superstitious pandering as the Left Behind mentalities and end-of-the-world frenzies. The Coming of Christ in Consciousness demands that we grow as a people, that we leave behind primitive tribalism and legalism and our preoccupation with material signs of status. That's hard work and leaves us no sense of superiority to those other humans whom we *need* to demonize in order to feel better about ourselves. It becomes much easier, then, to retreat into the idea of the Second Coming as an exterior event, like the climax of a Jerry Bruckheimer movie with all the special effects Hollywood could muster.

Many people use the biblical passage about Jesus coming in the clouds to suggest the physical and literal return of Christ to this planet to wage a huge cosmic war against the devil, whose works Scripture says He already came and destroyed. I used to view the Second Coming this way, and preached it with the rest of them. Yet what if this is not some futuristic event but one we can experience daily—and have been for the last two thousand years without recognizing it? What if the Second Coming of Christ is spiritual, not literal? What if the Apocalypse is Christ in Consciousness, coming not to destroy man's civilization but to destroy our old dualistic way of thinking, to destroy the religions that get in the way of the true message and meaning of the soul? Is this too boring to be true? It may not serve our hunger for significance and existential drama. But must we continue to ratify world war, global conflict, and the proliferation of human hatred and violence for the sake of feeling like life is more dramatic—or needs to be?

What if we reinterpreted the entire Second Coming scenario and saw it as a fresh and evolving revelation of the Christ Principle as well as the Christ Person? I pray for that new vision of God and Christ. I wish that we could see Jesus the Christ standing alone, without all the Old Testament visions of religious legalism and prophecies of doom that thunder from far too many pulpits in our country. This siege mentality and paranoia that the so-called religious right seems to relish (especially during election season) is an insult to the dignity and eloquence of God, humankind, and the universe.

YOUR SECOND COMING NOW

What if every time a cloud arises in your life, it is a kind of Second Coming for you, a fresh awakening?

In the Bible and in our lives, clouds portend difficult times, storms in life or nature, and the hiding of a clear path. Sometimes clouds represent glory and clarity. Yet it is through these very clouds, this Second Coming or "calming" of Christ, that the Spirit of God is teaching us how to walk by faith. Clouds or difficulties are opportunities to grow, to discover new strengths we didn't know we had, to evolve to new levels of love, will, worth, wealth, and health. Again, if there were never any clouds in our lives, we would have no need or use for faith in God or ourselves. The Old Testament prophet Nahum wrote, ". . . and clouds are the dust of His feet" (Nahum 1:3, KJV). Difficult times are a sign and often a reminder that God is there and good is possible and probable. What a revelation it is to know that sorrow, mystery, wonder, bereavement, and even suffering are actually the clouds that come along with the God Consciousness and are natural but not eternal. These clouds allow you the chance to have your own Second Coming—your own resurrection and enlightenment of self-discovery. They are the opportunity to both renew and re-know your self. They *rain* on you the life-giving moisture of self and soul realization.

We must learn to interpret the mysteries of life in the light of both our knowledge of God and our ignorance of divine realities. It is essential that we do not delude ourselves into thinking we know the mind of the Universe or the nature of the divine plan for each event in the world.

Rather than panicking over the present situation in the Middle East and jumping to some eschatological conclusion suggesting the literal end of the world (something we have done for decades, especially since 1948, when Israel was founded), perhaps we should learn to experience a Second Coming of mind and attitude as we repair our past misinterpretations. Leave the Rapture to fiction and create a world in which we would be happy and proud to be "left behind." One of my Jewish rabbinical friends is working on a book titled *Left Behind and Doing Just Fine*. I love his approach and agree with his premise.

Is there anyone except a Second Coming of Christ in your cloud? If so, it will only get darker until you get to the place where there is no one else there but God *with* you, *in* you, and *as* you. This is the Christ Principle and Consciousness, regardless of any religious affiliation or affirmation. I am not saying that Christ's resurrection will not occur, or hasn't—just that it will and can occur through you and, hopefully, in you. Resurrection from the dead simply means both metaphorically and metaphysically awakening to and arriving at your *authentic self*. It is not pie in the sky by and by. It is both the now and new you, fresh and sparkling in spirit, mind, and body.

When you stop asking for permission to "be," and you stop apologizing for who and what you are, you are born again and resurrected. You don't need to be a Christian or belong to any other religion to do this. In fact, it is better if you dismiss or suspend, at least temporarily, your religion in order to attain this reality in spirit. I do this consistently and find it to be life changing in the most powerful and positive ways.

I am closer to the place of fuller "being" than ever before in my life, and this is the happiest and most fulfilling time I've ever known. I've never loved or enjoyed being me this much before. Again, we are not human "doings," but human "beings"! Who is the unedited you, independent of dogma, fear, and oppressive teachings? To discover and recover that person is indeed resurrection from the dead, from spiritual amnesia. Resurrection is simply remembering who you are and forgetting who you aren't. If that isn't salvation, nothing is.

CHAPTER FIVE

IF I WANTED RELIGION IN MY BEDROOM, I'D GIVE IT A KEY

Sexuality poorly repressed unsettles some families; well repressed, it unsettles the whole world.

—Karl Kraus, Australian writer and journalist

In the religious community I grew up in, human sexuality was denounced as dangerous, threatening, and a major human liability. I became both aware and wary of it as early as I can remember.

According to Old Testament Scripture, God's first command to humankind was to be fruitful and multiply. The first assignment for man was to increase in number. This mission could be fulfilled only through the act of sexual intercourse. So from the very outset of the human race, there has been a divine mandate to be sexually active. God has sanctioned sexuality. Why, then, do Christians and most other religions have such a problem with sex?

There will always be something sexual about God and creation: procreation. In our subconscious reality, the act of doing the same through sexual intimacy is a replication of the divine act of creation and our connection to it. One of the other early Old Testament references to multiplying is recorded in Genesis 8:22: "As long as the earth endures, seedtime and harvest, cold and heat, summer and winter, day and night will never cease." Everything starts with the "seed." One way or another, intentionally or not, most religions equate sexuality and sensuality with spirituality.

GODDESS WORSHIP

The word *venerable* originates from the name Venus, the Roman goddess of love and sexuality. We get the word *venereal* from the same word. In the ancient religion of Rome, prior to its Christian-ization, one could say to the equivalent of a priest, or potentate, "Your Excellency, the Venereal Bishop," and be perfectly correct and not viewed as derogatory. In the worship of the goddess Venus, sexual acts were expected, respected, and revered. In many ancient religions, polygamy and incest were normal, and temple priests and priestesses participated in elaborate sexual rituals (like Rahab, in the Old Testament, who happened to be a distant relative of Jesus). In some cases, orgies in the temples were common acts of worship and were considered highly spiritual. To these people, life not only originated in spiritual genesis, but from physical genitals. Both were revered.

Christianity, however, repudiates such practices, considering them pagan, heathen, and immoral. The other Abrahamic faiths, Islam and Judaism, do so as well. Covering and hiding the body—especially the female body—is fervently practiced to this day among the more conservative and orthodox of these religions. But why did this become the case? Why was an act seen as not only fundamentally human but deeply spiritual turn into something shameful, unclean, and obscene? I believe it has a great deal to do with the ancient patriarchal society's desire to suppress the influence of women as healers and midwives, but that idea did not originate with me. To go beyond it, this unhealthy, unholy demonization of sexuality is yet another manifestation of our misunderstanding God, leading to a debased image of everything human. When we can separate the most essential acts and drives of humankind from our supposed divine selves and turn them into sins, we set the stage for self-hatred and for allowing others to control us based on our sense of shame.

This has led us to be ashamed of the sexual act and to condemn it in public, and for many self-proclaimed "moral leaders" to commit the most grievous acts of hypocrisy behind closed doors. It has also led to a vile, hateful campaign against homosexuals, who during the most challenging times in my ministerial life showed themselves to be the most giving and Christ-like of God's children. They reached out to me with compassion and healing love even though at times I may have caused deep hurt and insult to them, along with the fundamentalist positions I took and taught against anything I didn't understand or feared. Let's take sex out of the church closet, shall we?

Sex Among the Saints

In ancient Greece, athletic events such as gymnastics, track and field, and wrestling were performed in gymnasiums with the athletes often nude, or nearly so. In fact, the word *gymnasium* comes from the Greek word *gymnos,* which translates as "naked." When someone's performance was extraordinary, he was considered a son or child of the gods. Here again, physicality and sensuality were considered spiritual and often took the form not only of heterosexuality but also homosexuality and bisexuality. Originally, all of these acts were a form of spirituality—of godlikeness. They were considered religious. Remember, Mount Olympus was where the Greek gods and goddesses resided. The Olympics were performed in honor of the gods.

"No aspect of our humanity is invested with more anxieties, yearnings, emotions, and needs than is our sexual nature. So, sex is a major arena in which the prejudice of human beings finds expression," wrote Bishop John Shelby Spong in his book *Living in Sin?: A Bishop Rethinks Human Sexuality.*

As I wrote earlier, I learned early in life that my grandfather, a Pentecostal preacher, was a womanizer. We like to call men (and especially preachers) that, while we seem to ignore the fact that there had to be women—in his case, numerous women—to womanize. Why do we never hear the term "*man*izer"? It seems that sexual aggression is attributed exclusively to men. As a single man, which I was until the age of forty, I remember being incessantly pursued by what we called "spirit-filled" Christian women. I was baffled that they seemed attracted to me in such strange ways and large numbers. I was always uncomfortable with this part of my public ministry and my role as pastor, traveling evangelist, and TV preacher. I found it disappointing that as a so-called anointed vessel of God, I was not respected more in my ministerial office.

My denominational discipline taught against such carnality, as we called it. Sexual promiscuity and even discussion of sex was frowned upon—considered worldly, secular, fleshly, and sinful. I was told it was because of my inward and unsanctified carnality that these persons were drawn to me. It was one of those "these kind come not out but by prayer and fasting" issues that I needed to rectify. I attempted to do this incessantly through the years by fasting and praying anywhere from three to forty days at a time. I did this for two reasons: to obtain what we called the "anointing" and to gain and maintain control over what I saw as my innate human sinful nature, bringing it under subjection to the Holy Spirit.

As I grew up in my strict evangelical Pentecostal community, I heard frequent talk of sex scandals—scandals that, according to taboo, were never supposed to be discussed, but were. Sexual sins were addressed loudly and regularly from the pulpits, especially by women preachers, whom we called missionaries. Our religion was so convoluted in so many ways that most of us lived in constant denial of what most would consider common sense. "Being human" was simply *not* acceptable and was forcefully denounced. As a young person, I often wondered why the constant emphasis on sexual purity, especially among saved, sanctified, and spirit-filled "saints," as we called them. I was totally oblivious to the preponderance of sexual sins among the so-called saints. We preached holiness, so I assumed that we lived in a holy manner, but it was obviously an unending struggle for even the most anointed to suppress their natural sexual urges.

My maternal grandmother changed churches because, we later learned, she had been propositioned by a pastor, a bishop in our denomination. Her father, my great-grandfather, who also was a holiness preacher, had twenty-six children, ten of them outside marriage. When I learned of and met child number twenty-six, he was eighty-six years old. Few in our family knew him or knew of him. Talk about a rolling stone! I actually met this dear gentleman through an invitation from his daughter to minister in their home church. I remember being fascinated by how much he looked like my great-grandfather and my uncles. Even though I was an adult by the time I met him, I loved him instantly.

RELIGION IS SEXUAL

From the huge child molestation scandal that has rocked the Catholic Church to sex scandals involving Protestant preachers from Jimmy Swaggart to Ted Haggard (former president of the National Association of Evangelicals, and a former ORU college mate of mine), it seems that more than ever, the story of sexuality and Christianity has become a case of "Do as I say, not as I do." Why the proliferation of sexual misbehavior among "holiness people," and especially among ministers?

In religious circles, human sexuality is a profoundly delicate and passionately avoided taboo. Christian religion is subtly built around sexuality and sexism. After all, it begins with God supposedly impregnating a teenage virgin already pledged to, presumably, a much older man. (You would think God would have chosen an uncommitted, slightly older woman.)

From the outset of our cherished religion, the God we are taught to revere and worship all but breaks up a home and commits a form of adultery. Adultery is one of the sins banned by the Ten Commandments, so is this an act of holy hypocrisy? If so, it was perhaps the First Hypocrisy in a landscape littered with faith leaders and "fathers" who professed sexual purity in public, only to engage in lewd and lascivious acts behind closed doors—until they were found out.

Christian theology teaches that Jesus bore our sins, actually becoming sin while not necessarily sinning, and yet the Holy Spirit is said to have impregnated Mary while she was betrothed to another man. How this actually took place remains a mystery we are expected to accept by faith. We can either assume it to have been "spiritual insemination" or that somehow the third member of the Trinity actually had physical intimacy with a twelve- or thirteen-year-old girl. Today that would be considered statutory rape. The Holy Spirit would have to be arrested and prosecuted for such a crime. The thought seems preposterous indeed. Imagine the perp walk, the plea, the press conference: "I did not have sexual relations with that woman Mary . . ." And then we wonder why our subculture has such a preoccupation—a forbidden yet irresistible fascination—with sexuality and the sexual act. It's not a mystery. The Christian religion begins with a sex act that we have spiritualized and sanctified as holy and even wholesome. Our very salvation is tied to it.

Christianity, like most religions, is a fertility religion founded on the idea of the sacredness of life, beginning with its procreation and followed by its consecration and preservation. Fertility religions emphasize the importance of life and its origins, beginning with human genesis, sexual or spiritual. Both are revered as the beginnings of life. From the start of the human race, there has been a preoccupation with how we got here and where we go when we leave. Since life comes through male and female conjugal relations, our first reverence and forms of worship revolved around sex and its attributes. This practice or premise precedes Christianity by thousands of years.

We are taught that we Christians are God's spiritual seed and that we should be randomly scattered over the planet in order to extend God's family on earth. We even call Christ the Immaculate Conception. And even though Mary had at least six more children (presumably by Joseph), she is still revered and worshipped as a virgin. Did her many sexual acts with her husband in later years simply not count, or would we rather ignore them?

THE SON OF WHOM?

It is interesting that Jesus' favorite title for Himself was "Son of man," not "Son of God." Jesus never attempted to make Himself a god or idol to be worshipped. He seems to have tried to draw people to the divinity within themselves. He is recorded to have said, "Is it not written in your Law, 'I have said you are gods' " (John 10:34). He's actually quoting the Old Testament's Psalm 82:6. He said this while discussing with His detractors whether or not He was God's son. I doubt He saw Himself as *"The"* Son of God as much as just one of millions of God's children—albeit one considerably more enlightened.

This is a sticky theological point, but since we're talking about sex and offspring, it's one that needs to be discussed here. In most of the faith traditions, there is reverence for Jesus, both the man and the myth. While Christians regard him as the Son of God, Jews and Muslims regard him as a great prophet and/or spiritual teacher, even messianic, divinely inspired—but very human. This is not unusual. Many religions have some mythological ideology of their founder being messianic, be it Krishna, Buddha, Muhammad, or one of the ancient Egyptian or Sumerian gods or goddesses.

In Greek mythology, we have Zeus, who regularly impregnated human women and produced demigods. In Christianity, we have Jezeus or Jesus (Yeshua or Joshua in Hebrew tradition), the product of a union between God and human. The parallels are fascinating. Gods having sex with humans and battling one another over same is nothing new. The legends go back thousands of years before Christianity. Somehow there has always been a connection between deity and desire, Creator and procreating. Sex, sensuality, and spirituality are part of divinely human expression.

Christ's point seems to have been that we are all begotten of God and offspring of the Divine Parent. He never claimed superiority; He claimed only that He had a deep connection to God and that He was a representation or example to us of the innate divine nature that lies within us all but that many of us ignore or neglect. He is called in New Testament Scripture "the first born among many" (Romans 8:29). If Jesus was the New Testament firstborn, then we are His siblings; sons and daughters of God in the same way.

To ignore or denounce this reality is a kind of blasphemy against the elegance of our created humanness. Finding a healthy, happy, and holy balance in the expression of this reality is where the wisdom of the ancients may well be our finest teacher.

THE MANY TEMPTATIONS OF CHRIST

But, some will protest, the life of Jesus itself contains many statements that make sexuality a sinful, forbidden act. It is true that Jesus indicated to some of His Pharisaic and religious dissenters that looking upon a woman sensually was tantamount to committing adultery. He spoke this to people who ritualistically stoned to death women (but not men) caught in the act of adultery. In those days, there was little social interaction allowed between men and women in the prevailing religious culture, especially in public.

Jesus actually began by saying, "You have heard that it was said to the people long ago, but I say . . ." (Matthew 5). Notably, this was not one of those "It is written" moments. Jesus was referring to the oral traditions of the Hebrew culture and religion. He was addressing one of the Ten Commandments but did not identify His reference as such. He seemed to address this issue as something handed down through both mouth and memory, not so much as the inspired word of God. He is recorded to have made the statement at least five different times in the book of Matthew. He was dealing with cultural and religious taboos of sex among religious leaders who use sexual suppression as a rule of law and control.

However, Jesus was also a man of His times, affected and influenced by the social fabric of a society shaped by the intertwining of Jewish, Pharisaic, and Roman cultures. It is unlikely that He believed that sexual lust was inherently adulterous; rather, He was simply reaffirming the limited, shortsighted religious mores of the time. As we know today, social, sensual, and sexual attractions to other human beings are as natural as breathing, eating, and drinking water. Sexuality is a normal part of a healthy human nature, and to suppress or deny our need for sexual pleasure—whether procreation is involved or not—is dangerous and completely out of touch with reality. It can and usually does lead to all kinds of perversions, and disruptive and destructive behavior and habits.

This abnormal separation of spirit from flesh was not always the rule in Christian thought. Hebrews 4:15 says, "For we do not have a high priest [a reference to Jesus] who is unable to sympathize with our weaknesses, but we have one who has been tempted in every way, just as we are—yet was without sin." The suggestion that Jesus was tempted in every way "just as we are" is a rather so-bering thought. Most of us don't tend to view Jesus as being human or normal enough to be tempted. It is difficult for most people to conceive of Jesus being tempted as the rest of us are, and still more difficult to imagine Him struggling with His human impulses. Yet Jesus was a man of the flesh; presumably He had sexual urges, bouts of greed and rage, desires to wield His power over men to achieve selfish ends, and other normal human expressions, impressions, and experiences. How does admitting that Jesus was tempted by the flesh make Him any less divine or any less worthy of our re-spect or reverence? In my view, this deeply human side makes Him even more worthy of veneration.

It's like the distance many in our Pentecostal world imposed toward Dr. Martin Luther King Jr. and other civil rights activists and leaders once we learned they smoked, drank, or may have had romantic encounters outside the marriage covenant. Did such ac-tivities make their powerful and prophetic work or worth less real or effective? Does one have to be perfect to be divinely inspired? I think the fact that such enlightened ones are as *flawed* (or pre-sumed so) as we are elevates them even more, because if they can surpass their perceived flaws to achieve greatness, so can we.

The issue has been recently raised concerning a possible sexual attraction Jesus may have had to Mary Magdalene, and that He may have been married to her and conceived a child with her. While I don't necessarily subscribe to that position (there isn't much convincing evidence outside of the novel *The Da Vinci Code*), I am not offended or distracted by it. Unless Jesus was either asexual or homosexual, He would have had the same attractions to women as any other heterosexual man would have had.

Remember, He died in His early thirties, a time when most men are still quite virile and sexually active. I'm sure He would have noticed the beauty and bodies of the women that Scriptures say attended to Him (Matthew 27:55). I am not implying that Jesus lusted after these women, though He very well could have, since, as alluded to earlier, He was tempted just as we are. There is a difference, however, between admiring and desiring someone sexually and lusting after that person.

Jesus referred to Himself as the Son of man. That Jesus was the son of a human being is to recognize that Jesus had a definite human side, with lust, anger, greed, pride, jealousy, egocentricity, and all our manifest human propensities. The "yet without sin" clause means that even with all His temptations, He never offended God. It doesn't mean He never missed the mark in being a presumed "*perfect being.*" The Greek word for *sin* in this passage is *hamartia,* not *hamartano.* Hamartia means "to offend," while hamartano means "to miss the mark." Jesus probably couldn't offend God (none of us can), but He could—and no doubt did, in His humanness—miss the mark at least on occasion, as do we all. The perfect, bloodless, fleshless Jesus we insist upon and cling to today is a myth. The mythical being and the mystical man are not the same.

THOU SHALT NOT BE A HYPOCRITE

The divine connection between flesh and spirit should not be demonized, as we tend to do today in public. In fact, it is the empty pronouncements of sexual purity and abstinence by religious leaders, followed by their perversions and illegal, immoral acts in private, that are sinful, not the sex or sexuality itself. "Thou shalt not be a moral hypocrite" could have been the Eleventh Commandment. It is this suppression that gives rise to the fantasies and excesses within much of the religious community with regard to sexuality and sensuality. As said earlier, what you fight, you ignite, and what you resist, tends to persist! Denying one's sexuality or sensuality sometimes forces it to become the focus of attention in ways that can cause the development of unhealthy and destructive habits.

As referred to earlier, in John's Gospel, Jesus says, "I will not speak with you much longer, for the prince of this world is coming. He has no hold on me." He seems to be implying that the principal laws or laws and principles of His Jewish religion did not have the same sway over Him as they had on others within His community. It is also a reference to His resistance to the religious legalities of His faith community and how He did not necessarily feel beholden or subject to them. Notice again His words in Matthew 5, when He says, "You have heard that it was said, 'Do not commit adultery.' But I tell you that anyone who looks at a woman lustfully has already committed adultery with her in his heart."

The implication is that we in our humanness will break these religious laws either outwardly or inwardly, because this is how we function naturally. Jesus is not suggesting or encouraging promiscuity, just identifying the fact that, as humans, we like and lust sexually. He wanted to point out the reality of this human propensity especially to those Pharisees who were most unforgiving and violent toward anyone "caught" in such acts. Jesus insisted that His audience take a good look at their hearts and how they operated inwardly, rather than content themselves with self-righteous, false piety, something He obviously deplored.

We are bedeviled with false piety and sexual suppression today in the Christian, Islamic, and Orthodox Jewish worlds. Again, this has given rise to the abusive behaviors of many groups, especially the mistreatment and oppression of women in many fundamentalist Muslim regimes, as well as in some Jewish and Christian cultural disciplines. As a pastor, I remember counseling couples who complained that they felt they were treated as little more than sex toys in the marriage and that the only time their spouse showed them any intimacy was in bed.

One of my sisters had a fairly close social relationship with her beautician, who happened to be a gay man. When I questioned her about it, she simply said, "Oh, he's just one of the girls." I was amused at first and then curious about her casual response. It made for interesting conversation and observation.

An interesting observation I've noted in my further investigations into what was for me some rather delicate theological, social, and, to some, moral issues, is that often, gay men are socially attracted primarily to females but sexually attracted primarily or exclusively to males. It is often the opposite with straight men, who often prefer other males socially and turn to females only for the purpose of sex. Homosocial relationships are often stronger than homosexual ones and homosensual attractions are often as common as heterosexual attractions are.

This points to an even more insidious problem within both the evangelical culture and our society at large: the selective application of accusations of homosexuality. Most men tend to enjoy "hanging out with the boys." They attend sporting events, play golf, fish, and hunt. Some hang out in bars, clubs, and even church almost exclusively with other males. Again, this is often their social, not sexual, preference. Even Jesus seems to have spent most of His adult life with twelve rough and rugged men who were often away from their wives and families for sometimes weeks at a time while they traveled with this itinerant preacher for nearly three and a half years. Jesus presumably had no marital or parental obligations and may not have necessarily been sensitive to those of His disciples. Scripture makes no reference to any specific complaints regarding husbands' absences from home and family for the sake of the ministry, but I'm sure there were some, especially from the wives and mothers and possibly the children.

We can assume that when the disciples had or took the chance to leave the traveling posse and spend time with their wives, they would fulfill marital responsibilities, including sexual intimacy. It appears, however, that they were with Jesus for most of that three-and-a-half-year period. We can assume as well that they enjoyed being together: laughing, talking, teaching, and ministering with Jesus and one another. Scripture suggests that Jesus shared very close ties with Peter, James, and John, and that John—called the beloved disciple, and who was possibly a first cousin—would actually lay his head on the Lord's chest with a kind of more physical intimacy than the others. Few would assume this to be a suggestion of homosexuality, but it is obviously homosocial and homosensual.

There is little suggestion that a roomful of women looking at other females parading across walkways in fashion shows, often scantily dressed, is abnormal, sinful, or socially unacceptable. The same is true of men in weight-lifting or bodybuilding competitions. This is done around the world, where the sensual same-gender attractions and fascinations are expected and celebrated without suspicion. But in religiously suppressed communities, these practices are considered dangerously carnal, worldly, and tempting to our sinful nature. I heard this all my life and preached it as well. I was made to believe that if I didn't create a sense of shame and sin around the sexual impulse, the people would become lax, unguarded, and more prone to violate the moral codes of our religious discipline. In other words, they would disobey and yield. How dare they act like humans being human?

Sensual and sexual expressions are natural and created by God. But we, in our religious paranoia, are taught otherwise, causing us to deny and denounce this aspect of our fuller selves. The potency of sexual desire can become consuming, and in our fundamentalist communities—built around control of every aspect of the followers' lives—nothing can be allowed to become more powerful than the impulse to do what the leaders command. So "sects appeal" becomes more important than sex appeal. This demonization of what should be a sanctified act leads to secret fantasies and pathological, deviant, and destructive behaviors that might otherwise be avoided. It's time to bring sexuality out of the Christian and religiously oppressed closet. Homosectarianism is much more threatening to me than homosexuality. Same-sect relationships can be far more intimidating culturally than same-sex relationships.

On Homosexuality

And with that not-so-subtle segue, we move the discussion to the bête noire of today's religious right: homosexuality. As has happened throughout history, oppressive regimes find a group or cause on which to project their own insecurities, fears, and hatreds. The Nazis had the Jews. At one time in America, African-Americans were put in this category for abuse, discrimination, and mistreatment. Today's most pernicious, hateful Christian groups have gays, lesbians, bisexuals, and transgender people to pounce on.

The late Jerry Falwell encapsulated the Fundamentalist Christian view of homosexuals when he said after 9/11, "I really believe that the pagans, and the abortionists, and the feminists, and the gays and the lesbians who are actively trying to make that an alternative lifestyle, the ACLU, People for the American Way—all of them who have tried to secularize America—I point the finger in their face and say, 'You helped this happen.' " Sadly, there are millions of American Christians who believe this. I used to be one of them. But I cannot allow this chapter to conclude without taking this warped, unfair, and maligning view to task.

According to the Bible legend of creation, Adam was a kind of hermaphrodite, having within himself both male and female. In order for the female to have been extracted from him, she would have to have been part of his essence. And if God created Adam out of Himself, as Scripture suggests, then we must assume that God the Creator and Adam the created were bisexual or pansexual beings. We have said before that God is neither male nor female but beyond and above the idea of gender. God is It, or "I Am." Here again we tread upon shaky ground theologically, but isn't that what we're here to do? Clearly, when one talks about sexuality as an authentic expression of spirituality, one cannot exclude homosexuality.

Some Christians also draw their bigotry against gays and lesbians from the ancient story of Sodom, the corrupt city that God supposedly destroyed in the first recorded instance of urban renewal. Well, the historical context is rather different. The word *sodomite* is the Hebrew word *quadesh,* and it means holy, consecrated, or specially dedicated—a sacred person. It comes from the word *qadash,* which means "to pronounce or declare clean and sanctified, morally or ceremonially." *Qadesh* usually referred to a male devotee. Why? Because Sodom was a very religious city, though by Jewish standards idolatrous. There was no official Judaism at the time—no Moses, Ten Commandments, Pharisees, priests, or rabbis. Abraham himself came from a culture and family of mysticism, spiritualism, astrologers, and soothsayers.

This ancient world was spiritually rudimentary, superstitious, extremely religious, and feared and worshipped many deities. The Israelites had strong, though antiquated and rustic, concepts of deities, demons, and devils, called in the Old Testament "goat idols" or "goat gods," as discussed earlier. The cities of Sodom and Gomorrah themselves were not necessarily rife with homosexuals; they were cities that put great stock in the sexual and sensual as a form of spirituality. Sodom in particular was a smug, pious, religious town filled with arrogance, exclusion, pride, self-sufficiency, and self-righteousness. The people there were known to be inhospitable and intolerant of other religions. It was a hateful place that bears a strong resemblance to today's most delusional, exclusionary, bigoted Christian communities. So Sodom has far less to do with homosexuality, or even sex per se. It was actually a place of deep intolerance, religious bigotry, and anger. But in our Christian obsession with all things sexual, we have made it a symbol of what we see as homosexual perversion and sexual corruption. As always, we look in the mirror and see the demons we have created and fear most.

THE ERROR IS OURS

According to Bishop John Shelby Spong's book *Living in Sin?*, in which he discusses the scientific and theological sides of human sexuality, some primitive societies looked upon male same-gender eroticism as honorable, not a perversion. The homosexual man was often assigned the role of shaman, medicine man, or holy man. He was sometimes thought of as a kind of third sex and was given permission to wear female clothing and perform acts within the liturgy that outside the liturgy belonged to the female domain.

I am not suggesting this should be the acceptable norm today, but it is surely not a coincidence that the fine arts—especially music, theater, and dance, which we use so much in worship—should be populated by a large percentage of same-gender-loving people. I often wonder what the church would be like artistically, musically, and creatively if there were no same-gender-loving people. Many of our greatest and most sublime songs and music have been both written and performed by men and women of homosexual or bisexual orientation, even if they kept it hidden for fear of prejudice.

Some of the most gifted, gracious, and spiritual people I've known in the faith community have been people who identified themselves as gay and lesbian. I used to ask God myself how and why He chose to use people considered so profoundly defiant of the moral codes of the church. It was inexplicable, until I realized that the error was not God's. It was mine and the church's. I have come to the place where I no longer question but welcome, affirm, accept, celebrate—even consecrate—these dear and precious people both within and outside the church walls.

When I hear a religious leader or preacher proclaim that sexual orientation is a choice, not a birthright, I assume that the accusing person believes that he, too, has bisexual tendencies and has chosen to resist and reject them as he insists the gay person must. To insist that gay people choose to be gay is to assume that they (the accusers), too, have the same tendencies, temptations, and propensities but simply choose to concede to them. Perhaps they are actually identifying themselves and the validity or legitimacy of same-gender attractions as natural. Generally the ones who scream the loudest have the most pronounced issues with the thing they are denouncing so vociferously.

HANGING WITH SINNERS

One of the most gratifying aspects of my journey to Inclusion and my separation from the more reactionary elements of my beloved fundamental, evangelical, and Pentecostal communities has been how the "fringe" congregations of Christianity—the so-called New Thought, Unity, Unitarian, Religious Science (Science of Mind), gays, lesbians, transsexuals, and people with AIDS—have embraced me with open hearts. Shortly after I lost my megachurch, I attended a progressive-church conference meeting in Phoenix, Arizona, where most of the congregation were people in these rejected and condemned groups. At this lowest point in my life, after I spoke about Inclusion, the congregation rose as one and affirmed the washing of my feet at the altar by their bishop, a same-gender-loving woman. It remains one of the most deeply moving and healing moments I have ever experienced. The lack of judgment and the presence of pure love and belonging were extraordinary. That is what I feel for the gay community.

People like to accuse me of reaching out to them, something I do proudly; but in reality, they reached out to me, and I am simply and gladly responding to their warm and hospitable initiation of our growing mutual admiration, relationship, and covenant of respect. *They* were the Inclusionists I was claiming to be.

Jesus knew this feeling well and acted upon it. He had a long history of spending time with the perceived sinners of His day, those who were rejected and marginalized by the orthodoxy of their society, in the same way that homosexuals and others are rejected by many in today's Christianity. To illustrate:

> Jesus entered Jericho and was passing through. A man was there by the name of Zacchaeus; he was a chief tax collector and was wealthy.

Tax collectors were considered crooks and traitors who used their professional authority to bilk the people out of money by intimidation and thievery. It was the most despised profession of the ancient Jewish world, not unlike the IRS today.

> He [Zacchaeus] wanted to see who Jesus was, but being a short man, he could not, because of the crowd. So he ran ahead and climbed a sycamore-fig tree to see him, since Jesus was coming that way.

I think all religions are trees (or elements of truths) that people climb in order to get a better look at the transcendent, but few of them give or even have a clear view. Usually, people see just the leaves, or doctrines, of that particular brand of faith, filtering, screening, and often jading their view.

> When Jesus reached the spot, he looked up and said to him, "Zacchaeus, come down immediately. I must stay at your house

today." So he came down at once and welcomed him gladly. All the people saw this and began to mutter, "He has gone to be the guest of a 'sinner.' "

Today that is one of the proudest compliments someone could give me. Matthew records Jesus as saying: "It is not the healthy who need a doctor, but the sick." How will we ever reach the so-called sinners if we run away from them or run them away from us? We are not called to judge homosexuals or any other perceived "sinner," for we are no better than they are. But we *are* called to express the true Good News to them: their established and equal salvation in Christ and their participation in the Christ Principle, which exists for all human beings. By shunning gays, we communicate only disdain and hatred, isolation, alienation, and the rejection that has triggered reactions as violent and vicious as suicide or murder.

I am African-American. The overwhelming majority of the Pentecostal world is comprised of people who are also of African, or so-called Third World, descent. We, African-Americans in particular, have fought and suffered for *centuries* to be seen as equal to all others, not to be discriminated against or thought of as lesser beings because of our skin color, origins, or ethnicity. How, then, can we turn around and discriminate viciously against a group of men and women based on their inherent sexual orientation—based on *who they are or are not*? I cannot think of a more disappointing or obvious hypocrisy and betrayal of everything the civil rights movement, spirit, and principle stood for. Homosexuals should be judged, as all people, on the content of their character, and even then, loved nonetheless. Many African-Americans don't know that Bayard Rustin, the man who did most of the organizing of the great march on the National Mall in Washington, D.C., in 1963, where Martin Luther King Jr. gave his famous "I Have a Dream" speech, was openly gay. He also organized the earlier and lesser-known march on Washington in 1948. His sexual orientation had nothing to do with his purpose and destiny with regard to his influence on both Dr. King and the civil rights movement.

Casting the Last Stone

The choir at my former church, New Dimensions, in Tulsa, sang regularly at a community center that caters primarily to gay, lesbian, transgender, and bisexual people and families. We also extended a welcome to the new pastor of the Metropolitan Community Church in Tulsa, which ministers specifically, but not exclusively, to God's same-gender-loving children. Just as humans can have biological homosexual children, so can God.

If Dick Cheney's daughter, Newt Gingrich's sister, and Oral and Evelyn Roberts's son can be gay, so can millions of God's offspring. Because these people are born to straight parents, should they despise their parents or love them less than the heterosexual children born to these same parents? Should these parents love their gay children less? Should they subject them to the humiliating, abusive "conversion" programs that purport to turn gays back to heterosexuality, while succeeding only in creating corrosive self-hatred? This does happen in some families, and I have certainly seen some deeply Christian families torn apart because a child "came out." But in most cases in my experience, the parents tend to love their gay children all the more because they realize their child stands to be marginalized, persecuted, and discriminated against. When TV talk-show host Larry King asked Billy Graham how he would respond to having a gay child, Reverend Graham's response was, "I would love a gay child all the more."

I began to realize the dangers of the Christian intolerance for homosexuality when I received a letter in February 2007 from a couple who were leaving my church and decided to write me to explain why:

Pastor, my wife and I will be leaving the church. I did not like what happened in service last Sunday. If we are not going to call sin a sin, then why preach God's word? I know we are not perfect, but I do not practice sinning. The gay lifestyle is a sin according to God's word. I love you, Pastor Carlton, and my church, but we can't act as if the gay lifestyle is ok. It's not ok. I will keep you and the church in my prayers.

Here was my response:

I was surprised and disappointed to receive your short note advising me of your decision to leave the church. You have walked with us thru so very much and have been so warm and faithful over the years. You have served faithfully with us, and we will always be grateful to you. You will be missed and always loved, sin or no sin.

Jesus said the wheat and tares must grow together. He was gentle with sinners, and His blood was and is powerful to remit them all. He always loved sinners, including you, and so do I. Jesus taught to love and forgive, not judge and resent. I thought you were far more advanced spiritually than you are.

I'm sure you will find a place where your spirit feels more at ease with those you view as righteous. I hope you don't happen upon any sinners there, especially gay ones. If you do, I hope you will do as Jesus instructed us to do: love and forgive. That's what He always did.

I am glad He didn't run away from all the sinners He encountered or resent those who loved them. He said, "You who are without sin cast the first stone!"

Scripture, or as you call it, the word of God, also says: Let everything (I'm sure that also means everyone) that has breath praise the Lord. It didn't say "unless, of course, you're gay." Your attitude disappoints me, as obviously mine and the church's disappoint you. All I can say is go in peace and serve your Lord. God bless you. I pray that you will one day have a change of heart and love unconditionally. Remember, Paul said, "Where sin abounds, grace abounds all the more."

I still feel nothing but love for that former parishioner and the others who have left my church over the years in conflict with my teachings, which identify what I see as the often narrow, destructive, and false teachings of conservative Christianity. But I also see that attitude for what it is: placing one's own wisdom over God's. In Scripture, we are commanded to love all people, regardless, including sexual orientation or activity, because we are all flawed, as some would perceive us, and yet God's children. Human parents love their children even as those children, as criminals, march to the gas chamber or electric chair. Nothing is greater than parental love. Yet some of us would rather cherry-pick passages from Leviticus, a book filled with absurd dictates and prohibitions about human activity, as a justification for deciding that we will love and accept just *some* of God's children. The book of Leviticus also forbids us from eating lobster and shrimp. What shall we do with all the shrimp and lobster lovers in our churches? What makes a homosexual person less inherently moral or just than a straight one? In my opinion, homosexuality and human sexuality are first cousins. We are so busy casting stones that we fail to see them falling back on us. I would like to live to see the last stones cast at our same-gender-loving siblings. Just as being born with darker-colored skin doesn't make me cursed, being born with what many consider an out-of-the-norm sexual orientation doesn't make one cursed.

THE PRICE OF PRINCIPLES

The Metropolitan Community Church was founded by a Pentecostal man who could not find acceptance within the regular Pentecostal churches of the 1960s, so he sought to create a place where same-gender-loving people could find a common nonjudgmental forum and worship God without being vilified. The people of New Dimensions went over to welcome the new pastor of MCC, and it was because of that act that I received the Dear John letter from my parishioner. It is precisely this attitude that makes the MCC church, assemblies, and organizations like them vital. Not only do some people not want gays in their churches, they don't want them in any church! They don't want them to exist. What in that attitude is remotely like Jesus or the Christ Spirit?

The denial of homosexuality ties in with the denial of human sexuality in general, a common practice in Christian and fundamentalist churches. It contributes to a litany of societal ills: high rates of divorce and teen pregnancy, the suppression of sensible sex education, the closeting of sexual or homosexual impulses by adults who wind up suffering either public disgrace or legal penalty, as happened to Jimmy Swaggart and Ted Haggard, among others. In fact, I would say that the more a preacher or moral leader talks about the evils of sex or homosexuality, the more likely it is that he's engaging in exactly that behavior in the shadows.

Remember Zacchaeus the tax collector? That story has more to say:

> But Zacchaeus stood up and said to the Lord, "Look, Lord! Here and now I give half of my possessions to the poor, and if I have cheated anybody out of anything, I will pay back four times the amount."

He didn't say that he would cease to be a tax collector; he just said he'd be an honest, sensitive, generous, and benevolent one. Jesus did not require that he give half his possessions to the poor, but the man's heart was evidently pricked by his encounter with the Christ Principle manifested in Jesus, and this inspired benevolence in the man, as it does in all of us when we encounter Christ in consciousness, which indeed is a much deeper experience than simply becoming, as it were, a "Christian."

> Jesus said to him, "Today salvation [*soteria,* meaning "rescue and safety"] has come to this house, because this man, too, is a son of Abraham. For the Son of man came to seek and to save what was lost."

What Jesus came to restore was the preciousness and sacredness of all life and of all living beings, saint and sinner together. He said that the man was also a son of Abraham. To Jews, that was the same as saying He was a son of God the Creator, a fellow brother of the same spiritual worth. The inference is, of course, that they were both (as we are all) children of the Ultimate Parent.

This is what happens when we hang out with *sinners*—in this case, people whom the majority of the Christian Church considers to be sinful. Instead of judging and excluding (or pontificating to gays how wrong they are and how the proper therapy can "fix" them), our goals should be love, understanding, and inclusion. I'd rather lose friends and parishioners than lose my mystical and mysterious love for all of humankind equally, even those who reject that love out of what seems right to them.

I don't feel sorry for homosexuals. I feel sorry for those who simply cannot find it in their hearts to love and accept them—or anyone else who disagrees with their desperately held beliefs. I don't expect people to affirm everyone or everything. But, as followers of the Christ Principle and Person, we have a mission to perceive and accept everyone as loved by God and redeemed by His Christ. We don't have to love someone's lifestyle, hobbies, habits, or hungers; we just get to love the person. It is a privilege to do so.

Salvation has nothing to do with accepting Christ. Salvation is Jesus coming to our house without an invitation. The Christ Principle existed long before the Christ Person appeared in the flesh as Jesus. We are told in Scripture that Christ is the lamb slain before the foundation of the world. This would mean that the idea of Christ was pre-incarnate. In other words and worlds, the problem was solved before it ever appeared! The question was answered before it was ever asked! We are all saved (safe) and loved in oneness with God, including those who violate what we see as "right" in the bedroom, ballroom, or boardroom.

SAME-SPIRIT MARRIAGE

Homosexuality is not going away. To those who see it as a moral issue, I remind you that you cannot *legislate* or teach morality. The best you can do is to *demonstrate* it. When it comes to heterosexual marriage in America, we haven't done a very good job of demonstrating moral fidelity or covenant—not even Christians, who reportedly have a higher divorce rate than atheists. It seems that rather than preach about the perceived evils of others, we need to be getting our own sexual and spiritual houses in order.

The knee-jerk reaction of many religious people to same-sex marriage is indicative of the innate paranoia present in our theology. Is God freaking out over homosexuals or the divorce rate in America? If so, can't He do something about it without state legislation or a constitutional amendment? So far, He hasn't brought down hellfire on courthouses where gay men and women are lining up for marriage licenses.

The more attention you bring to an issue, the more tension you create. In other words, what you make the issue, becomes your idol. Thousands of same-sex partners live in our neighborhoods, and have done so for years, and we would have never known if attention had not been drawn to it. Scripture suggests it is better to marry than to burn with lust. I have always assumed that verse to be a reference to a heterosexual covenant, but in principle, it can as easily apply to same-sex lust or love, which can be and often is a love as covenantal in spirit as that of heterosexuals.

If we kick the homosexual community to the curb, insisting that they ignore their sexuality, we will be contributing to the proliferation of some of the most destructive practices imaginable in our culture. I, too, am more comfortable with marriage remaining a covenant between a man and a woman, but to "get real," I'd rather see same-gender-loving people enter a monogamous commitment than live the promiscuous and noncommitted life in which many people, both gay and straight, engage. How in the world could an increase in stable, loving families in this country be anything but a blessing?

Traditional marriage is in no way threatened by the growing homosexual culture any more than gay people eating in the same restaurant with straight people affects the service, taste, or nutritional value of the meal. Same-gender-loving people making a civil or marital commitment are no more a threat to the larger society than interracial marriage or live-in lovers enjoying the benefits of common-law marriage are. Marriage is more threatened by Christianity's own unhealthy repression of normal sexuality and its willful ignorance of issues such as pregnancy, birth control, and marital fidelity. We should be getting our own house in order before trying to order the sex lives and love lives of those who are our brothers and sisters in spirit if not in orientation.

Laws allowing same-sex marriage or civil unions are already being passed, and life will go on as it has since women's suffrage, Prohibition, school desegregation, African-American voting rights, and abortion on demand. Perfect love casts out fear. Love, not sex, should be the center of our lives. Sometimes our reactions are more derisive than our actions.

PART TWO
WHO'S CREATED IN WHOSE IMAGE?

God makes three requests of his children: Do the best
you can, where you are, with what you have, now.

—African-American proverb

CHAPTER SIX

NEW VISIONS AND VERSIONS OF GOD

Dream lofty dreams, and as you dream, so you shall become.
Your vision is the promise of what you shall one day be;
your ideal is the prophecy of what you shall at last unveil.
—James Allen, eighteenth-century English writer,
poet, and philosopher

Don't allow all my sometimes cynical—and to some, critical—comments about my fundamentalist evangelical Pentecostal upbringing to leave you with the impression that I regret my experience or in some way disregard it or even disrespect it. I both love and respect deeply my religious and cultural background and its inherent values and virtues, even as I am learning to adjust what seems extreme, inaccurate, or inappropriate about much of it.

I trust that perhaps by now you are beginning to see faith not as something static that you adopt when you're young and then defend with eyes and mind closed until you die, but as a dynamic system of evolving knowledge; an ongoing experience of divinity and transformation. Or maybe you just think I'm bound for hell, and you dismissed this book hours ago but can't put it down altogether. I can live with either result as long as I'm true to myself and my vision. And vision is the heart of this chapter, because what I am trying to impart to you as a part of our dynamic journey is the truth that it is your responsibility to discover your own vision and version of God.

Remember that we said God was different for each of us based on our experience but identical for all as the Original Consciousness? Your perception of God is that unique vision, and its unique quality gives your life meaning. If your perception of God and your own divinity compel you to become an artist, a police officer, or a political or religious leader, then you are fulfilling your personal vision according to your personal version of God. You're not necessarily living according to someone else's estimation or appraisal, and that is freedom. So let's take a look at how to develop your own vision and version of God by starting with a look at what it means to be awakened—or as some evangelicals would term it, "born again." It's a phrase we hear all the time, but what does it really mean?

BORN FREE?

Part of being born again is obtaining a newer vision and version not only of God but of yourself in relationship to Divinity, including your own. The Greek word for "again," as used by Jesus with reference to being born again, is *anothen,* the source of our English word *another.* It means to be born anew or from the beginning. We are obtaining or experiencing *another* opportunity, choice, and challenge for change and evolution.

"Born" is the Greek word *gennao,* from which we get our English word *genetics.* Adopting a new vision and version of God is a *regenerative* act of, and in, consciousness. It means that, in effect, we get to know God and ourselves all over again for the first time, thereby breaking the rule that says you never get a second chance for a first impression. In this sense, I disagree. It is one thing to experience God through an intermediary as I did in my youth—through rites, rituals, rules, prayers, prohibitions, and a loving but smothering culture. It is quite another to reexperience God anew or from the beginning, before there were laws, rules and regulations, temples, cathedrals, shrines, synagogues, and mosques. This happens not as a matter of time but of personal spirit or consciousness. It would be not only a reconciliation but also a recall or reconnection—perhaps even a reconstruction spiritually. The new vision of God is a version without religious rituals and rites, one beyond ceremony and performance-oriented pieties. It is God direct and unfiltered, live, coast-to-coast, and conscience to conscience.

God from the first is the alpha God that existed before our Bibles and other sacred writings put Him (It) into a form humans could comprehend and mold according to our fears and fantasies. That brings up a few thoughts about the Bible. With this book and my last, I received many comments and questions from people who were taken aback that I would defy all of Christian tradition using the very book that is at the heart of the faith. My very good reason for that is this: the Bible is not a Christian book. It may (in part) tell the story of the life of Christ, the principle and the person, but it is not Christian in the sense that it does not promote the myths and doctrines that have become more central to the Christian religion than Christ Himself. The Bible is a book of history and allegory. It is a book of myth, magic, and miracles that sheds light on our varying interpretations of God and the actual, unfiltered wisdom of Jesus. That is why it has value—not to mention its unquestionable impact on world and, especially, on Western culture. I respect the Bible, but inspect it as well.

It must be noted that the God the biblical Adam knew existed before there was anything to read. This nameless God, the "I Am That I Am" One, existed before words, ideas, or images could be put into language or literature. This is the God that we rediscover when we become born again, not into Christianity, but into Christ Consciousness—a human aspect of God and the purest form of our concept of good. This is also why our powerful rational minds are barriers to knowing this God and why we are much closer to Him or to our divinity when we are in a state of noncognitive prayer or meditation. Our reasoning minds are all about words, symbols, and images. Language and literature are hallmarks of our civilization, and we are rightly proud of them. However, we tend to focus on what words can describe but not necessarily define. The true reality that we call God is beyond words and man-made images, so our rational minds falter when we try to grasp Ultimate Divinity or Its expression in terms of names or descriptions.

AN OBSOLETE GOD

I was having a conversation with the daughter-in-law of one of the most prominent Jewish businessmen in the state of Oklahoma. She made a statement to me that I never thought I'd hear coming from a person born in Israel and very committed to its culture, spirit, and continued existence. She informed me in no uncertain terms that she'd never taught her children about the hateful, fearsome, and terrorizing God of her religion; she had "fired" that God (her words). I was first amused and then deeply moved by her passionate and unexpected confession.

I remember reading a passage in the newsletter of Dr. Darnise Martin, founder and CEO of the Quest for Meaning Institute in Los Angeles, that said, "Spiritual wisdom, inner knowing, nondualist thinking, and faith itself cannot be proven through empirical reason. These gifts come from cultivating a relationship with the Divine, and surrendering to it."

It is impossible to know God totally or absolutely, but we *can* know Him, Her, or It individually as particles and participants in and of Divine Essence. We can know or experience the Divine or less divine in us on a unique and personal level, far beyond another person's experience or philosophical leanings—and indeed we must.

To know God is to experience your true and authentic self. Such knowledge is the only way we can move forever beyond the limited, hateful, intolerant, controlling modes of religion that dominate our world stage and compel us to do things to ourselves and one another that a dispassionate observer would find insane. Only when we leave behind childish fairy-tale visions and versions of God can we be free and grow beyond self-imposed human limitations.

Just as we changed the gender reference of God from male to female, we will now begin to refer to God by the depersonalized "It." Doing so will make room for greater imagination and ethereal expansion and growth.

The old version of God has grown obsolete and irrelevant. We need to accept the new one. Not a different God in reality, because God is beyond time, space, age, and change, but a clear and truthful interpretation. This new vision and version of God needs to occur in the sense of our personal image (imagination) and perception. It is a kinder, gentler God, one without wrath, with whom we can walk and talk in the cool of the day, as the first Adam is said to have. This is a God who forces us to grow up just like a parent lets his or her children make their own mistakes in order to mature and come into their own. We must let go of the idea that God will be there to pick us up and intervene when we make poor choices; that is not Its role. If this were actually God's role, It would look rather incompetent, given all the misfortune in the world (an argument that some atheists use to claim God's nonexistence). Instead we are expected to be grown-ups, to rely on God for inspiration and wisdom, energy and guidance, but to build our own futures and co-create our own realities. This God is not a genie ready to emerge from a lamp to grant our wishes or to punish those who disagree with us—or It.

According to the Christian and Jewish Bible, Adam and Eve hid from the personal God after they disobeyed Him, but God came looking for them anyway. He didn't abandon them. The only reason they were banished from the garden was so they wouldn't eat from the "tree of Life" and live forever in that fallen state of consciousness. Again, these stories and legends are mostly allegories written to make a larger and more practical point. To read them any other way is almost nonsensical and irrelevant.

BE STILL AND KNOW

Psalm 46:10 reads, "Be still, and know that I am God; I will be exalted among the nations, I will be exalted in the earth. The Lord Almighty is with us; the God of Jacob is our fortress." The past few years have been times of transition for me and the people who have chosen to speak affirmatively about Inclusion. Transition is always jarring, sometimes wrenching, and painful. Much has taken place that I'm still learning to fully understand and appreciate. It has been my experience that wisdom never stops coming to us, honing and humbling us, even if we live to be one hundred. So, rather than try to puzzle out all the intricate workings of the Divine intent that has set me on my path, I gain greater insight and peace if I allow myself to be still and know while not being afraid of *not* knowing.

Author Erwin Lutzer wrote, "Often we assume that God is unable to work in spite of our weaknesses, mistakes, and sins. We forget that God is a specialist; and is well able to work our failures into Its plans. All things work together for good to those who love God and to those who are called according to Its purpose. Realizing this is the first step to our healing." As we see, there is much to be learned from analyzing the original language of the Bible, first Hebrew or Aramaic, then Greek. The Bible was supposedly written by the people who lived in the time of Christ, the Apostles, and the Old Testament prophets.

The word *still* is *raòphaòh,* a derivative of the primitive root *rapha,* which means to "mend," "cure," "heal," "repair," or "make whole." The figurative context is one of lying down, resting, relaxing, being passive, and listening to one's inner voice. You can never really know God inwardly (the only way you really can "experience" God) until you heal your self from the wounds of frictional, fictional, and fractional living—wounds typically inflicted by our conflicted religious culture that tells us we are inherently unworthy, unloved, and bound for hell unless we're lucky enough to hit the faith lottery by doing something to appease our capricious God.

Bishop E. Bernard Jordan says in his book *The Laws of Thinking: 20 Secrets to Using the Divine Power of Your Mind to Manifest Prosperity,* "The understanding of who we are starts with the understanding of Who I Am." We are all created in the image and likeness of God as Consciousnesses having a physical experience. Many of us think human form is the essence of man, but the real you is *not* form. The real you is without form. It is a spark of Divine Consciousness emanating from God; you are Divine in nature. Your human form is a physical shell for that consciousness, and it differs only slightly from other human beings based on genetics. However, the true essence of who we are is "I Am," and that is eternal and unchanging. Rediscovering that truth and embracing it is the beginning of healing, or "being still." Being still is reconnecting to the Original Intention, which is God.

This is why it is so important that we be still to know. To know what? Well, the vision that comes from opening our intuitive, non-linear mind to the Mind of God gives us a panoramic vision of all things and possibilities. Consider how narrow your mind can be when you limit your perception by binding it to a single form of thought. If you see everything through the prism of a limited, conservative religious viewpoint, you may see only a small sliver of reality: your church, your community, fellow believers, the politicians who ascribe to your views. This is abstractly restrictive. But when you let go of such controlled and manipulated views and see all of existence not as a threat to your beliefs but as a confirmation of healthier, freer thinking, you are given liberty to view all existence from 360 degrees. From this clearer vantage point of wholeness and accuracy, you will know "I Am God," or that indeed you are god.

KNOWLEDGE IS FREEDOM

Knowing God, or thinking you do, doesn't mean labeling Him, It, or Divinity. Naming God is confining It to the parameters of the name or label you have selected. The author of the New Testament letter to the Hebrew Christians wrote that he who comes to God must believe that He is and that He rewards them who diligently seek Him (Hebrews 6:11). In the Hebrew Bible, the word *know* comes from the Hebrew *yaòda,* meaning "to ascertain by seeing." The term suggests intimacy, to know, by observation, care, recognition, designation, instruction, and consideration.

In the book of Genesis, God is recorded to have said to Adam and Eve that they were free to eat from any tree in the garden, except the one that suggests any of the other trees are bad, wrong, or inappropriate: "The Lord God took the man and put him in the Garden of Eden to work it and take care of it. And the Lord God commanded the man, 'You are free to eat from any tree in the garden, but you must not eat from the tree of the knowledge of good and evil, for when you eat of it, you will surely die.' " Metaphysically, trees represent truths, so God was commanding Adam and Eve not to adopt a belief system that placed one truth over another or make covenant with opposing allegiances and loyalties. When God, in the narrative, told them they would die, I interpret that to mean, "You will start judging each other based on your human evaluations and estimations of right and wrong, good and bad, black and white, duos and duals . . ." and that would be the beginning of their end as spiritually sensitive and satiated beings.

Duality is death, because it implies conflict. Once you chain your consciousness within a prison of opposing forces, you lose sight of the inherent oneness of all things and people. It becomes much easier to oppress, persecute, or kill your brother when you think he is not your flesh at all but a detached being who has nothing to do with you or you with him. The same is true of all other living things.

According to Scripture, freedom is not a suggestion; it is a birthright. It was the first biblical command to humankind from God, who wanted us to be free of our limited manner and means of thought. However, our carnal, unenlightened Adamic nature feels compelled to defend the image we have of God and good, and trying to manage these images has caused us to systematically put the planet in peril. This is why science, for all its wonders, cannot save us from ourselves. It is a system of knowledge in which meaning and essence play no part. Whether you believe in God or are an atheist, you cannot deny that the empirical facts of science have nothing to do with whether or not freedom and good are real or worth destroying ourselves for. Meaning must come from the individual in touch with his or her own soul. To discover how to recover our sanity and freedom, we must know ourselves from within.

ON BIBLICAL LITERALISM

One of the hallmarks of the limited mode of thought by which we define God and therefore restrict our freedom is an obsession with interpreting the words of our holy books or Scripture to be absolute truth. Anytime that knowledge and a version of the truth are considered to be absolute, fundamentalism is the result, whether the arena is Christianity, Islam, Judaism, or any other religious faith, as well as atheism, conservative or liberal political views, even evolution or intelligent design. Anytime our minds are closed and there is no room for dissent, we are on a slippery slope toward stagnation.

Consider this biblical verse from Galatians 5 in the KJV along with my clarifications about the ideas in their original language:

> Stand [*steko,* "persevere"] fast therefore in the liberty [*eleutheria,* "freedom, chiefly moral or ceremonial liberty, to go about without restraint, exempt from rules and regulations") wherewith Christ has made us free and be not again entangled [*enecho,* "possessed by, quarrel with"] with a yoke [*zugos,* "obligation"] of bondage [*douleia,* "enslavement"].

There are myriad ways one could interpret that passage, depending on one's prior biases, fears, and desires. That is the nature of sacred texts: they serve as a mirror held up to the nature of the society that beholds them. In a New Thought interpretation from the perspective of Christ and God as Consciousness, not superheroes, this text exhorts us to remain free of ritual and dogma that define and constrict our spiritual lives or selves. Most Christians (me included, prior to my personal awakening) tend to interpret the passage in one way, especially if they are unaware of the more accurate translation of the original Greek. You could interpret it thusly: "Be born again and do not become a slave to sin or other belief systems and religions outside Christianity." This passage could be seen from a perspective of duality and fear as a call to reject faith traditions that do not match one's own, something that is all too common today.

New Thought is about rethinking God and how you relate to universal divinity. That means rethinking how your sacred texts influence your life—and if they should influence it at all. Even if you reject any literalism or direct interpretation of the Bible, Koran,

Torah, or other text, other people who may come into your orbit
will be influenced by them, so you must know how to make your
case and stand your ground. Here's another Christian passage that
is more revealing than some might think:

> The ministry [*leitourgia,* "liturgy"] Jesus has received is as supe-
> rior to theirs as the covenant of which he is mediator is superior
> [*diaphoros,* "differing, surpassing"] to the old one, and it is
> founded on better [*kreitton,* "stronger, more noble"] promises
> [divine pledges or vows]. For if there had been nothing wrong
> with that first covenant, no place would have been sought for
> another. But God found fault with the people and said, "Look!
> The days are coming, declares the Lord, when I will establish a
> new covenant with the house of Israel and with the house of
> Judah."

RELIGION'S OWNER'S MANUAL

It is the perception of many people (not just Christians and Jews)
that God tells us what's best for us and then it is up to us to do
it—or else! That sort of enslaved thinking is the source behind
those bumper stickers that read, "The Bible [God] says it, I believe
it, that settles it." That type of closed-minded, willful ignorance is
chilling for the future of our world. God wants us to abdicate the
thinking and reasoning abilities with which we were created? That
makes as little sense as the idea that God shares wisdom and knowledge with us not inwardly or individually but only through a book
or Bible—sacred writings written by flawed men long after the
fact, colored by prejudice and exaggeration—and that we are supposed to live by these writings exclusively as inviolable writ and
eventually be judged according to them.

I often wonder why people who claim to have a relationship
with God through their acceptance of Christ presume that this

God with whom they have this wonderful and intimate relationship is confined and even initiated by a document several thousand years old, written by men who had no concept of a world outside their own and no idea that their words would be read and revered thousands of years later by people who weren't Jews. The same would be true of other religious disciplines, such as Islam: its sacred writings are read and revered by a billion or so people, but are less regarded by some five billion others.

It seems daring to say it, but that is nonsense. Each religion has its book or sacred script, and each church or denomination has its rules, regulations, and rites to further emphasize and execute the "instructions" laid out in the sacred books. The rituals exist for two reasons: to make the man-made versions of the perceived divine word seem more real, and to hold the adherents of the religion in bondage to the rituals themselves because they feel comforting and transcendent. But this is all illusion. In the broader spiritual realities, no rites or rituals are necessary to know God. *None.* Any religion that insists you can come to intimate knowledge of the Divine by any means other than stillness, self-awareness, and unity with Consciousness is deceptive. So-called holy texts are about religion, not necessarily about God. They are really owner's manuals for faith traditions. I am not denouncing them altogether, as I love the Bible and have studied it reverently all my life. But I don't view the Bible as the inspired word of God as much as the inspired word of men *about* God, as they perceive God through their often jaded, human perspectives. Again, I respect these so-called sacred writings. I would just like to see them read and placed in their proper, less idolatrous, place.

In the holy books of the Abrahamic faiths, we've been taught that we were created in God's image and likeness, born in sin and shaped in iniquity. Certain interpretations of these words suggest that we are intrinsically bad, sinners from birth, born with an automatic death sentence followed by eternal torture, weeping, wailing, and gnashing of teeth—the whole grim picture. Yet this same book teaches that God created us in *His* likeness? The standard seems double, unless God's likeness is one of eternal cruelty and evil. This perception of God makes us openly fear Him and inwardly hate Him. No wonder we hate one another; we're proxies for a God at whom we can never strike and for whom we feel a deep, unspoken, and often unacknowledged animosity.

We Christians, as do followers of other religions, presume that what we believe about God is relevant to all belief systems, and that ultimately our system of faith and religion will prove to be the correct one, by which all others should and will be evaluated and judged. This ideology is instilled within us from birth and has been deeply entrenched in Western culture for two thousand years. If you include Old Testament Jewish thought, add three thousand or four thousand years to that number. In any case, the operative idea here is that there is right and wrong theology—a right God and a wrong God. But this is an invalid premise. All versions of God are the same thing: *a human interpretation of the Universal Consciousness.*

The ultimate reality that some refer to as God exists in the most remote and extravagant reaches of Consciousness, the deepest recesses of the soul. This is the God and good beyond human limitations. It is the transcendent awareness of being, the peace that surpasses understanding. Judeo-Christian thought and philosophy are ancient and quite institutionalized. Yet finally, this ancient theology is being challenged in ways it could not have been challenged just a few decades ago. Its own adherents are challenging its relevance, and the result could be a faith tradition that is stronger, more relevant, more holistic, and more adult—*if* we can get past our primitive, childish, and superstitious ways of thinking.

THE GOSPEL ACCORDING TO . . . NOBODY?

The eight-hundred-pound gorilla standing in the middle of the church (at least in the Western world) these days is, "Did we get it wrong?" In other words, could the doctrinal positions that we have been so sure about be no more than an effort to impose order upon that which cannot be ordered except by Itself? Would God have allowed us to get the whole thing so wrong? I think the answer to that is, "Of course," but not ultimately. The next passages of Scripture suggest that for at least four thousand years, the Jews and early Christians who created Scripture got it wrong. Note this passage from the Old Testament, our Hebrew Bible:

> "It will not be like the covenant I made with their forefathers when I took them by the hand to lead them out of Egypt, because they did not remain faithful to my covenant, and I turned away from them," declares the Lord.

Declares the Lord? Says who? The Prophet said this, so how can we be sure it was God speaking? Only by faith, which makes it true only to the ones who believe and possibly irrelevant to those who don't. The passage continues:

> "This is the covenant I will make with the house of Israel after that time," declares the Lord. "I will put my laws in their minds and write them on their hearts. I will be their God, and they will be my people."

If you are a biblical literalist, you will view these words as applicable *only* to Old Testament Jews and no one else, including New Testament Christians. Then you have the Christians who presume these words from Galatians 3:29 refer to Christians as New Covenant Jews and therefore the heirs of Abraham's promise: "If you belong to Christ, then you are Abraham's seed, and heirs according to the promise." How convenient. On one hand, the Jews praise themselves as God's chosen, while on the other, the Christians insist through some linguistic parsing that *they* are the chosen. But what if neither was true?

These are the words of the Apostle Paul, a staunch and formerly Pharisaic Jew who was trying to connect his new non-Jewish European Christians to his Jewish religious heritage, which he links inextricably to his Jewish understanding of God: a separate, bad-tempered being who sits in judgment and plays favorites. For the sake of argument, let's assume that these next words, from Jeremiah 31:34, refer to all of humanity, not just Christians and Jews. Remember, they were spoken some five hundred years before Christ, and are presumed by most to be a prophetic reference to the New Testament age:

> "No longer will a man teach his neighbor, or a man his brother, saying, 'Know the Lord,' because they will all know me, from the least of them to the greatest. For I will forgive their wickedness and will remember their sins no more," declares the Lord.

What is to stop us from interpreting that passage in the most generous way possible: as an exhortation to set aside the mission to evangelize and to "teach neighbors" something they innately already know about—namely, God? From this perspective, which would completely shatter the evangelical concept of saving others (and good riddance to it), no one is a spiritual scholar. No one's interpretation of the Bible or any other book, including this one, is superior to anyone else's. We all possess the secret knowledge, only it's no secret, just forgotten. It is both sacred and secret, and yet we all know it in the deepest part of our selves and souls.

Only our hunger for temporal power compels some to go on

turning the phrases in books produced by men into eternal "calls to arms" supposedly proclaimed by God.

OVERCOMING LEGALISM

Literalism is one sin we must cast over the side of our spiritual ship; legalism is another. Legalism is a theological position that focuses on adherence to dogma, rules, regulations, and codes of conduct over all else, including love, grace, mercy, compassion, spiritual growth, and a personal relationship with the Divine. As practiced by the Pharisees, legalism was the principle behind Jesus' eventual arrest and execution. This was not necessarily an exclusively Jewish, racial, or cultural malady; it was a religious one. It was Pharisaic (separatism), something most religions are guilty of whether identified as such or not.

Clearly, when we are trying to grow beyond petty, destructive practices of religion toward more pure spirituality, legalism is a death sentence. Instead of inspiring the believers in a certain faith to follow certain moral precepts because they are central to personal spiritual development (in Christianity, these are supposed to include compassion, care for the poor, mercy, love, and justice), legalism simply demands obedience to the religion's "rule book" and "thou shalt not" prohibitive actions. It is a deeply controlling philosophy that precludes free thought and self-interpretation of a faith tradition and instead seeks to perpetuate itself by making people dependent on the man-made system of the religious organization rather than the unfiltered Deity.

I think legalism is especially dangerous to Inclusion and the kind of unmediated knowing or experiencing of God that I am talking about, because it makes spiritual life all about actions that take place in the outside world, whether that means fasting, praying, studying Scripture, or observing the Sabbath. Those are important actions for some people, but make no mistake: they are about human needs, not spiritual realities. Like labels, they are filters through which we allow ourselves to perceive a narrow slice of the spiritual whole. Theologian Keri Harvey writes, "Legalism is to seek to achieve forgiveness from God and acceptance by God through my obedience to God." But that statement is full of fallacies that represent the outmoded view of God that is tearing apart the world—as well as the lives of individual, conflicted Christians.

We do not need to be forgiven by God or accepted by God; that would be like you looking at your foot and saying, "You need to walk five miles today for me to forgive you for tripping last night." We are a part of the One Consciousness that is God, so there is no forgiveness or acceptance to be had. We simply are in God, with God, as God. As for obedience, living by constricted, legalistic rules is not obedience to God but to man *proposing to represent God.* For millennia, weak and impressionable humans across the planet have mistaken the words of a person who *says* he is speaking or writing for God in God's voice. With all due respect, Muslims who claim that they became suicide bombers because an imam told them that Allah told *him* to blow up the enemies of Islam are not on a holy mission; they are simply brainwashed into obeying authority without question. It is cultish and careless, ignorant and arrogant. The same would be true of a group of fundamentalist Christians who feel they are assigned by God to bomb abortion clinics or antagonize gay youths to the point of desperation and suicide. That is the danger of legalism. It is a tool of human power and human self-deception. If there were ever anything to be associated with what some call demonic, legalism is surely it.

If rituals clear your mind, bring you peace, and enable you to feel closer to God without anyone or any dogma standing between you, then that can be considered positive and perhaps helpful. But if you obey church instructions or follow intrusive teachings out of fear of damnation or blind obedience to habit, ask yourself, "Who am I obeying?" Chances are it's not God.

GOD 2.0

Clearly, if we are to move past this perilous time in history, a new image of God must come to the fore. This new image of God will transfer us in consciousness from the God we have invented (who can't even conquer a devil He created, and who cannot bring peace to our world, even though His son is billed as the Prince of Peace) to the awareness and presence of a holistic God who doesn't require doctrines or even churches: God within us, flowing into our consciousness without the need for clerics or holy books. Yes, this would completely upend the established system of churches and related institutions, and they won't go without a fight. Among other things, today's religious institutions represent trillions of dollars of economic activity and personal wealth as well as tremendous temporal power for those who run them. But a revolution every now and then is a good thing, even if it puts me out of a job, so to speak.

We have all the religious platitudes, accolades, and superlatives we can stand, but we don't see or experience the realities they suggest. In his book *Tomorrow's God: Our Greatest Spiritual Challenge*, Neale Donald Walsch writes, "All truth begins as blasphemy. The time to challenge our most sacred beliefs is at hand. If we don't challenge our beliefs soon, our beliefs are going to challenge us."

Today I assign you to freedom of thought; new thought about God and how you relate to divinity. Most of what we see today in our scientific and material world is the result of someone's idea materialized. It is inextricably connected to the original idea and is not necessarily perfect, just evolved to its present form. Tables, chairs, lightbulbs, automobiles, computers—the list goes on—are all lesser forms of more perfect ideas that have been reduced to materiality. So is the case with you. You don't have to be perfect to experience your inherent connection to God, the Original Idea. In fact, perfection is the last thing you should be seeking, because it implies an end to growth. Instead seek awareness and connection and evolution. I have been accused, mostly by Christians, of preaching a false gospel, but that is untrue. I am preaching the original Gospel, the one preached before religion corrupted it. The word *Gospel* doesn't just mean "message," it actually means, from its Greek translation, "good news" or "glad tidings." No, I am not preaching another Gospel, but I *am* preaching another God, one different from the God presented to billions for millennia. I am preaching a new vision and version of God. This reimagined God is not mean and paranoid. *He* is not nervous and jittery (God on too much caffeine?). *He* is not angry, vicious, and violent. *He* is not worried about the universe He created and has no plans to destroy it like a petulant child wrecking his Tinkertoy creation because it displeases him and starting over. This "God 2.0" is more like the one Jesus preached about and attempted to re-present (more than represent) in His day.

As Walsch wrote in his book, most of humanity believes that God decides which humans are included in the Word. We humans then form groups or clusters around what we perceive God has decided, and we call them religions or faiths. God then supposedly, through His word or our perceptions of His words, assures us that He will bring those he approves of back to Him in heaven, by telling them what is best for them. We then preach that what we perceive Him to be telling us is best. Those humans who are not included in our perception of those chosen by God become *them.* They become the *other,* the adversaries. They will not, under any circumstances, be part of the elect that God brings back to heaven. Nor will they be part of the chosen people *if* they don't do what is in accordance with what is best for the doctrine that *we* have created out of what we *think* God has said to us. So if you don't accept Christ, get baptized, and all the rest, you're suddenly unworthy to be part of the chosen or loved of God? Says who?

ON PANPSYCHISM AND PANTHEISM

We are not victims of creation, destiny, or God. We are cocreators or, as Scripture says, "joint heirs" with Christ. I like the way George Bernard Shaw once put it: "Life is not about finding yourself, it's about creating yourself." I would add that life is also about recovering ourselves, the part of us we misplaced at birth, thinking it didn't fit or flow here.

In the book *Can We Talk to God?*, Ernest Holmes writes, "We are on the verge of disclosing a spiritual universe and will ultimately conclude that what we call the material universe is a spontaneous emergence, through evolution, of inner forces which cannot be explained, but which must be accepted. How, then, can we doubt that the very mind which we now use is the Intelligent Principle from which all that lives draws its power to be and to express?"

Scripture teaches that all of humankind is created in the image or imagination and likeness of the Creator. This could mean that we are all images of an imagined divinity or divinities. If, in fact, God is omnipresent, then I Am is everywhere, everything, and ultimately everyone. God is the ultimate reality, the ground state of everything that is. In Judeo-Christian theology, God is considered One. Most perceive that to mean one single consummate entity, being, or essence. But I perceive God's Oneness to mean something more; something that does not actually conflict with traditional religious thinking. According to dogma, God is everywhere. That would also mean that God is in you, me, and everything, from the rocks to the book that you're holding. *Omnipresent* is not an ambiguous word. The broader truth of God may well lie in the concepts of panpsychism and pantheism that have existed for millennia.

As an Inclusionist, I find it both important and necessary to entertain the validity of an uncontained, unrestrained reality called God, a God that expresses Itself in all states, things, and beings. I once heard a pastor friend say that he didn't necessarily believe in one God but in over six billion gods all vying to be worshipped. This is deep wisdom in a sense, because the reality of God is that while there may be billions of ideas, ideologies, personifications, and expressions of the "Original Operative Intelligence," they all circle back to the same truth: *God is everything.* God and the cosmos are one, and everything in that cosmos is a different and important expression of God. That is pantheism, the marvelous idea that God is everywhere and every*when.* Panpsychism is a companion philosophy that says that as God is Consciousness, all things must share in some form of that conscious energy. This does not mean that rocks can think, at least as far as we know. It does mean that rocks and everything else are linked to the Consciousness that underlies existence. The entire universe is sacred; all the world is a church.

When I say that God is not a Christian, I mean that God cannot be limited or defined in reality by Christian rules or perceptions any more than It can be defined by the dogmas and stories of any other faith. This God can be experienced and expressed but not necessarily known. The experience is to me more valuable than the knowledge. What you claim to know can be debated. What you experience is yours and yours alone. It is not necessarily up for debate, nor does it need proof.

Again, we can neither prove nor disprove scientifically that the image of God most of us have exists in reality, and I no longer believe it is necessary to do so.

The closest to God any of us will likely ever get in this life is the

God who *we* are and who we hopefully will continue to become more fully. We are remarkably complex and intricate entities, with many mysterious aspects to our bodies and minds yet undiscovered. These mysteries are part of our elusive divinity. Yes, even our purported divinity is an illusion of sorts. Maybe everything is. If this is true, I am intrigued by it and am enjoying it immensely. Truth is not a destination, just a journey. Enjoy the trip.

LOVING THE MYSTERY

Human beings are mysterious. Being human is a challenge. Together they make up the magnificent mystery of our conscious existence. We have documented in our history books how human beings have affected the world, especially those we presume to be inspired by God. It is more difficult to do the same with regard to how *God* affects the world, except perhaps by humans presumably inspired by divine influence. This is because human beings can experience God, but they cannot truly know or define God.

The exercise often is one in futility. It's like trying to understand all the technical and scientific facts about the Internet while using it. We can experience and enjoy the Internet, but to know it intricately is, in most cases, neither possible nor necessary. Even many professionals seem to know the intricacies only in part; no one seems to know it all. The human mind cannot embrace what it means to be God, as most of us perceive God. We barely know how to express what it means to be human. We cannot view the world from God's perspective, though many preachers—especially Pentecostal charismatics, like me—have often presumed to do so.

We rarely admit it, but we cannot absolutely show where God's intervention was precise or decisive. We presume to know it based on Scripture, but in reality, it's speculative. If we could prove God's intervention absolutely, we would presumably be able to explain why God sometimes presumably doesn't intervene. This has always been a question in my presumed-faith-filled mind. I've always claimed to have strong faith, but my faith, which faith-filled minds presume, has always had serious and, I think, legitimate questions. I am not alone.

If God can be appealed to for intervention in only some instances, then we must also raise the question as to why He presumably doesn't in all cases, especially when asked or expected to. Can God stop a hurricane from barreling down on New Orleans? Can God stop a tsunami in the Indian Ocean before it kills three hundred thousand people? Can God stop the inevitable spread of an incurable disease? Can God dispose of a rival deity that millions of people revere? If God *can* do that, why would He not?

What seems more plausible is that we do not understand how God works any more than we understand what God is. I no longer see God as a "being" like us, just without human limits. God is not a genie who bursts forth from a lamp to grant wishes, no matter how much we would like to believe this. I am beginning to see all human beings as divinities like God, carrying within us the embodiment of a permeating presence, a living and thriving faith and force, love and grace, an energy operating through us via our intelligence, wisdom, vision, healing, and self-awareness. To me this is the epitome of faith, pure and nonreligious.

As Dan Allender wrote in *The Healing Path: How the Hurts in Your Path Can Lead You to a More Abundant Life*, "What then is faith? It is the childlike wonder in a story so good it can't be true, but deep down to our toes, we know that if it is not true then we don't exist."

TOMORROW'S GOD

If God is the same yesterday, today, and forever, then we don't necessarily need a new God, just a new understanding of the old one. We need an expanded concept, a deeper awareness of the Divine

Reality. We don't need an Old Testament God or a New Testament God or a Then and Now God; we need a clear and real God, unencumbered by the baggage we have heaped on It for so many years. We need to see clearly our human reasons for obscuring God then do away with them.

Our new version and vision of God is the same God who always was, is, and will be. It is simply not the God with which we have been presented over the centuries via our various religious inventions or conventions. It is the God we have forgotten, misplaced, or replaced with the human construct we have branded as God. We must recall the difference between God's creations and our own illusions—to know truth as God created it and as the Christ Principle embodies it rather than as man, in his fearful fantasies, has invented it. Only then can we know and/or experience God more totally, rather than selectively.

There is another way to live. Our differences do not have to divide us. Our contrasts do not have to become conflicts. We don't have to go along to get along. We can mind the same things without having the same mind about everything. This is the basis of Inclusion Consciousness. Walsch insists, "There is another way, yet we won't find it by looking for it." We will find it only if and when we create it. And we will most certainly not create it by remaining steeped in the old superstitions and insisting on adherence to empty and imposing rites. We will only get to our goal by opening ourselves to new ideas, new frequencies, and new levels of awareness and consciousness. New visions and versions of God and life can truly enlighten and re-enliven the world.

CHAPTER SEVEN

THE IDEA THAT CREATED A UNIVERSE

> When I admire the wonder of a sunset or the beauty of the moon, my soul expands in worship of the Creator.
>
> —Gandhi

C. S. Lewis writes in his novel *The Great Divorce:* "Our opinions were not honestly come by. We simply found ourselves in contact with a certain current of ideas and plunged into it because it seemed modern and successful."

When I say that God is not a Christian, I am also suggesting that It is neither Jewish, Hindu, Muslim, nor any other religion. Religion is a human product. Spirit is what we *are.* I am a follower of Christ in Person and Principle. That does not mean I am Christian in the sense that I believe the myths that I have already busted. I used to pride myself on being called a Christian, but no longer. Christianity has atrophied to become something far different from what I had hoped and believed as a child. I used to want the entire world to become Christian because I thought this would guarantee its salvation and make the world a happier and better place. These ideas were inculcated into me from infancy, as they are for millions of others, mostly by well-meaning people. I felt they were "right" because I had never known anything else and was never encouraged to question. I was plunged into a current of cascading religious and theological ideas and never asked if I could swim, but was expected to nonetheless. The same was true of my parents, their parents, and so forth, back to our slave ancestors and even before.

Obviously, adherents to other faith traditions and disciplines feel the same way that I did. Their version of reality is the right one because it's theirs. I think that most religious traditions tend to work toward peace and oneness in theory, but because of the duality in our psyche, the belief that no religion is better than another is incredibly rare. The opposite—smug self-righteousness and arrogance—leads to hatred, conflict, and war. But all dogma is just a human construct. Spirituality has little if anything to do with religion in any form. Religion can find expression through spirituality, but the opposite is rarely true.

Resurrection, or "resurrected consciousness," introduces you to a freethinking existence totally absent of fear, intimidation, paranoia, and hopelessness. Could it be that we so-called born-again Christians are not as free as we think or perhaps not genuinely born anew?

We have taken a rough and emotionally wrenching ride over some outdated ideas about God, Christ, and Christianity. Now that those are behind us and some childish myths about Christian thinking (for some of us) have been put to rest, it's time to move on to the next step in our evolution: examining new ways that we can explore the questions of reality and of God. For as you might expect, once you free yourself from dogma and power structures that constrict your ability to reason, you will see more clearly that God's essence is far more complex and subtle than what you've been taught in Sunday school.

IN THE HANDS OF AN ANGRY GOD?

When we come to God from this perspective, we see that our ideas about His supposed anger and rage are absurd. Does God kill, maim, and blame? Does He throw temper tantrums? Is He psychotic, with serious anger management problems? Do we need Jesus to protect us from Him, like a mother holding back an abusive father? If so, how is this God worthy of our worship? He's not. This confusing, frighteningly malign yet supposedly benevolent male entity is a dangerous lunatic who needs to be locked up or given some professional psychological therapy. Yet the evidence of our experience with the transcendent does not suggest that. The frightening image that has been misrepresented to most of the world is not the God of our hearts and hopes; it is our childish misperception of Him.

Yet this idea retains incredible power. The word *judgment* comes from the Greek word *krisis;* we get our English word *crisis* from it. The foremost crisis in Western religious conscience is said to be God's judgment. We struggle constantly between the image of a God of unconditional love and the image of a God of eternal judgment and damnation. But of the two, most of us clearly prefer to dwell on the latter. I saw much of this after Hurricane Katrina hit New Orleans in 2005, and I wrote an editorial in the *Tulsa World:*

> The recent disaster in the Gulf Coast states has put both America and the world on alert to the awesome and independent power and volition of nature. It is important to note that neither Hurricane Katrina nor any other natural disaster is or was an act of God, as some would erroneously insist.
>
> The hurricane itself was an act of nature; the breaking of the levees, which caused the terrible flooding of the city, was an act of human error and neglect. Again, neither should be considered

an act of God any more than normal or even abnormal bodily functions would be considered an act of God rather than an act of nature.

In Luke 13, Jesus dealt with those who insisted a particular tragedy in his day was an act of God, when he said: "Do you think that these Galileans were worse sinners than all the other Galileans because they suffered this way? I tell you, no! But unless you repent [rethink], you too will all perish. Or those eighteen who died when the tower in Siloam fell on them—do you think they were more guilty than all the others living in Jerusalem? I tell you, no! But unless you repent, you too will all perish."

Perception is the ultimate reality, but not necessarily the ultimate truth. If you perceive God as vindictive, vengeful, and merciless, then to you, God will always be just that, and this will become your pitiful reality. God is a good God and doesn't have or need to throw temper tantrums like a spoiled and undisciplined child in order to get His way or because He appears not to have it.

We should not attempt to reduce God to such mundane human variables. We were made in His image and likeness, not the other way around. What seems to have been a disaster of unspeakable proportions may very well turn out to be one of the greatest occurrences in the lives of the dear people affected by it. Tough times don't last, tough people do. This is not the time to point the finger. This is the time to extend the hand; not just a hand out, but a hand up!

I would now change one aspect of that commentary: I do think that we have remade God in our own image, casting It as rage-filled and violent, and that image is reflected back upon us in the world we have created. I think many Americans, especially right-wing conservatives and religious fundamentalists (I was one of them at the time), thought that by our putting George W. Bush in office and emphasizing family and/or moral values, God might have mercy on America and preserve us from His inevitable judgment. This expected or suspected judgment wasn't averted. Even 9/11 happened on his watch, not to mention the worst national financial crisis since the Depression. We've been at war for years and lost thousands of soldiers and suffered more than thirty-one thousand serious injuries. The eventual cost of the Iraq war is expected to be in the *trillions*. (Evidently, the other side's Islamic faith has not necessarily saved them from the horrors their supposed righteousness should guarantee, either.)

The only explanation many perceive is that God must be judging this sinful nation and world harshly, right? Wrong. *We* created this world, and we created its crises. As stated earlier, most evangelical preachers don't necessarily preach Christ, they preach crisis. They don't preach Good News, they preach judgment. They preach anger and retribution by God and reduce their congregations to shivering, terrified masses begging for forgiveness in the face of imminent damnation. This is abuse! Wars and natural disasters are not products of God but of man or natural forces like wind and waves. To conflate or confuse them with some sort of judgment is an act of evil manipulation and paranoia. It is also a slander against God, one that we will work to counter in this chapter. Who knows but that the negative energy our wars and hatred send out into the universe may somehow directly or indirectly affect the forces of nature. Remember, we're all energy, including our thoughts, attitudes, and actions, and we have impact whether we know it or not.

THE WORD IS NOT GOD

In an op-ed for *The New York Times* on May 13, 2008, columnist David Brooks wrote about the new transformation at the boundary of science and spirituality: "In unexpected ways, science and mysticism are joining hands and reinforcing each other. That's bound to lead to new movements that emphasize self-transcendence but put little stock in divine law or revelation. Orthodox believers are going to have to defend particular doctrines and particular biblical teachings. They're going to have to defend the idea of a personal God, and explain why specific theologies are true guides for behavior day to day. I'm not qualified to take sides, believe me. I'm just trying to anticipate which way the debate is headed. We're in the middle of a scientific revolution. It's going to have big cultural effects."

I think that kind of clarity of thought and expression in the face of such massive conflict and mystery deserves an "Amen!" I was certainly glad to see such innovative thinking go mainstream, because parochialism and territorialism are the bane of our spiritual growth. I'm also encouraged to see things like the John Templeton Foundation's ongoing effort to ask scientists, skeptics, philosophers, and theologians, "Does science make belief in God obsolete?" (You can view the fascinating answers at www.templeton .org/belief.) I'm delighted that questions like these are simply being asked. There was a time when asking them would have resulted in prison, loss of status and property, and even death in both this country and Europe. The new open-mindedness is a wonderful antidote for our long-term blindness.

In my self-appointed mission to reenlighten people to the reality of Inclusion and a God that defies our limited human perceptions, the word *God* has become a major stumbling block. In our very human tendency to give things labels and for those labels to become reality (*liberal, conservative,* and so on), we often forget that the label is *not* the reality. It is merely a kind of mental shorthand we use when spending an hour awkwardly describing our thoughts simply will not do.

We in this country and culture have chosen to give the name *God* to the Consciousness that we believe underlies all things. But

God can be a difficult and vexing term and an obstacle to clear thinking. This is in part because the English origin of the word comes from our concept of good, which demands a concept of bad to balance it out, and thus the battle begins. But just as difficult is the fact that the word is freighted with a multimillennia-long train of emotional and intellectual baggage that often derails attempts to engage in informed dialogue about the nature of God, especially between believers and secular people. Neither side can seem to shed the idea that God is an old bearded *white* man in the sky—a personal, anthropomorphic Deity—and so atheists can easily ridicule this concept, while believers cling to it. Any greater idea of God is quickly lost in the battle of religious concepts that follows.

But *God* is really just our word for that which cannot be named or fully grasped intellectually. When we talk about the Andromeda Galaxy, that is not its actual name, merely our small human label for something so titanic that it is truly beyond our comprehension. The same is true of God. God is a name, as is Allah, Jehovah, Yahweh, Brahma, Buddha, Krishna, or Christ. God is not *God*. God is That Which Is, and using the male pronoun *He* is just as vague and limited a description. God the being is not a word, but *He* or *It* is the Word. And in that distinction lies the beginning of our new, greater understanding of God as far more than an angry, frightening being who lives in the sky. It is the outset of our awareness of God the Force, God the Idea, God the Substrate of Consciousness. That is where we are headed in our understanding.

WHAT'S IN A NAME?

The word *God* suggests "good" in English and implies that all else is bad. That is precisely the kind of duality that represents our primitive nature. Good and bad gods, people, things, ideas, and realities leave those of us who value and evaluate all aspects of human spirituality—who see all interpretations of God as noble attempts to parse and comprehend the very nature of existence—in a constant argument, a quiet riot that eventually gets noisy and even nauseating.

Even now as I write this sequel to my book *The Gospel of Inclusion,* I feel somewhat guilty because I am happier than I felt I would be at this stage of my life, in light of the profoundly radical change and transition I've made toward both Christianity and God. At the same time, I find myself frustrated with the limitations of language to describe and discuss the concept and Is-ness of God, something in which I strongly believe. We are limited creatures who communicate in limited ways, so we are stuck with language and often by it. But what language does one use to convey the truth that God is all and everything, not a being who reflects our minuscule and comparably mundane nature? Do we talk about the One, a Presence, the Divine, or does it matter? Once we know that we are talking about a being who is more than being but reality itself, perhaps the words are irrelevant. Arriving at that understanding is our challenge.

Christianity is a religion and, according to the Christian Bible, God isn't. Jesus said that God is Spirit. The word *spirit* is *pneuma* in Greek and simply means "breath," "wind," or "air." The Hebrew or Aramaic (colloquial street Hebrew) term would be *ruach. Strong's Exhaustive Concordance of the Bible* defines *ruach* as "wind" or "breath"—figuratively, life, anger, or insubstantiality. It also means to smell or perceive. The concept of God being breath, life, or spirit is connected with the idea of invisible movement or motion. God, to the early Jews and to ancient humans, was something rational, alive, alert, and usually alarmed about something or someone.

The portrayal of God in human terms is a deeply natural phenomenon. However, it is also as much a relic of ancient ignorance as the idea that the sun moves around the earth. It is this abstract and immature concept of God that I am getting further away from, while hoping others will join me in the journey. It's not so much abandoning as it is expanding the notion and knowledge of the God concept. It is as President Bill Clinton said with regard to affirmative action in light of the advancements in race relations, especially with regard to African-Americans: don't end it, just amend it.

Our attribution of base emotions and human behaviors to the Creative Power inherent within the universe does nothing but debase God and mislead us about Its true nature and our true calling. Basically, God may be an Idea and a Word, but It is not any name or small anthropocentric concept we have attached to it. The sooner we let go of such a bankrupt concept of the Divine and accept how little we truly know, the better off we will be.

GOOD GOD ALMIGHTY

"Good Lord" is an expression we English-speaking Westerners use sometimes in disgust, irritation, astonishment, and disbelief. It carries many differing connotations and perceptions. I often say, "It's all good because it's all God," which is to suggest that the ideas are inseparable, something I tend to believe. However, *good* and *God* are relative words that have different meanings based on who you are and your particular moral code, which is always based on whatever customs you are most familiar with. To suggest that God is good is itself a kind of reduction. To suggest that God *is* may be more accurate, if less satisfying.

As former president Bill Clinton could attest, the word *is* can be fraught with difficulty. Yet while this description may sound a bit generic, this is how I am beginning to view God—or the Ultimate Reality we call God. I now view God as less personal and more comprehensive than I would have before my transition. Once, I would have been deeply threatened by this assessment, because I clung to the juvenile idea of God as Big Daddy in the Sky, not only standing for good but for *my* version of good, something I think most mainstream Christians feel. But because I feel so close to this Reality, this new idea has become both comfortable and comforting for me. Because I no longer view God as emotional, pathological, or even personal, I no longer see myself as confined to such caricatures. So liberating!

In effect, to say that God is good, bad, glad, sad, angry, anxious, loving, hateful, and so on is to utterly diminish Him. If God is the Oneness of all Consciousness present within us as Christ Consciousness (as I and many New Thinkers believe; more on this in chapter 8), then God simultaneously contains all emotions and states of being and is *beyond them.* God is the totality of all we can and indeed can't comprehend.

This distinction is important because our varying descriptions of God are based on such temporal associations. Every time we attempt to confine our version of God to the need of the moment—invoking God's name to lend benediction to war, for instance—we stifle our souls by denying God's true state as well as our own. We establish ourselves in mind as servants; pawns of a cosmic being who could erase us at a whim. At best, we should simply say that God Is. To go further is to personalize and trivialize God, and it's not far from there to insist that your personalized version of the Deity should be everyone else's as well. I'm sure some may insist that this book can be accused of doing that, though this is not my intent.

THE EXPERIENCE OF DIVINITY

As we evolve as a species in spiritual understanding, my fondest wish is that our relationship to God evolves so that we become less inclined to judge one another based on the qualities we attribute to God—the differences which create tensions that threaten our world's stability.

How you experience God in consciousness may be totally different from the way someone else does. Your experience of God is not universal; quite the opposite. No one will experience God in the same subjective way that you do. The mistake we make is in taking this unique subliminal interaction with the Divine and projecting it onto others, religiously. God is simultaneously unique to you, yet divine essence remains identical for all people regardless of faith or belief. Think about breathing: you may have a completely different sensation upon drawing breath than someone else—strained if you have asthma, cooling if you live in the mountains, scented by herbs if you live near a garden. Yet you are drawing in the same air as everyone else, except for a few small regional variations. Air is air—unique to you because of your perceptions, but the same for all in objective reality.

God is the same way. Your God is not *the* God. But because of a human proclivity to try convincing others that our way is the right way, we tend to try foisting our conception of God—or our lack of belief in a God at all—upon others and become angry if opposed. On the other hand, God can be everyone's perception and limited to none of them. If God is infinite and formless and yet pervades everything—indeed, is everything—then how can we so arrogantly assume that any of us knows Its ultimate nature? I don't presume in this book to do so. All I hope to do is point out what I consider to be the fallacies in our thinking and, hopefully, point the way to a new understanding or consideration that reflects what I believe to be a clearer picture of reality—and maybe of divinity.

GOD THE IDEA

I am infinitely free in a tiny sliver of infinite space. Free will and real thinking occur only in the space between me, the chooser, and what I am experiencing. Only *I* observe that I am having certain thoughts or feelings. The moment I observe that I am having them, then that tiny sliver of infinite space is created. My freedom lies there, in that clearing where I choose how I am going to respond to my thoughts and feelings. I call this Logos, the logic and reasoning of our being and being here. It is spontaneous spontaneity. When you are existing in Logos, or God Thought, the one thing you *can* control is what you do with your thoughts and feelings.

Logos is Greek for "word," or "reason/reasoning" (logic), and it is often used to represent the Word that expresses what some perceive to be the mind of God. To explain, I will paraphrase John 1:1: In the beginning was the Word [Logos or Reason], and Reason was with God and Reason/Logic was God. Logos also refers to the meaning of a word. Therefore, Logos can also mean universal reality. This is what the Greek philosopher Heracleitus meant by it. He was the first to use this word philosophically. For him, Logos was the law that determines the movements of all reality.

The Logos is God or the Divine manifesting to Itself in Itself. Therefore, whenever God appears, either to Itself or to others outside Itself, it is the Logos that appears. In Christian theology, this Logos is in Jesus as the Christ, the Self-Manifestation of God, the Self-Manifestation of Being. In what some call New Thought, this Logos is manifest in humankind, as we, too, are Self-Manifestations of God. To carry this idea to its conclusion, God is an idea, a meaning, an abstract and extravagant essence. So are we. You are a body expressing an idea that carries a meaning and an essence.

Then there's the translation of Erasmus. He didn't translate *Logos* as "reason" like the Greek philosophers. He translated it as "conversation." That lends a completely different meaning to the discussion: "In the beginning was the Conversation and the Conversation was with God and the Conversation was God." If *Logos* is not simply Word but Conversation, what does that mean? First, God is a Being who converses (communicates) in a relationship with someone else. We inherit this conversation and are free to invent our own conversations—our own Reason. In essence, the

life we live is the continuation of a conversation between the divine
in us and God, in and through which we continually re-create
ourselves.

God is never more than a conversation (a reasoned thought)
away. I am able to see what It has revealed about Itself and com-
mune with It if I choose to live in the conversation. What if God *is*
the very language we are speaking? What intimacy could be possible? How are we making ourselves manifest in our conversations
with God and with others?

What if Jesus Christ symbolizes the spoken promise who
through His life and presumed resurrection made eternity available to all in Himself, the Christ Consciousness, Principle, and
Purpose? Jesus declared Himself as "the Way, the Truth, and the
Light." What would be possible if we join Him in His truthful,
light-filled conversation with Divinity? Would it be possible for us
to live in this temporal world while engaged in an eternal conversation with Ultimate Logic and Infinite Reasoning? This kind of
Christ logic (perhaps even Christianity) is to me much more reasonable and *logical* than the traditional more infantile perceptions and
projections.

Let's go one step further: What if the Scriptures and the theology we make of them were never intended to be used to prove the
existence of God or to validate what Jesus said? What if they are
meant as a doorway, a tiny piece of God revealing Itself to us so
that we might relate—find a way to consider and converse—with
the Divine? What if we were given the Logos through the medium
of wise men and Prophets so that we can relate to all people of all
races, colors, cultures, and creeds? If interpreted in this way, instead of as excuses for brutality and oppression, might this Logos
open divine possibilities to us? What if our system of relating to
God is only a sliver of what exists in Divinity? What if we are mea-
suring God as a particle, when there is a principle, or a wavelength
aspect of God that we are not seeing?

GOD IN CONSCIOUSNESS

Scientists tell us that huge parts of the universe cannot be seen. The latest estimate is that we can perceive only about 4 percent of the matter and energy in the cosmos, the small part that emits light or radiation. The rest of existence, a whopping 96 percent of the universe, is beyond our view because it is said to be composed of either "dark matter" or "dark energy." (Dark does not imply evil but simply unseen or unperceivable.) There is no direct evidence to date for either of these exotic forms, but they are suggested by observation and mathematical models of the universe. This we know: there is something else driving the expansion and evolution of the cosmos that we do not know and cannot perceive. That doesn't mean it's God; I'm not a subscriber to the rather puerile "God of the gaps" mode of thinking. It does mean that even in areas where we have accepted science, our knowledge is severely limited.

My friend Philippe Matthews, of the Shock Philosophy Institute, writes: "All that you could ever want, need, or desire is already housed in the database of the Holy Quantum Spirit." Quantum comes from the Latin word *quantus,* meaning "how much" or "how great." We know a lot, but how much don't we know? I call this the "quantum question." How much God is there? The word *quantum* is thrown around a lot these days in media (like in the film *What the Bleep Do We Know?,* which thoroughly intrigued me), and many similarly interesting books, but to many, it ends up being just a lot of nonsense to explain New Age beliefs that don't seem to be supported by evidence. What does quantum really mean for us? It means that there is an inherent uncertainty in all existence, and this uncertainty is not resolved until a conscious observer perceives the aspect of reality in question. As conscious human beings, we change, choose, and create reality out of probability every waking moment.

But before there were humans or any conscious life, what was there to observe reality and make it real? God Consciousness, the essence of life and light. This is why many New Thinkers now believe that God is the universal *panconsciousness* that has existed since the beginning of time, the substrate of all reality that then shaped material existence out of conscious thought. We have seen in experiments that human intention can affect the material world (from mental telepathy to the world of inventions). How would that be possible if the fabric of reality were not based on consciousness instead of electrons and protons? God is the Consciousness upon which all things were founded. We gave Him a name and form and emotions that reflected our own nature and fears, but the mystery we call God is beyond such concepts.

Both my being and my body are twins of purpose in this realm of consciousness. Christ Consciousness is the bridge between ordinary reality and spiritual reality. As I am beginning to more thoroughly embrace this consciousness, my world has begun to change profoundly in both the physical and metaphysical realm. It has caused me to relocate, take on a new ministry, make repeated appearances on national secular television, sign a publishing deal with the largest publishing company in the world, and even have a movie about my life's journey in the works. You can experience the same shift. Do you understand that personal dominion was given to you before you showed up on this planet or plane of existence? Do you realize that there is not and can never be any separation between Creator and created? Separation, isolation, and alienation from God are illusions fueled and fed by erroneous human theological constructs, which are based on fear and ignorance.

Do you understand that every thought is a prayer of potential manifestation, or that questions are nothing more than the seeds of answers or answers in seed form? We all have divine DNA in us, which means that we are all divine consciousnesses in nature. Nurturing this nature is part of this book's emphasis.

The most vital part of transformation is getting beyond the human realm of sin consciousness and going on to maturity of consciousness—consciousness of your original and authentic self rather than the wounded accidental self that you have been convinced is the real you. For years, my relationship with Christ the Person was about physicality and emotion, focused as much on separation and desperation as inspiration; I was preoccupied more with physical resurrection, mine and Christ's, than I was with spiritual and mental elevation. I did not have the sense that Christ and I were parts of the same Being. Today my relationship is with Christ the Principle, more than with the person or historical figure, yet it is a hundred times more fulfilling. I am beginning to grasp my own place, space, and pace in Consciousness—to feel, experience, and express God's DNA within me.

THE NATURE OF THE SOUL

Oh, we love taking on big questions, don't we? It's not enough that we tackle Christianity; now we're going to get down and dirty with the soul. There are no experts in this field, so we'll trust inspired speculation and logic and profound curiosity.

The word *soul* is another human linguistic approximation of something huge and eternal, something our minds at this stage cannot contain or fully explain. But we can reach out with our intellect and intuition and, as with God, at least try to understand what we do not understand and grasp what the soul *might* be.

There is a constantly evolving world of consciousness that is full of fresh new ideologies of experience and experimentation. This new world is both spiritual and scientific. It is occurring even as we communicate at the quantum, subatomic level with the visible and invisible universe around and within us. What wonderful speculations exist now. It is a high privilege to live in such a world where fundamental assumptions are being questioned. There are so many paths to knowledge, even if they are not always comfortable due to our preconceptions—such as the idea that we have an immortal, immeasurable, and possibly immutable soul. I call this "essence."

This idea, of course, is what Christianity is based on: that there is something ineffable in humankind that makes us more than the sum of our parts; something that leaves our bodies at death and is forever. Renowned New Thinker and best-selling author Deepak Chopra says, "The soul is a living, dynamic part of each person. It exists as consciousness and therefore must be found, discovered, or recovered in consciousness." This appears to be a more accurate assessment than many realize. You see, the idea of the soul is yet another label that we use to describe that which we cannot explain, especially given the materialistic, reductionist mind-set so prevalent today. Put simply, the soul is a name that we give to experiences that momentarily connect us to the Consciousness that is our underlying reality—that state that we habitually ignore most of the time in order to continue with our daily, comparatively mundane lives. Rather than acknowledge the grand beauty of the One Mind of which we are all part, we retreat into simplistic doctrines and religious beliefs often based on fear of the unknown.

This state of being is truly unconsciousness, and it is via this religion-induced unconsciousness that we have created such a threatening, tenuous world. Religious fundamentalism has all but paralyzed the emotions and spirit of the masses, deadening their awareness of the Ultimate Reality: God Consciousness. Religion has taken the place of God or spirituality. People are hungry and angry, but many don't know for what. They know they're missing something: their authentic and essential selves. They are like me, homesick for me, not the falsely pious impersonator our society expects me to be. King David the biblical psalmist said, "My Soul shall make her boast in the Lord!" When was the last time your soul (not your ego) boasted?

Deepak says, "Everything the brain experiences is a manifestation of the Soul." The Hebrew word for *soul* is *nephesh,* the animal sentient in you, the alive or animated self that is constantly in motion toward wholeness. Your *soul*. The soul is not an immaterial "ghost in the machine" that dwells in us and then separates at death. The soul is us; our essence as participants in consciousness. It is always one with the entire fabric of the greater consciousness that is God or Spirit. The idea that it is separate is an illusion, something we see because we are in a state of unconsciousness.

LIVING IN TRUTH

It is worth arguing that one cannot live every moment of the day aware and in awe of this reality, of our inseparable connection to the Ultimate Consciousness that we call God. Those who live this way are usually monks who spend forty years contemplating the tips of their noses (pardon the irreverence). That's fine if you don't have a wife, kids, or a job, but what if you do? My answer is that you—we—must find a balance where we are aware of our participation in Consciousness but also manage to operate fully in our illusion of separateness; to dwell at once in both worlds. Matter is an emergent property, a consequence of Consciousness, not the other way around.

In our minds, we all live on different planes of consciousness and reality. We see ourselves as separate from one another. This excuses actions of disrespect, disregard, and harm to others. But though perception is the ultimate reality, as said earlier, it is not necessarily the ultimate truth. People who live deceptive lives suffer from spiritual amnesia. They have forgotten or refuse to remember who and what they really are. This usually is the result of living a life of impersonation. They live as who they think they need to be in order to survive emotionally, garner acceptance from others, and fit into whatever concept of God and Spirit they have come to accept. But there is another way: stepping away from the limitations of outside thought and accepting the greater reality that Consciousness is who and what we are.

This is authentic living, and it is not something you learn as much as it is something you "remember." You reconnect with it, and by doing so, you recover your fuller, more accurate, and sustained self. This is how I interpret what Scripture calls reconciliation. When Scripture says that Christ will reconcile all to God, I perceive that to mean that people's reawakening to the Christ Principle or innate spirituality will reconcile us all to our true natures and our oneness with what we call God, including the God in us all. This awareness has depth, and the deeper you go, the more your reality will change. Reality is dependent on your state of consciousness. As your consciousness goes deeper, it acquires more power and influence on the self and the broader reality. To quote Deepak again: "There are no facts that cannot be influenced by awareness. Ultimately, your awareness *and perceptions* create everything you experience. We must all learn to pay attention to the impulses of the soul. The impulses of the soul don't lie to you. Don't be afraid of the seriousness of the soul. Pay attention to your soul, and you will be guided more specifically."

CHAPTER EIGHT

WHO AND WHAT IS JESUS CHRIST?

Being a Christian is more than just an instantaneous conversion—it is a daily process whereby you grow to be more and more like Christ.

—Billy Graham

In 2007 a team of archaeologists, working with filmmaker James Cameron, announced a find that they said would turn the world's faith community upside down: they claimed they had found what they called the "James ossuary." An ossuary is a small stone receptacle built to hold the bones of family members. What made this find exceptional was that an inscription supposedly read that the chamber held the bones of James, brother of Jesus. This is in addition to the 1980 discovery of the so-called Talpiot tomb, a collection of ossuaries that discoverers claimed had once held the body of Mary Magdalene as well as, according to an inscription, "Jesus, son of Joseph."

Now, the whole affair is colored by blatant publicity seekers as well as questionable biblical and archaeological scholarship, so it really doesn't bear getting into from an accuracy standpoint. However, several scholars of the region and its history have stated that there were many men named Jesus at the time of the New Testament who were prominent enough to be buried in an ornate tomb. But the issue is not with science; it is with our fascination with the continuing exploration into the life of Jesus. Even people who are devout Christians and completely accept the divinity of Christ seem to continually seek validation from science or evidence, defying the fact that faith cannot be falsified and so cannot be scientific. It seems that we are insecure about our beliefs, even when they are central to our lives. We all somehow want proof.

None of this would happen if it were not for our blind focus, as Christians, on Jesus as the Christ, the divine being who was ordained by God as the Messiah. By misreading the importance of Christ we put ourselves in the position of being subordinate to Him, constantly seeing ourselves as falling short of some Christian ideal that does not and cannot exist. It would be much better for Christians and Christianity if we took a more realistic view of Jesus Christ—even if we stepped into what many see as unthinkable and argued that He was not necessarily resurrected but died like every other man has and will. Now, wait before you blow a fuse!

There are forces that will viciously, vigorously defend the "standard model" (to borrow a physics term) of the Trinity, the resurrected, Divine Christ, and the whole mythical construct. But the more desperate the defense—the more it denies our advances in knowledge and greater awareness both of science and spirit—the more the "old" Christianity will become a relic of the past. I submit that would be a positive, life-affirming event for the entire human family. So let's see what we can do to speed up the transition and take a critical look at the various aspects of Christ: man, myth, principle, and consciousness.

CHRIST THE PERSON

Peter, the New Testament apostle and direct follower of Jesus, writes, "His [Christ's] Divine power has given us everything we need for life and godliness through our knowledge of him who called us by his own glory and goodness." What does that mean? It means that we already have everything we need to become everything we wish to be and have in life. Note an important point about this passage: Peter wrote, "our knowledge of him" rather than "our belief in him." But aren't belief and unconditional acceptance of Christ supposed to be cornerstones of conservative Christianity today? Yes, but it would appear that for a man who actually knew Jesus, knowledge of Him was all that mattered.

In other words, to know the Christ Person was to see through His actions and come to the understanding that we share in the same godliness (God-likeness) as He did. Knowledge of Christ the Man led to consciousness of Christ the Principle. Jesus never emphasized His person over His principles. Jesus was the man, Christ was the Principle. I perceive Jesus as a mystic, operating in the Christ Presence and Principle, who was in touch with and taught us to be in touch with our spiritual center, our souls, our preincarnate selves. This is Christ Consciousness, something so much more potent, plausible, and viable than the religion bearing the name. The same would be true of all religions.

Our knowledge of God in the Christ Person is not learned, it is *remembered.* This is the difference between faith and knowing. Most people think that the opposite of faith is fear or doubt, but I say the opposite of faith is certainty, confidence, or safety. Faith is speculative. Though perceived as faith, most of what we believe about Jesus is myth and legend—indeed, religious and cultural folklore and gossip. We believe, but we don't know. We read the biblical stories and barely understand their context, and we internalize a few highlights, like a movie trailer of Jesus' life: water into wine, loaves and fishes, casting out the money changers, healing the lepers, Gethsemane and Judas and Calvary. Jesus' Greatest Hits. These are all about the history but little about the mystery of Christ. That is what underpins the Christian faith for most believers: ignorance of what and who Jesus really was or wasn't. That may seem tactless and, for some, a distasteful way to approach the subject, but if you are going to build an oppressive, globe-spanning culture out of your mythology, you'd better know fact from fiction!

What we know or experience inwardly about Christ is completely different because we have not learned it from a thousand Bible studies and church lessons. Jesus was a man like any other: He slept, ate, had bodily functions, became lonely, experienced sexual desire. From this perspective, He was wonderfully human, which I find inspiring. He does not have to be a cosmic being or heavenly bellhop to be worthy of reverence and abiding love. His Gospel was to the poor, spiritual beggars who were somehow convinced that they lacked something or that they were depraved and marginalized and thus deprived of their better selves. Jesus healed them not necessarily through some miraculous divine power but by opening their eyes to their better nature—by revealing to them that they were all they needed to be complete. He taught them they were gods or divinities. He reminded them of their immutable selves and their priceless worth.

We all seem to struggle with low self-esteem. We all have a wounded and warped self-concept, usually handed down to us from parents or people with the same issues of self-worth and self-wealth. Jesus called them "poor in spirit." Part of the problem for Christians is that we are constantly comparing ourselves to Jesus the preacher as a divine being who was without sin and so on. But how do we know Jesus the Person wasn't just like us? The Gospels don't tell the full story because they were written in part to popularize the new religion. So we have no way of knowing if the concept that Jesus was some sort of superman is anything more than church propaganda. But our hearts and minds feel the effects of the flawless Jesus when we compare ourselves to Him and find ourselves wanting while subconsciously or unconsciously "being."

As mentioned earlier, the Jewish book of Hebrews says that

Christ was in touch with the feelings of our human weaknesses and was in all ways tempted like we are, but without sin (Hebrews 4:15). This is the part of Jesus we rarely hear about. He was so much of a man that it is difficult to believe He was what many perceive God to be and so Godlike that it is difficult for many to believe He was actually a man.

We spoke earlier of natural, or human, reality and spiritual reality. They are similar but not identical. Your lower nature is earthbound, your spiritual or spirit nature is without boundaries, limitless, ageless, timeless, indeed infinite—like God. Through it you have everything you need, because you are in fact everything that is necessary according to your created intention. This was part of the mission and message of Jesus. He healed those who were in a state of forgetfulness by reminding them of their true and whole selves including their sophisticated human selves, at one with nature.

Jesus the Person was and is all about helping us recover from our spiritual amnesia and recover the true immutable, immortal, and immeasurable selves that we have always been.

THE LAST ADAM

When I say recovery, I mean regaining and recollecting your essential self, your pre-Adamic and pre-incarnate self, the one that was around before the legendary fall and failure of the first Adam. In a metaphysical observation, Adam was the first model for the incarnate version of man, and he existed in unity with God as the One Consciousness until his fall into the caves and covens of duality, which was the emergence of the illusion of separateness; the tribal sense of duality in which things are opposed and warring at all times. The first Adam represents self-expulsion from God's presence in the sense that we no longer live in an effortless state of universal self-awareness in which the self is sufficient for any miracle. Over the millennia, we have allowed Adam's story to influence us into believing the illusion of aloneness and disunity and suspicion that religion tells us is our natural state.

In Christian theology, Jesus is perceived to have taken form as the last Adam, the latest incarnation of man. He was perfected, though not in the sense that Christ was without a single impure thought. I personally do not think He was, because it makes no sense. I don't think it's possible for a human being to live for thirty-two years and not curse out of frustration, have a lustful thought, or entertain feelings of anger, greed, or envy. That some people will insist Jesus did not have such impulses just shows how far we have fallen into mindless idol worship, something Jesus would repudiate. I prefer Jesus the flawed human being who was perfect in the most important way of all: He was fully, completely aware of His divine nature and existed in total harmony with the eternal self that He had always been. He knew that He was one with God in consciousness—that He was a Son of God. Not *the* Son, but *a* son of the One Divinity, a concept and reality He sought to awaken His followers to. That is a vital distinction, because we are all sons and daughters, or as Scripture says in Acts 17:24–29, offspring of God.

What made Jesus extraordinary was not His presumed divinity but His very real humanity. As the presumed last Adam, He completed the circle, chosen by God to reawaken us to the reality of our transcendent nature and reunite us with the oneness that the first Adam cost us when he cast us into a false consciousness of duality and separation. That illusionary state is the stagnation we call death. Only a man, with flaws and faults but with a stronger knowledge of His own eternal nature, could inspire so many to find that truth in themselves. That, to me, is the greatness of Christianity in its original form: man as God more than God as man.

CHRIST THE PRINCIPLE

In the Second Epistle of Peter, Scripture reads, "For this very reason, make every effort to add to your faith goodness; and to goodness, knowledge; and to knowledge, self-control; and to self-control, perseverance; and to perseverance, godliness; and to godliness, brotherly kindness; and to brotherly kindness, love. For if you possess these qualities in increasing measure, they will keep you from being ineffective and unproductive in your knowledge of our Lord Jesus Christ."

This is not a reference to physical or even religious knowledge. The Christ Principle preceded the Christ Person by at least three thousand to four thousand years. Indeed, the Christ Principle, or Messianic Principle, has existed since the beginning of humankind. It is the creative and procreative force in consciousness and spiritual culture, and the second part of what some could consider the Holy Trinity of the unified Christ Consciousness. If Christ the Person is the New Testament foundational part of the whole, the Christ Principle is what He stood for, fought for, and died for.

The Christ Principle is, in effect, the concept and reality that Jesus taught through His life and works: that we all partake of the Divine Oneness that is God, that we are all God in physical form, sufficient for creation of whatever we want to experience in our reality.

The inventions of modern technology we enjoy today, from airplanes and satellites to microwaves and cyberspace, all would have been more than miraculous, and, indeed, inconceivably so, just a hundred years ago, not to mention two thousand years ago. We experience our creative divinity scientifically every day and those who hinted of it in centuries past, like Galileo, Copernicus, and other scientists, artists, and inventors, were demonized, tortured, and executed, simply because religion didn't allow for or understand true Christlikeness and its creative ambiance.

We are not debased or sinful beings; that is a myth imposed upon us by a religious power structure. Those who believe they are sinners from birth begin acting out that sinfulness almost from birth. When that concept is ingrained in your psyche all your life, it becomes both habitual, actual, and, on a terrestrial and carnal level, factual.

The reverse awareness is that we each carry within us the potential to be equal to Christ in spirit if only we can awaken to that state of being and embrace our divine nature. Such an awakening is the true born-again experience. If God was the Idea or Logos that created the universe, Christ the Principle is the idea that created us.

EVERYONE IS CHRISTLIKE

In Luke 12:8–10, Jesus says: "I tell you, whoever acknowledges me before men, the Son of Man will also acknowledge him before the angels of God. But he who disowns me before men will be disowned before the angels of God. And everyone who speaks a word against the Son of Man will be forgiven, but anyone who blasphemes [*blasphemeo,* "to vilify"] against the Holy Spirit will not be forgiven."

Note that Jesus is not referring here to the common Jew. He is confronting the doubts, denunciations, and hypocrisy of the Pharisees, the conservative religious fundamentalists of His day. He warns in verse 1, "Be on your guard against the yeast of the Pharisees, which is [basically ultra-right-wing religious] hypocrisy. There is nothing concealed that will not be disclosed, or hidden that will not be made known. What you have said in the dark will be heard in the daylight, and what you have whispered in the ear in the inner rooms will be proclaimed from the roofs."

He was letting the Pharisees know that their hypocritical words of religious paranoia would ultimately be revealed for what they were: manipulation. He was also hinting to these people that this same group would one day be responsible for the destruction of His body, but that God was the only one to be truly reverenced, not religious rules, rituals, or regulations! Jesus wasn't playing games or in anyway disingenuous with His mission: to communicate the Christ Principle to humankind through the example of His life and light. In fact, according to Scripture, it was His refusal to back down from that mission that resulted in His crucifixion!

In verses 11 and 12 of Luke 12, He continues by warning them of what is to come from this particular religious faction: "When you are brought before synagogues [were He a Christian, He'd have said "churches"], rulers, and authorities, do not worry about how you will defend yourselves or what you will say, for the Holy Spirit will teach you at that time what you should say." Jesus is referred to as the "Righteous Judge," meaning that He is fair and equitable toward all of humanity. He was indeed a sacred humanist activist. Jesus was so inclusive in spirit that the separatists (the true definition of the word *Pharisee*) both resented and resisted Him. Unfortunately, this same Pharisaic spirit also manifested itself even among His disciples when they thought someone was ministering in Jesus' name without their endorsement. Does that sound at all like someone preaching the Gospel without the sanction of the institutional church? It's precisely what yours truly has experienced. Notice Mark 9:33–39:

They came to Capernaum. When he was in the house, he asked them, "What were you arguing about on the road?" But they kept quiet because on the way they had argued about who was the greatest. Sitting down, Jesus called the Twelve and said, "If anyone wants to be first, he must be the very last, and the servant of all."

He took a little child and had him stand among them. Taking him in his arms, he said to them, "Whoever welcomes one of these little children in my name welcomes me; and whoever welcomes me does not welcome me but the one who sent me."

"Teacher," said John, "we saw a man driving out demons in your name and we told him to stop, because he was not one of us."

"Do not stop him," Jesus said. "No one who does a miracle in my name can in the next moment say anything bad about me, for whoever is not against us is for us. I tell you the truth, anyone who gives you a cup of water in my name because you belong to Christ will certainly not lose his reward."

It seems that it was (and is) human nature to instantly self-divide into tribes, clans, or gangs based on the presumption of sacred knowledge, to presume that some have it and some do not, and those who do not are somehow less than those who do. Some of Jesus' contemporaries, wise men who shared in His living example, did that. The irony is that this is a false dichotomy, as there is no one who does not possess the sacred knowledge that made the disciples stop the man driving out demons. This was the message Jesus came to speak, that no one is more or less divinely privileged than anyone else! Every one of us is Christ waiting to be reborn into that inheritance. In our better and best selves, we are all innately messianic—anointed and sent to this plane and planet to help recover "that" which was lost (Matthew 18:11). "That" is nothing more or less than the virtue and value of "being" human. Human beings being human is not a sin, but institutionalized religion insists it is. We don't need religion; we need recovery from it. I like to refer to myself as a "recovering fundamentalist."

THE CHURCH AS DRUG DEALER

It's impossible to know how many leaders of the world's churches possess knowledge of the Christ Principle and how many are living in ignorance of it. I can speak from my own experience: before my reawakening to Inclusion, I had heard of the principle that all men were gods and that Christ was a state of being rather than a super-hero to whom we had to pledge our subservience or else hell would open up and claim us. I found it heretical because it conflicted with the teachings I had learned since my childhood. Truth was not important to me at that time; I was more interested in the mental comfort that came with having what I thought I knew reaffirmed, and with sticking to the doctrine that had made me successful, respected, and admired in most evangelical circles. In other words, I was more concerned with being accepted and approved of by the people and powers that exist in that world than in the next plane of consciousness, as it were. I think many religious leaders in the Christian Church and others are guilty of this same crime against their followers and themselves; I hear from them all the time.

Yet we tolerate this sort of abdication of our responsibility not just to tell the truth to our congregations but also to *be and bear* the truth of the Christ Principle to ourselves. We tolerate the obfuscation of the Christ Principle and Christ Consciousness. You will never change what you develop a tolerance for. Tolerable recovery—partial and incomplete salvation or limited deliverance—is all that institutionalized religion offers. Religion is suspicious of anything or anyone who declares freedom from it, because its purpose is not to save anyone, but just to play and in some ways placate.

Let me say that again: *the purpose of the organized, institutionalized church is not to save anyone!* The purpose of any organization, from churches to governments, is to perpetuate its own existence. It runs counter to the interest of any Christian, Jewish, Muslim, or any other formal faith tradition to declare that you can be free simply by adopting the Christ Principle, because then you will not need the church, and it will have no reason to exist. Mind you, all of the Abrahamic faiths—Judaism, Christianity, and Islam—believe some form of Christology (Christ logic). It is Christ, the principle not the religion, that humans love and aspire to, at least conceptually.

What has become known as the Albigensian Crusade or Cathar Crusade, carried out by the Catholic Church from 1209 to 1229, came about because a group of nobles in southern France, the Cathars of Languedoc, had begun a movement that insisted that the church was not necessary and that people should be free to speak to God on their own terms. Threatened by this perceived heresy, the church wiped out the Cathars, killing from two hundred thousand to one million people in God's name.

George Orwell wrote in *1984,* "The object of power is power." That is the idea that the Christ Principle threatens. Christ was never about religion; He did not come here to found one. He was about personal awareness and self-discovery, the church that lies and lives within each of us. Organized religion is designed to compel its adherents to become addicted to *the church,* not God or Christ. Religion is a drug, and its most intolerant proponents are drug dealers who push ignorance. The addiction that millions have to religion has caused many destructive and abusive habits and criminality within human culture. Instead of the church being a spiritual rehab center for drug-free living, it has become the crack house where addicts get their hits. Going cold turkey, as I did, is painful, but there are better and less painful ways to get free. I offer some in this book.

Religion cannot and will not survive true Christ Consciousness. That is why it cannot tolerate Inclusion. The less religious you are, the more radically inclusive you become.

Christians tolerate sin and sinfulness because we are convinced by our religious presuppositions that we are and will always be sinners. This is why Paul said, "Where there is no law, sin is not taken into account" (Romans 5:13). Religion is built on its own legal system of right and wrong, dos and "don't you dares," but these wither when faced with the simple grandeur of the Christ Principle.

GOD'S DISCIPLINE

Well, that was some provocative language. But we are fighting the tide of two millennia of entrenched belief, indoctrination, and self-imposed blindness, and sometimes it takes shocking ideas to penetrate the shields of delusion that we erect around ourselves. The simple truth is that the Christ Principle, not Christ the Person, should be what Christianity is built around. Not the resurrected Savior who ascended into heaven and will return to beat the daylights out of Satan, but the higher self that Christ came to earth to teach us to become. Both resurrection and the resurrected Christ are consciousness. You are free to literalize it if you like, but unless you arise in consciousness, both you and Christ will remain dead.

Jesus, while on this earth, sought to confront and dismantle the legalistic religion of His time. In 1 Corinthians 15:56, the Apostle Paul writes: "The sting of death is sin, and the power of sin is the law. But thanks be to God! He gives us the victory through our Lord Jesus Christ." But religion insists that you "stick with it" and "wait till your change comes," as recorded in the book of Job. That would be like Jesus saying to the lame beggar on the side of the road, "Do you want to be half as opposed to whole? Then take up your bed and limp." It would be like him saying to the crippled man, "Here, take these braces, use this walker or wheelchair; or take two *gos*-pills and call me in the morning. Or read a couple of Scriptures, and I'll see you in church next Sunday." Imagine Jesus saying to humanity, "Would thou be made whole? Then here, join my support group. Join my hospice called Christianity."

I operated by that mentality for nearly forty years of ministry; many of my colleagues still do. I understand this mentality, as I have been a victim of it as well as a victimizer of people with it. But

Paul wrote, in his letter to the church in Rome, as just stated (Romans 5:13 NIV), "Sin is not taken into account when there is no law." He also wrote to the church at Colosse that Jesus abolished the written code (the religious legal system) with His blood (life), nailing it to the cross: "Having canceled the written code, with its regulations, that was against us and that stood opposed to us; he took it away, nailing it to the cross. And having disarmed the powers and authorities, he made a public spectacle of them, triumphing over them by the cross" (Colossians 2:14).

Apparently Jesus saw His mission as one of living and teaching the Christ Principle and perhaps defending it by giving His life. The universe knew that a martyr who lived according to the principle and then laid down His life for refusing to bow to oppressive, legalistic religious authority would cement the idea of the Christ Principle in the minds of the people forever. This was God reconciling the world to Himself through Christ, bringing people back into oneness. Unfortunately, that state did not last long, as a new religion was created that was just as oppressive as the old one.

Passing judgment on the very people for whom Christ is believed to have died is *blasphemous,* or anti-Christ, if anything is. In Christian tradition and theology, though not acknowledged, it is a rejection of the Holy Spirit's power to convince everyone of what Christians supposedly believe, that Jesus is Lord. Remember, according to Christian Scripture, every knee will bow and every tongue confess that Jesus is Lord in heaven, earth, and under it. This does not mean that we must worship the human person Jesus of Nazareth. It means that we recognize that He was the principle embodied, that His sacrifice in the name of that principle was about making it possible at least positionally for us to be restored in consciousness to our pre-Adamic state in what I call the "grace place." Recognizing this is an opportunity for Christians or the church to rethink our position about Christ and the role of the church. We must remember that unfortunate things happening to other people around the world or here in America are not a sign of God's judgment but more of a universal corrective principle based on love. Christians tend to see God as a stern, paternal disciplinarian who wants them to grow in wisdom and succeed. This is based in part on interpretations of scripture such as Hebrews 12:5–7, which was written to a Jewish congregation and reflects the supposed new Jewish concept of a Father God:

> And you have forgotten that word of encouragement that addresses you as sons: "My son, do not make light of the Lord's discipline, and do not lose heart when he rebukes you, because the Lord disciplines those he loves, and he punishes everyone he accepts as a son."
>
> Endure hardship as discipline; God is treating you as sons. For what son is not disciplined by his father? If you are not disciplined (and everyone undergoes discipline), then you are illegitimate children and not true sons. Moreover, we have all had human fathers who disciplined us and we respected them for it. How much more should we submit to the Father of our spirits and live!

Knowing and living by the Christ Principle is not easy, but the rewards are beyond measure, and the greatest of these is knowing God—in you, with you, around you, as you.

CHRIST AS CONSCIOUSNESS

Philippe Matthews of the Shock Philosophy Institute writes,

> Your car, church, clothes, furniture, food, home, family, and *you* all come from Source, the Divine, the Quantum, the Holy Spirit, the All in All. It is our point of observation or level of consciousness that collapses the quantum molecules into the

atom of currency, clothing, homes, churches, and material possessions. The more people keep looking and seeing the very same thing, the larger and more real the illusion of the effect, but the cause is always created and housed in Spirit . . .

. . . You may not be rich financially, but there is an area in your life where you are rich. You must defragmentize your consciousness and develop intention and focus to summon the forces of the universe to produce the effect of wealth or money in a tangible form. Right now, your wealth may be in your relationships, your imagination, your education, and your material possessions. So if you want more of the physical appearance of monetary wealth as opposed to the fragmented wealth that you already have, you must create an intention and focus that will collapse the subatomic field into that expression. It will only manifest, however, to the degree of your concentrated consciousness. If you cannot discipline yourself to focus on the Allness of Spirit for extended points in time, then you will manifest fragmented, hit-and-miss outcomes and manifestations.

This is ancient wisdom expressing itself in "New Thought."

To elaborate further: Christ Consciousness is the third state of Christ, and the one that makes the vital transition from His being to ours. In Christian theology, the Christ Person is, of course, Jesus the man, who was born and died on earth. The Christ Principle is a philosophical idea that expresses a spiritual reality that we partake in the wholeness of divinity. Christ Consciousness completes our evolution and represents the final stage in the brand of salvation that Christ was really bringing to humanity: the state of "being," in which one is like Christ, a fully realized being of thought and divine energy, able to manifest whatever realities one wishes out of pure thought and intention. Christ Consciousness is our full and complete destiny from an Ultimate Intention many call God.

However, the degrading, power-hungry conventions of mainstream religion make it impossible for the average believer to embrace this point of view. We are told for decades that we are evil at heart, damned at birth, barely tolerated by a rageaholic God who would as soon throw us into hell as look at us. Coming as they do from that place of thought, it's simply too great a mental and spiritual leap for most people to see themselves not just as holy beings but as equal in spirit to Christ Himself. With the constant messages of unworthiness flowing from today's Christian fundamentalist churches, it's a wonder that the average believer can lift his or her head in church, much less equate himself or herself with God! We suffer from a self-esteem crisis that organized religion has inflicted upon us for its own purposes. Accepting Christ as a consciousness that we can attain, rather than a cosmic good guy coming to rescue us from our iniquity, requires some major personal, spiritual evolution.

OUR TRUE DESTINY

1 Peter 2:9–10 reads, "But you are a chosen [*eklektos*, "elected, uniquely called or summoned into existence"] people, a royal priesthood, a holy nation, a people belonging to God, that you may declare the praises of him who called you out of darkness into his wonderful light." This is the purpose of the church: to declare—better yet, to demonstrate—Christ Consciousness to the world and make everyone aware of his or her wonderful spiritual destiny. But we have come so far from this awareness that at times it seems impossible that we will ever find our way back.

How can we declare the praises of Him who brought us out of darkness, obscurity, and defeat if we are not there? If freedom is not our experience, only our doctrine, will we transcend that doctrine or merely rise to heights of anger and violence to defend the status quo, as we have so far done? How can we effectively and truthfully preach deliverance if we are not delivered free and whole or if we don't perceive ourselves as such? Do we really perceive that we are saved, or do we simply preach it out of habit and tradition? Do we even know what salvation is anymore, beyond our cartoonish notions of a Superman-style Christ and a devil with horns, hoofs, and a tail?

The Gospel of Inclusion has changed what I believe and why I believe it. It has changed what I know about why I am here and what my role is in the universe. My sin-and-saved consciousness no longer exists. I no longer see myself as a struggling, crawling creature whose only hope is a capricious God; I now know that I am already free or redeemed from the curse of the law (religious legalism), as Scripture declares. I chose to live in this new reality as opposed to the tired old one of my past religious bondage, with its innate terror. I have also chosen my challenging path in order to bring this same *new* Good News to others—to let everyone know that the lies of our current pseudo-understanding of Christianity cannot and will not bring peace to anyone, because that is not their purpose. Only through the realization that all humans carry Christ or "God" Consciousness within us and that we are all already saved and safe can we move beyond our doomed state of mind to a world of peace and healing.

Between our realities and God's absolutes, there is an obscure place where most of us tend to get trapped. Sorting our way through those obscure, opaque places in life becomes the primary occupation of our existence on this planet. Healing our minds' trouble and trauma due to the years of misinformation and misrepresentation becomes our preoccupation when we should be spending our time loving and helping to encourage others to bring and be light in the world, including embracing all of our global brothers and sisters.

Inclusion and Christ Consciousness are inextricably linked. When we strip away the trappings and psychological chains of organized religion and its myths, we can see clearly that it was never meant for us to perceive ourselves as slaves to God's whims and to perceive our human selves as base creations barely above the ants and rodents scurrying along on the ground. We created that perception from our own need to elevate some humans above others. Establishing a hierarchy is in our most primitive nature, it seems. Once we can accept the possibility that we are beloved children and heirs of creation, partaking of the same substance and spirit that gives God being, we can begin to see the other truth: *we are already saved*, and, more importantly, we're safe! Inclusion recognizes that all people are divine in nature, which was what Jesus felt He was sent here to tell us. We have perverted that message, but that does not make it any less true. There is no need to pray for salvation or ask Jesus to be your personal savior. You don't need a savior; the Christ Consciousness makes you realize you are safe in God, with God, and as God. When you recognize this, you don't allow fears or the wrathful unregenerate or unconscious self to create a hell for yourself or anyone else on earth.

Again in 1 Peter, the Apostle of Christ writes: "Once you were not a people of God, but now you are the people of God. Once you had not received mercy [*eleos,* "divine grace, unwarranted favor"], but now you have received mercy." God the Creator, through His Christ, has identified with your humanness and the complexities of your duality—your sense of right and wrong, good and bad, black and white, male and female—and shown you the path back to the unity that you once enjoyed as your birthright.

Through Christ and *as* "I" in us, God relates to this duplicitous aspect of our being. Yes, God recognizes our complexities but is not perplexed by them. The father-parent consciousness of God sits universally where we sit and feels what we feel. This Divine Grace is more than unmerited favor, it is empowerment, understanding, and enablement. It is wholeness, healing, and success of being. God doesn't forgive because It doesn't have to. God is love, and love cannot be offended, nor does it need defense. We do not need God to forgive us because there is nothing to forgive. We have been carrying out the nature that God placed within us when we were created. Any other image is an illusion. As God is a complex Reality of many aspects, so are we. Duality is but one aspect of humanity. Unity and Christ Consciousness are yet others. Which will you choose?

My ministry is not just about training, it is about enlightenment! I invite you out of darkness and into His marvelous light. Not only the light of God but also the light of you, both the light in you and the Light you are in God!

CHRIST, MAN?

A new vision and version of God includes one whose love cannot be changed or challenged. A love that cannot be envied or become jealous. A love that doesn't know indifference or pain. A love beyond hurt and that cannot be hurt. God is love, but not as we perceive love. God's love is perfect: full grown and fully expressed. It is infinite and therefore cannot be defined. Our love is finite, but it has the potential to be infinite, as do we.

Christ as Consciousness is the most exalted state in which Christ can exist. You have felt this state at times even if you are currently straitjacketed by limited thinking and dogma-induced fear. When you meditate, and you feel your mind moving beyond its physical limitations, when you feel at one with all things, when you intend something with a pure heart, and it comes to pass—those are all manifestations of Christ Consciousness. You may call it something else, but this is what I call it. Some may simply call it consciousness, spirituality, or God and I am fine with that. My objective is to encourage all to recognize the transcendent in and around us. I see this as a peace operative that will greatly enhance and benefit the world.

It is the state of being in which the mind, focused with pure and total faith and awareness of its own divine nature, creates reality. You've heard it referred to as the law of attraction, a good marketing scheme that has people rethinking, but it is even more. Christ Consciousness is not about what you have but who you are becoming: a healer, a peacemaker, a bringer of light and love to the world. You can create this world with your mind and spirit when you exist in Christ Consciousness. You can be Christian, Jewish, Muslim—even atheist—and still employ and enjoy this consciousness in spirit.

In this context, I would like to ask one more question of seismic implications: does it matter if Jesus called Christ was a divine being? We have seen the speculations of films like *The Da Vinci Code* and the news cycles filled up with stories about the James ossuary and how they "debunk" the historical Jesus. But does it all really matter? Would the importance of Christ the Person, Principle, and Consciousness be any less if Jesus had been as the Muslims see Him: a prophet and a great visionary, but mortal? Does Jesus have to be *the* Son of God to be *a* son of God?

I would argue that it does not matter. If Jesus came to earth as a man, inspired by and connected to God as few have been, to share with humanity the truth of the Christ Principle and bring us back into conscious oneness with the Creator, how could it matter one way or another whether He was resurrected from the dead or was a divine being Himself? In this context, the man does not matter; the motive and idea is everything. If Jesus were only a divinely ordained prophet who expressed the words and thoughts of God and lived them in His daily life, His message would remain just as powerful and relevant, and the Christianity that is based on His teachings would actually be healthier, because it would be focused on self-awareness, compassion, and unity with God, not on legalism and dogma. Martin Luther King Jr. did not have to be physically resurrected in order for the civil rights movement he helped inspire to become effective.

I harbor no illusions about the Christian religion accepting this utterly heretical notion; it is built too solidly on a foundation of "Christ is born, Christ is risen, Christ will come again." But if this speculation were to be true, it would change little except to put *us* at the center of our religious tradition, rather than the Prophet or even God. If you insist that your God desires and requires blood sacrifice in order to accept and forgive, or that love can be expressed that way only, then that may be where you remain, but it does not make it true or necessary. I believe that it is completely possible to perceive God and love apart from and/or without the need for brutality, violence, and repression. I can still call Jesus Lord and not be cannibalistic or executionary in my perception of him. Blood is precious; why make it the focus of love rather than just a function of life? God is love; why is anything else necessary, and why must death as we perceive it be part of its equation or expression?

Human or divine, Jesus came to this earth as a messenger, perhaps more than a savior, at least as one saving us from God or *His* perceived "wrath." Christ's message was that we are the architects of our own salvation by the nature of our being, and that if we choose to create a hell in our consciousness by virtue of our fears or hatreds, that becomes our imaginary reality. That is our choosing, not necessarily God's. God does not judge us or stop us; we choose. We are free to make our own decisions, headed toward the place when we will see the truth and reconnect in consciousness to God's boundless love. That is Inclusion, and Inclusion is the very essence of what makes Jesus as Christ—man or God—such a towering figure in our history. Because as person, principle, and consciousness, He does what all great teachers should and must do: show us by thought and example what we ourselves can become. Jesus did not come to protect us from God but to reconnect us *to* God in consciousness.

PART THREE
JOURNEY TO TRANSCENDENCE

Service without ideal of self trains you to transcend
all the artificial distinctions imposed by history and
geography, and to realize that the human community
is one and indivisible.

—Sri Sathya Sai Baba

CHAPTER NINE

YOUR PRE-INCARNATE SELF

The words "I am" are potent words; be careful what you
hitch them to. The thing you're claiming has a way of
reaching back and claiming you.

—A. L. Kitselman

Memory is the cabinet of imagination, the treasury of
reason, the registry of conscience, and the council chamber
of thought.

—Saint Basil

It is estimated that in a lifetime, a brain can store one
million billion "bits" of information.

—Isaac Asimov

What if we could somehow go further back than the lifetime
we remember? What if we could connect or reconnect with
or to the life or lifetime we have forgotten? Do you ever think
you're hearing music that you can't trace, or have thoughts or see
images that seem strangely familiar? You recognize them but can't
identify where they come from, or when or where you experienced
them last.

We have trodden some profoundly controversial ground, you
and I. We have discussed questions that were previously asked only

in secret: the divinity of Christ, the political motives of the Christian Church, the nature of God Himself or Itself. But to this point, the journey has been largely a look outward at the concepts and realities of God and Divinity, as well as the human-made church. Now I want to take the journey inward, into your powerful potential as spirit. We have discussed the Christ Principle that Jesus came to earth to remind us of: the reality that we have within us a deep and everlasting connection to the substance of God that requires no church or dogmatic mediation for us to experience and know. But what about Christ Consciousness? What does it mean to live in Christ Consciousness—to be like Jesus? I can tell you, it's got nothing to do with rules, rites, or rituals, and even less to do with judging others or taking away their rights, as so many conservative Christians and other religious zealots seem to think these days. It doesn't even have anything to do with "Christianity" per se.

There comes a time in your journey toward self-actualization when you don't need anyone else's permission to "be." You stop asking for permission and stop apologizing for "being." I am closer to that place than ever before in my life, and this is the most happy and fulfilling time I've ever known. I've never loved or enjoyed being me this much before. Nothing can move me more deeply than this realization. I am happily a human being being human. In this final section of *God Is Not a Christian,* we will look at what it means to live and experience the Christ mind and spirit. In doing so, we will transform the popular question from "What would Jesus do?" to "Who would Jesus be?" and, more importantly, who are *you*?

THE YOU THAT HAS ALWAYS BEEN

Obviously, I still love the Bible. In Jeremiah 1:5, Scripture reveals to us a hint of the wisdom that we have been missing for so long: "Before I formed [*yatsar,* "fashioned, determined"] you in the womb, I knew [*yada,* "recognized, identified, and chosen from among others"] you, before you were born I set you apart; I appointed you as a prophet [*nabiy,* "inspired person, seer, visionary"] to the nations."

I am a big proponent of what I call pre-incarnate consciousness—that is, what you knew and were before you were incarnated (infleshed) in your human form. In ancient history, shamans and mystics in all cultures used herbs and plants to recall what the mind had forgotten but the spirit had stored. Recovering that sense of transcendence has to be the great ambition of the soul. We have largely forgotten about our pre-incarnate self, the eternal you that is a part of God's essence and cannot die or lie. It's been obscured behind the layers of religious law and the prohibitive policies (police) that we hide behind or which hide and hinder us. But to be at your happiest and most complete, it is essential that you reconnect with your transcendent self.

To remember this pre-material being is to recall the Original Intent that led to your incarnation. Think about that and you'll ask, what makes me any different from Jesus? He was, in essence, an immaterial and eternal soul that took incarnate form when He came to earth. The answer is, nothing makes you different from Jesus in essence. You and Jesus are both "Sons of men," or human offspring. Essentially, we are all both children of men and children of God. However, Jesus' favorite reference to Himself was "Son of man." He loved to refer to us all as children of God.

In this process or progress we call life, we are all going back to our future, back to our (perceived) pre-Adamic fall or existence. The fall of man is only a perception. It is imaginary. There is no such thing as original sin. Sin was and is not original, only God is. Sin is a human religious construct. In effect, there is only God; anything else is an illusion.

We have been taught that we are fallen creatures—that we are sinful by nature and therefore have no choice but to sin, for which Christ must bail us out of God's court before judgment can fall. This is an illusion we are taught and have believed, and thus we act it out. We impersonate sin and sinning, at least our human brand of it. But in reality, our future is our past: we are meant and created to be as one with God, sinless and cocreators of existence. This reality is profoundly liberating and renewing to me, because for the first time in over fifty years, I no longer feel it is my responsibility or calling to protect humanity from the wrath of an invincible and invisible villainous God who hates them enough to kill and torture them forever. I no longer believe in such a love/hate relationship or mentality. What an unbearable weight off my shoulders and anyone else's.

We have forgotten that we were and are made in the image and likeness of the Creator/God; anything else is an impersonation. Death is a process of forgetting, of digressing into less than our highest consciousness. To remember is to reconnect to spiritual accuracy and precision of person and purpose—to repair or replace the accidental you with the flawless *essential you.* It is renewing and reknowing yourself all over again!

THANKS AND RESURRECTION

In Christian theology, we are taught that this return to original essence was accomplished in the Christ Person or Purpose. Note the words of Jude, purportedly the half-brother of Jesus: "Now unto him who is able to keep you from falling [from your original purpose] and to present you faultless, before his presence with exceeding Joy" (Jude 1:24). This is the essence of the Gospel as it is typically preached, and I understand it and appreciate it. However, in reality, we have never fully understood the issue. Jesus did not have to keep us from falling from God's eternal and unconditional love and favor. We only fell in consciousness because we failed to remember who we were. Sin and sin consciousness are spiritual amnesia. Jesus was a way of reminding us what we had forgotten and bringing us back to God in our original cognizance (awareness).

There is much talk of thanksgiving in Christianity, and I find the attitude about that *thanks* (not thankfulness itself) to be debasing and humiliating. We are often expected to present our meager thanks to God as supplicants on our knees, beggars in desperation, happy for any little blessing God bestows upon us, his cowering little servants. That is nothing more than a continuation of the toxic dynamic that is diminishing and destroying our world: God as master, believers as slaves. Instead I would like to put a new spin on thanksgiving. To be thankful is to recognize that everything, including every experience and circumstance, is interrelated, interconnected, and ultimately beautiful and benevolent. To thank is simply to think, and be conscious of the benefits and blessings of "being."

This to me is the metaphysical meaning of the resurrection to which Paul was referring when he said in Philippians 3:10–11: "I want to know Christ and the power of his resurrection and the fellowship of sharing in his sufferings, becoming like him in his death, and so, somehow, to attain to the resurrection from the dead." Resurrection from the dead simply means awakening to and arriving at your authentic self. Who is the unedited you? To discover and recover that person is indeed resurrection from the dead—from spiritual amnesia and stagnation.

Resurrection is simply remembering who you are and forgetting who you aren't. It is forgetting the lie and the impersonator and replacing that false persona with the real you, the transcendent you who has always been part *of* God—and, indeed, part God. If that is not salvation, nothing is. This was the message of the Christ Person we call Jesus. His suffering and death occurred because religious leadership refused His teaching about self-discovery and spiritual recovery. Arriving at the place we are discussing here does not happen without taking risks, as Jesus did.

Old Testament thanksgiving was always considered an offering. It was never casual. It was ceremonial, somewhat austere, and involved many rites designed to avoid offending the God to whom the thanks was being offered. This was an outward performance of an inward reality. It was like the difference between praise and worship. We praise God for what He does, but we worship God for who He is! Old Testament Scripture says that God "showed the children of Israel his deeds and Moses his ways." Once you recognize the ways of God or the divine way or construct, you will never be unthankful again.

Again, to be thankful (thinkful) means to be conscious of benefits and beneficence of existence and thus grateful. To appreciate something is to grasp its nature and its worth and value it accordingly. We tend to be thankful based on surface awareness. So if we are truly thankful for our being—not for our jobs or bank accounts or health or family but for our spiritual state and reality of existence—it follows that we could not help but appreciate them as the truly transcendent states of reality that they are. So, what if you were always thankful? What would that be like? Would that not be total, complete, and/or complementary awareness of our own perfection, purity, and accuracy of self? Could we remain in a sublime state of being for life and beyond life as we know it? I honestly don't have an answer to that question, but it sure is worth investigating and experiencing.

THE REALITY OF ABUNDANCE

There is a trap here, however. To give thanks also implies that some outside agency was responsible for giving you what you could not get for yourself. This agency, of course, would be God. The word *want* in Hebrew is *chacer* (khaw-sare), which translates "to lack, fail, be diminished, or decrease." If you exist in Christ Consciousness, where thought becomes reality, and yet you give thanks to God for

what you have in your life, does that not mean that you are ac-
knowledging want or need; that you were not able to produce abundance through your own consciousness or that you lacked anything?
Can't that line of thought rebound to bring you lack and poverty? I
am referring here to ritual thanksgiving in contrast to spiritual gratitude, which is conscious wellness. It is a reference to that question
that God is said to have posed to Adam: Who told you that you
were naked (uncovered or incomplete)? Who convinced you that
you were less than?

All poverty is artificial. Lack and want are delusions. They are
produced out of spiritual amnesia. In a more severe sense, poverty
is a form of insanity. Millions live in and by that delusion; it has
become their *superficial* reality. Yet it is an illusion that can be dis-
pelled with simple, pure awareness: *You have always been wealthy.*
You do not need to rely on anything or anyone, including God, as
the source of the riches in your life, whether those riches are in the
form of material wealth, love, creativity, or joy. You alone are sufficient to meet every need. You were created, lacking nothing. To
perceive yourself as lacking anything is a delusion you have been
taught to believe and accept. Poverty is only your state of mind in
the present. As Neville Goddard, a well-known New Thought lec-
turer and writer, wrote, "Poverty is wealth asleep." Jesus reminded
his disciples to "consider the lilies of the field," and how they were
adorned by creation to be beautiful, as were we all.

Poverty or wealth has nothing to do with material things. Some
of the richest people on the planet have less, materially, than 90
percent of Americans. They live comfortably in huts, tents, or
yurts. They have no running water, barely any clothing, no electric-
ity, and little technology. They have little sense of the past or future. They work, hunt, plant and harvest, and use the plants around
them as medicine. They have sex, make babies, raise families, worship their gods, and experience no sense of lack, need, or inferior-
ity. Their children seem rich with innocence, trust, joy, and freedom

from fear, worry, ambition, competition, and conflict. In many ways, these are the most sane and satiated people on the planet.

When I talk about spiritual amnesia, I mean forgetfulness of the essence of who and what we are; the spiritual and metaphysical essentials of ordained human existence. We somehow agreed to come here from our pre-incarnate state, and if we pause long enough, we will remember that we said yes, and eventually we will know why we said yes! You are *not* here against your will, so stop telling yourself that, and you will find a peace and security you've not known. Stop protesting, contesting, resenting, or resisting your existence on earth. Enjoy saying and perhaps singing "yes," and the universe will organize itself around your "yes"! Welcome yourself and celebrate your presence on and in the earth. When you do that, others will celebrate your presence as well. It is an honor to be here and human, while maintaining your spirituality.

THANKS FOR THE MEMORIES

I have said that this process is really not one of discovery but of recovery, which is simply "remembering": recalling the immaterial self that we were before our Minds were locked into cognitive processors and became minds (small *m*). But since neuroscience can now explain how terrestrial memories are formed, where they are stored, how they are recalled, why are we so sure that we can ignore our trace memories of our pre-incarnation? Those are the memories that come to us when we are at peace, silent, relinquishing anxiety and worry, and allowing the tranquillity of God to wash over us. At those times, we can know the omniscience and unsurpassed love and joy of our previous state. We can feel at one with everything and everyone.

Here again, I slip on my Bible teacher cap. Students of the Bible will find this part more appealing than others, but please indulge me: the Apostle Paul spoke of this kind of remembering when he wrote, as I referred to earlier, "I want to know Christ and the power of his resurrection and the fellowship of sharing in his sufferings, becoming like him in his death, and so, somehow, to attain to the resurrection from the dead." The reason this is such an important statement is that Paul believed in two kinds of resurrections: a general resurrection of both the just and unjust, or righteous and less righteous, and a special resurrection that was more personal and individualistic. He hints at this resurrection in his letter to the Philippian church (Philippians 3:12): "Not that I have already obtained all this, or have already been made perfect, but I press on to take hold of that for which Christ Jesus took hold of me."

The Apostle was experiencing a type of metaphysical recall here. Paul's driving question was, "Why did Christ take hold of me?" Not "Why did I take hold of Christ?" I know that answer, because once you encounter the Christ Consciousness (what we can also call enlightenment)—especially when it is as dramatic as Paul's encounter is reported to have been—anybody in his right mind would take hold of Christ, the Person, Principle, and Presence. But why would Christ take hold of us? Paul wonders this even as he recalls in numerous letters his days as a religious zealot.

Notice what Paul says in his letter to the church at Galatia: "I want you to know, brothers, that the Gospel I preached is not something that man made up. I did not receive it from any man, nor was I taught it; rather, I received it by revelation from Jesus Christ. For you have heard of my previous way of life in Judaism, how intensely I persecuted the church of God and tried to destroy it. I was advancing in Judaism beyond many Jews of my own age and was extremely zealous for the traditions of my fathers. But when God, who set me apart from birth and called me by His grace, was pleased to reveal His Son in me so that I might preach Him among the Gentiles, I did not consult any man."

Did Paul's mother tell him this as a child? Doubtful. Was this a "memorial moment," in which Paul recalled his elected nature as a child of God? More likely, this was his mental recollection, reconnection, and reconciliation with his original self and the Sponsoring Thought in the mind of his Creator. Paul was remembering his higher order and destiny. It became clear to him at that time why Christ took hold of him: he remembered who and what he was when other men did not. The Universe knew that It could make great progress toward a new world with such a man, as imperfect (so to speak) as he was and claimed to be. It seems somehow that all God (the Universe) has as human instruments are cracked or imperfect vessels. Other than as a matter of semantics, I think all great leaders—philosophers, artists, scientists, entertainers, etc.—regardless of religious affiliation or identity, in some ways feel this strange "significance."

In a transcendent reality, we have always been here spiritually, because we are in and of God. In God Consciousness, we are created in and of the image, substance, and stuff of Divinity. We were all in the Creator's mind and on the divine agenda from the beginning, whatever that is. In God Consciousness, we always were, have been, and will be. Divinity is the same yesterday, today, and forever. Jesus understood this when He said, "Before Abraham was, I am" (John 8:58). Awareness of this in memory is the most comforting and consoling reality I know. It is one of the primary reasons I am thankful. The thought that I am of God, with God, and as God is the most satisfying concept, and it gives me the greatest sense of hope and safety I've ever known in my nearly sixty years of life. Opening up to such a memory and glorying in its truth is the perfect antidote to all the legalistic religious trappings of our society that try to make us unworthy in mind and spirit and convince us we need them to get into heaven. We are already there. Everything is consciousness, and consciousness is not stagnant, it is creative and ever evolving. Both heaven and hell are created, perceived, and experienced in consciousness. Neither may be an eternal reality as we perceive it, but both can be realized here and now—if and however we choose them, if and whenever we do so.

INTENT, NOT ACCIDENT

It seems to me that we tend to forget the essentials of life. I don't mean our physical or biological essence; I mean the spiritual and metaphysical essentials of human existence. We tend to remember the accidents and dwell on them rather than seeing everything as synchronous, working together to create a dynamic whole that is always becoming something new or more. All things work together for good and God—there are no real mistakes, just misinterpretations of certain realities. As Polly Berrien Berends, the author of *Whole Child, Whole Parent,* writes, "Everything that happens to you is your teacher . . . the secret is to learn to sit at the feet of your own life and be taught by it."

Life—or people in your life—will attempt to edit who you are by delusionary and circumstantial evidence. We all have a memory of God or of our innate divinity deeply woven into our spiritual DNA. It is a kind of cellular recall that is awakened when we encounter something or someone in tune with this particular reality or spiritual frequency. As Spirit having an earthly encounter, we are supposed to be walking memorials or memorandums to the Divinity to which we are all connected and in which we find our relevance.

There is in all of us a pre-incarnate formless, skinless, sinless, endless, and nameless self. This self may be untitled, but it is *entitled*! I call this "divine entitlement." We all feel it, and inwardly we all know it. We know there is something more to us and for us than we are being told or than we are experiencing on a daily basis. According to the Old Testament prophetic writings, as referred to earlier, God acknowledged this pre-incarnate reality and called to Jeremiah saying, "Before I formed you in the womb, I knew you [*chose* and *called* you]." This was Jeremiah's response: "Ah, Sovereign Lord, I do not know how to speak; I am only a child." That was Jeremiah's way of admitting that he saw himself as an underdeveloped soul, spiritually immature. There was no basis for him to feel this way; it was what had been handed down to him through the spirit of dualism and lack.

Here is the response of Spirit to Jeremiah's lamentation: "Do not say to me, 'I am only a child.' You must go to everyone I send you to and say whatever I command you. Do not be afraid of them, for I am with you and will rescue you." In other words, Spirit would lift up Jeremiah and remind him of his true self, which had the courage and will to go out among the people and realize the destiny we are all called and enabled to realize. Holy Spirit did not make this choice lightly, or wrongly. Jeremiah was worth such trust, even though he did not believe it at first. We all dwell in that same state. What God wills is not that we believe in Him as much as in ourselves. To believe in yourself is in essence to believe in God, the ultimate energy, ambiance, and intelligence out of and through which you were created and exist.

DIVINE DISCONTENT

It seems that every day is another day in the winter of our spiritual discontent. I have experienced it with regularity since being estranged from my beloved Pentecostal and evangelical communities. It feels like righteous indignation, but it's something more. Divine discontent can be defined as that irritating impulse that persists after you awaken in consciousness to the fact that there is more to life than meets the eye. This realization results in a restless spirit that demands that you search more aggressively for deeper understanding. It's a feeling that makes run-of-the-mill spirituality, with its bromides (boring, spiritless sedatives) and anti-intellectualism, unsatisfying.

Divine discontent comes from losing your spiritual amnesia and remembering who you are (and who you are not) and from desiring to be what you were originally designed to be: a cocreator with God. You become homesick for your pre-incarnate consciousness. In a sense, we are all homesick for our higher consciousness, culture, and character—our higher self. It represents the best of what we can become, and when we realize it is there, beaming from us like sunlight, we cannot turn off that awareness. Psychological testing has shown that once someone sees a pattern in a seemingly random collection of shapes, he or she cannot go back to *not* seeing the pattern. Thus it is with perceiving pre-incarnation. All of our anger, resentment, and conflict come from our anguish and ignorance over needing to reclaim the love, security, and freedom that we know is our birthright.

With this memory of pre-incarnate reality comes an unavoidable sense of entitlement. You realize what belongs to you; to your very essence and spirit. You come to know that you have inalienable rights and virtues of unconditional love, peace, prosperity, personal satisfaction, and security. These virtues are your spiritual birthrights, and you realize that they not only belong to you but *are* you. They are your immortal, immeasurable rights and reality.

Ultimately, all you really know is God, because all there really is to know is God. All is Consciousness and Spirit, and since you are an aspect of the creative power of Consciousness that is God, you are an innate and intimate part of all that is.

You have and are a high destiny and vibration in the earth, and that awareness makes the mean and petty concerns of man-made religion seem insignificant and unsatisfying, like the poorly recalled dreams you have just before waking. Once you fully come into your inheritance of this divine awareness, you know you are capable of so much more than what any superficial and superstitious religious culture claims. Some of my most sublime letters about God or spirituality come from people claiming to be either atheists or agnostics. They have somehow attained a state of consciousness that most so-called people of faith dare to even think about. They seem to be free, confident, uninhibited, and generous in spirit and benevolence. They perceive and experience God outside the religiously imposed paradigms and seem much more satisfied and grounded.

When spiritual discontent disappears, it is replaced by a flood of self-awareness, the desire to atone (be "at-one") with or for the past, and the drive to become what our divine destiny suggests we can be and indeed are.

ON SPIRIT

Let me remind you of the higher truths and trusts of Spirit! The word is *vodun* in Creole French, the source of the word *voodoo* as it is misinterpreted and misrepresented in English and Western thought. *Vodun* means "spirit," "ghost," or "deity," and the Bible refers to the Holy Spirit because people from time immemorial have, in their dual consciousness and concepts, believed in both holy and unholy spirits or ghosts.

Oh goodness, you say, is Bishop Pearson now going to tell us that voodoo is holy and ordained by God? Does the man have no shame? Yes I am, and, no, I do not. The truth is too important for limited ideas like shame or sham. So: people have always believed in spirits, because people are essentially that—spirit. But when I say that people believed, I really mean they *remembered*. People have always remembered that there is Spirit and that we *are* spirit. Misunderstanding or misinterpreting this reality has given rise to religion and religiosity, which seem to be more palatable than spirit or spirituality. It seems easier to wrap your brain around religion than around spirit. But while religion is a product of man, spirit is the child of the universe.

The African culture has maintained its original spirituality longer than most other cultures, for reasons I will examine here as part of our discussion of spirituality. It is important to note that archaeologists trace the origins of the human race to Africa. The oldest recorded human skeletal remains were found in Africa. It is believed that the Garden of Eden was somewhere in northern Africa or modern-day Iraq, where the Tigris and Euphrates rivers originate. To Africans, and a few other cultures, the soul or spirit is just as important as the mundane physical body. Both are constant presences in life, as are the *perceived* dead. I recognize that there are perversions in all estimations and religious excursions of the spiritual, but I believe there is ultimately "pure Spirit," and we are all hungry and hopeful for it.

However, the further away the human race got from its original African roots, the further away from the historical spirituality it became and varying perversions replaced it. In an attempt to regain some sense of that lost spirituality, we invented extravagant forms of superficial spirituality that we now call religion and divide into denominations whose sole purpose at times seems to be to wage war upon one another. All the religions have their brand of reconciliation and their modes and models to obtain it. They compete and compare rituals; some more exotic and dramatic than others. Remember, I call this "penance envy" (pardon the pun).

There are three words for religion in the Greek New Testament. One is *Iouadimos,* meaning "Judaism," and the second is *threskeia,* meaning "ceremonial observance or piety," from the base *threomai,* "to wail, clamor, frighten, or be frightened." Religion has always been about fear of gods, of nature, of chaos, of death. In religion, the gods are and have always been angry. To please or appease them, we've created sacrifices, sacraments, rites, rituals, rules, doctrines, dogmas, and disciplines. We call it the "faith-based community," but in essence it is the fear-based and faith-biased community.

The third word for religion is *deisidaimonia* (KJV has it as "superstition"), from *deilos,* meaning "fear, dread (deus), or reverence for *daimonia* . . . demons or spirits." 1 Corinthians 2:10 says much about this:

> The Spirit searches all things, even the deep [*bathos,* "profound, introspective"] things of God. For who among men knows the thoughts of a man except the man's spirit within him? In the same way, no one knows the thoughts of God except the Spirit of God. We have not received the spirit of the world but the Spirit who is from God, that we may understand what God has freely given us.
>
> This is what we speak, not in words taught us by human wisdom but in words [*Logos,* "divine expression or concepts"] taught by the Spirit, expressing spiritual truths in spiritual words. The man without the Spirit [not operating in Spirit or the spiritual] does not accept the things that come from the Spirit of God, for they are foolishness to him, and he cannot understand them, because they are spiritually discerned. The spiritual man makes judgments about all things, but he himself is not subject to any man's judgment.

I invite you to recapture something that religion has lost and in many ways the human race has lost: *our transcendence.* We have abdicated the high altar of spirituality and compromised our authentic selves and souls to religious regulations and man-made rites and rituals. We have become foreigners in the land of spirit, or as evangelicals call it, the Kingdom of God. The Kingdom of God is not a gated community guarded by Saint Peter and accessible only to those who beg Jesus to absolve them of sins they never committed. The Kingdom of God is a state of mind. Jesus prayed, "Thy

Kingdom come, Thy Will be done on earth as it is in heaven"—in effect, heaven is the higher reaches of consciousness, the world of trances and transcendence.

THE TRANSCENDENT SELF

A trance is an altered state of consciousness. To transcend is to go beyond and penetrate the mundane into a deeper truth or trust. Transcendence is the application and realization of the extended self and soul. It is a form of ecstasy. Ecstasy is made of two Greek words: *Ek,* meaning "out of," and *stasis,* which means "state" or "status." Ecstasy is standing outside the self, the normal stagnant self. It is penetrating the impenetrable reality, the self beyond the self.

The writer of the book of Hebrews admonishes the church to leave the elementary teachings about Christ and go on to maturity. I could not agree more. He didn't say abandon the teachings of Christ, he just said to go beyond them; leave the elementary or in effect fundamentalist religious teachings about Christ and transcend them; forget about the childish mythological teachings and interpretations of Christ for the greater and more mature and mystical vision and version. The verses (Hebrews 6:1–3) read like this:

> Therefore let us leave the elementary teachings about Christ and go on to maturity, not laying again the foundation of repentance from acts that lead to death [meaning "useless rituals"] and of faith in God, instruction about baptisms, the laying on of hands, the resurrection of the dead, and eternal judgment. And God permitting, we will do so.

The author was encouraging his readers to move toward transcendent thinking! To transcend is also to move from the sense level to the spirit level; to enter the "transcendental field"—that area of the mind or mystical awareness that lies beyond rational knowing, in which we can rely on our intuitive minds and eternal awareness to reveal great truths.

Eastern religion calls this Transcendental Meditation, a form of discovery that laudably emphasizes both human potential and scientific evaluation. It is the Eastern rendition of the Pentecostal rite of glossolalia, or speaking in tongues. Both involve repetitive mantras and messages in order to transform the consciousness and take the mind from the mundane state of the material world to the esoteric place of extraordinary knowing and being.

Sound has an intimate relationship to consciousness and spirituality, especially in the worship experience, both public and private. Notice the sound *ah* and how it repeatedly shows up in names or references to the Divine: Buddha, Krishna, Judah, Yehovah, Isaiah, Yeshuah, Allah, Chayah ("life" in Hebrew), and so forth.

The Christian religion and faith in general should be prepared to accept this holistic path to knowledge that respects both science and personal awareness, setting aside its role as ordained mediator. It is not. Yet that does not mean you cannot pursue transcendence and the rediscovery of your pre-incarnate awareness and self. This "essential recall" will reconnect you with your essential self, the ultimate you, the immortal, immeasurable, immutable you. Life will attempt to edit who you are by delusionary, artificial, circumstantial evidence. Step into a church, and you will see it for yourself. Step out of the church, back into the bounty, beauty, and energy of the world, and you will enter the cathedral of your self, your own immortal mosque, your extraterrestrial temple or synagogue, the immersion into your own YOU-niverse.

CHAPTER TEN

HEALING THE WOUNDED YOU

The only work that will ultimately bring any good to any of us is the work of contributing to the healing of the world.

—Marianne Williamson

The last several years of my life have been dominated by a healing process, especially with regard to how I perceive God, myself, and the universe. This is not so much healing from the hurt of the dissolution of much of the achievements of the first half of my life, but of the crippling stagnation of soul that my religious upbringing had caused me. I am not referring to the rich spiritual heritage to which I was exposed almost from infancy, in which I was raised, and which I will always cherish, revere, and regard highly. I am referring to the ignorance and arrogance of misinformation that lead to bondage and paranoia rather than freedom of being. This was a kind of illness, a psychological malady.

I did not know I was sick until I began to heal. I think this is the case for millions of people in the Christian community and other religious disciplines. We as people spend a lot of time and energy preparing for what we hope is a better future, but I am discovering daily that reparation is as important and in some ways more important that preparation for a fuller and more fulfilling future.

We all came here prepared for (paired to) God and good. Somewhere between the womb and the tomb we tend to forget that truth and need to be repaired to God and Good. This is the only healing or salvation really needed, and it all occurs in consciousness.

After living a certain way for decades, you begin to consider your pain a natural part of your life, and you lose any concept of the possibility of a pain-free life. It's a bit like the story of the two prospectors' mules tied up at the front of a saloon in the Old West. One mule looks normal, carrying a normal amount of gear. The other mule is laden with so much heavy equipment that his back is horribly bowed; his belly nearly touches the ground. The normal mule asks him, "How can you stand to carry that load?" The other mule answers, "What load?" In a Christian community preoccupied with our own smallness, we are not conscious of the load anymore. Human beings have become experts at perpetual pain management. We can be free, but freedom is not for cowards.

For years, I've believed and preached that a sick church produces a sick society, a sick society produces pain in its people, and hurting people hurt other people.

As a Pentecostal preacher in the holiness tradition, I can say that we don't look kindly on sin—especially marital infidelity—and as Christians we are taught to distance ourselves from all sinners, especially those who claim to be Christians yet continue in practices that we consider sinful. We learn this from the basic tenets of the Christian faith, one of which is that all humanity was born in sin and thus unacceptable to God, and another that we need to be forgiven of our sins and redeemed to God by Christ. Then we must remain free from any practices or people associated with sin in order to be saved or remain so. In effect, our faith is saying that God hates sin and sinners and ultimately tortures them in hell. There's really no room for forgiveness of flaws; there is either total capitulation (enslave yourself to Me) or total annihilation (welcome to hell).

Avoiding God's judgment and thus evading His wrath is the ongoing priority in that fundamentalist discipline, tradition, and life. Since God hates sin and sinners, we Christians are expected to do likewise, even if this means hating ourselves for sinning or even being tempted to sin, which we all are. Being human is to be tempted, and as we discussed in our chapter about sex, sometimes the temptations are by something that in any sane culture would be considered healthy and normal. In reality, all the Abrahamic religions (Judaism, Christianity, and Islam) embrace this basic philosophy and theology, but we Christians tend to think our system of dealing with the sin problem is better than any other. We consider ours ordained by God Himself and handed down to us through both Scripture and history. Since Christ is perceived not only as God's son but God in human form, then God is not only Christ but essentially (and perhaps subconsciously) a Christian. It is this mentality that has crippled love and life for billions of people and caused the greatest tensions in our world. We are wounded at the soul level because of this erroneous and dangerous religious presupposition.

This chapter is based on a sermon I preached at a large Atlanta church with which I've had a relationship since the late 1970s. It was one of the largest megachurches in the country for years. This changed when the founder and senior pastor was accused of moral improprieties and had to step down as senior minister (now deceased) and archbishop. At the time I shared this particular message there, the congregation had shrunk to a fraction of its prescandal size of over fifteen thousand, and the people were wounded by the rigors of the scrutiny, embarrassment, and persecution of the religious and secular public due to their pastor's impropriety. They had discovered the ugly truth about our inflexible brand of faith: that in a religion where man is at the bottom of the spiritual food chain, there is no tolerance for someone being merely human or, as it were, imperfectly human. If we are not able to sur-

pass our inherent nature—a task that is categorically impossible—
then we are worthless. No wonder we are a wounded people!

I hope to convey to you what I communicated to that congregation in pain. Because of our religious moorings and upbringing,
just about all of us are wounded, weary, weatherworn pilgrims,
straining to maintain a courteous relationship with whatever we
see as God. We may be traditional Christians chafing under years
of being told we are unworthy to sit in God's presence; or spiritual
seekers finding no man-made denomination satisfying and instead
nursing a fierce spiritual hunger or anger; or adherents to some alternative religious creed that is rejected by the dominant culture.
Then there are those simply tired of being told by nonbelievers
that faith in anything is a pernicious delusion, yet still learning and
perhaps needing to believe in *something*.

Gaining and maintaining a relationship with a spiritual presence is the focus of billions of people, many of whom have become
emotionally and spiritually bankrupt because of the sick, sad ways
that God is misrepresented. I see this as a global sickness that affects most cultures and continents, Christian and otherwise. I hope
that by drawing attention to this false image of Deity, many will
rethink what they believe about God and why they believe it. In
the first chapter of this section, we talked about coming back into
ownership of your transcendent self. In this chapter, we look at
what you must do to heal your earthly self at the same time and
level of consciousness.

BEING TRULY BORN AGAIN

Some will accuse me of debunking or denouncing a religious system by using its manual—the Bible—to prove that both are falli-
ble. They make a legitimate point. In a sense, it's like using venom
to cure a snakebite. Vaccines are exactly that. They are small por-

tions of the disease they treat. Faith can be used the same way and often is.

Some accuse me of twisting and perverting Scripture to support my presumed erroneous doctrines, but to the contrary, I respect and regard Scripture as important to make my claims that it has been used erroneously for millennia to obscure and obstruct the broader wisdom of the ages. Here again I refer to it to make an important point.

The New Testament Gospel of Luke (4:18–19) quotes Jesus as reading the words of the Old Testament Prophet Isaiah: "The Spirit of the Lord is upon me, because he hath anointed me to preach the gospel to the poor; he hath sent me to heal the brokenhearted, to preach deliverance to the captives, and recovering of sight to the blind, to set at liberty them that are bruised, to preach the acceptable year of the Lord." (KJV)

The wound in you is the broken heart you experienced when you decided (or perhaps discovered) that you allowed someone or something, including recent circumstances, to convince you that you were someone other than the person that God originally intended and created you to be. We read in Scripture that God so loved the world that He gave his only begotten son, and that whosoever believes in Him will not perish but have everlasting life. Most Christians have taken this literally. They insist that we have to somehow believe that Jesus was the Son of God in order to obtain salvation. Here's another way to interpret that passage: the begotten son is a metaphor for the begotten or forgotten self or soul—namely, you. You and all of us are begotten of God. When you believe in and embrace the principle and reality of Christ Consciousness—the truth that you are a transcendent child of God who has no need for further salvation, except perhaps from the clogs and blogs of your mind—it liberates you and makes you both a free person and a free spirit.

As for perishing, we will all die or transition physically. That's nature. But there are worse ways to experience destruction or death: the death or dissolution of spirit, and hope, self-worth, and spiritual wealth; the death or even murder of love and graciousness; and the false sense of alienation and isolation from God. That is the kind of death Scripture speaks of. Total enlightenment rescues us from that death; that sense of doom, damnation, and stagnation. A religion-free zone may be the best thing that can happen to the planet as we move forward into global destiny.

Sadly, for many Christians, the "begotten you" has become the "forgotten you," as we have become consumed with our modern Christian consciousness of sin and unworthiness before God. My goal is to remind you who you are, the begotten of God. You are an integral, eternal part of the One Consciousness. Nothing else anyone can say to you will have the ring of truth like this.

Being born again means being born anew into another consciousness. It does not mean deluding yourself into thinking that you can say you accept Christ and then waiting for Him to change you. That's not His job. It's *yours*.

In the context of birth, it means being reborn in awareness into a higher level of consciousness and reality. It's as if you have awakened to a new wonder, awareness, and world; it's very much like resurrection from the dead, when you awaken to a new state of being. But the transformation is from within, not from without. Being born again simply means to recover the begotten you that was part of God from the beginning and fell behind a curtain of forgetfulness. Scripture calls Christ the firstborn (not the only born) of God and of many. As the Apostle Paul says in Acts 17, we are all God's offspring. He wasn't talking to or referring exclusively to Christians. Any faith tradition that hides from you your unique connection to God and to all of life is stealing your birthright and misleading you.

Sons of God are as old as the concept of God being fatherly, preceding Christianity by millennia. First there was the Sun of God, then the sons or Son of God. Sun worship is one of the first and most ancient forms of worship. As noted earlier, even today billions emphasize worship of God on *Sun*days followed by Moon-day, or Monday. Sun worship and Son worship are as old as humankind. Jesus worshipped Yehovah, as did His Jewish contemporaries. He never even implied that He Himself should be worshipped and would be both embarrassed and appalled that billions do so. Following someone's teacher and worshipping the teacher or the teachings are different objectives altogether.

ETERNAL LIFE 101

Scripture suggests that God begat only one Son, Christ, but eternity itself is forever begetting. Eternity is the ever and ether of God. The "Only Begotten" is a spiritual being, it is the Christ Principle, and the principle of the divinity of man. The "only begotten son" is that which is begotten *only* of God, not of flesh, religion, or superstition. Jesus is quoted in John 3 as saying, "Flesh gives birth to flesh, but the Spirit gives birth to spirit." He came to save *that* which was lost, not *those* who were lost (Matthew 18:11, KJV). So you and indeed every human being who has ever walked this earth or ever will walk this earth is begotten of God in Spirit, which is where our true or pure selves originate, dwell, and thrive or you wouldn't be here. The Gospel, or Good News (evangelism), reminds them of this wonderful postulate. Those who believe this— that is, those who accept it and come to full awareness of it—will live or enjoy conscious eternity in and as their spiritual selves, God with us, God in us, and God as us! This is both eternal salvation and internal sanctuary.

The difference between perishing and having everlasting life is *memory.* Eternal life is the ability to recall and reconnect with the Original Idea that brought you to this life; the Sponsoring Thought that spawned your existence in the first place. In one sense, we are already in eternity; we are only experiencing it in the dimension of time, a concept created by humans to accommodate our linear minds. In reality, many leading theoretical physicists have speculated that time may not really exist; that the appearance of things happening in a linear, nonreversible order may be a reality—or perhaps illusion—in our minds only; that all things and all times really are one. The fact is that we were part eternity in our pre-incarnate selves, the selves we were before we entered the realm of flesh or earth consciousness and its physical costume, called a body.

We have a mind, we have a body, but we *are* spirit. King Solomon of old wrote that God has placed eternity in our hearts and that He (God) knows the end from the beginning. Eternity is nothing more than encountering the infinite you, ever evolving and growing from glory to glory (to use a biblical phrase!). Among other things, this means that there is an indefinable you. We are told so often these days by dogmatic science (which is just as fundamentalist as dogmatic religion) that our inner lives are meaningless side effects of brain activity. But clearly, this is not the case. Could that be also the case with air, light, and sediment? There is a universe (or perhaps a YOU-niverse) inside you that keeps transcending itself and realizing greater divinity and spontaneity. This is the you in which you must learn to believe and abide: the you that cannot be hurt, that lives, moves, and has its being as a part of the wholeness of God, invisible, invincible, and indivisible.

WHY BE SEPARATE?

So why are we allowed to experience this illusion of separation? Why did God not keep us with Itself in the first place, rather than create man and set us on this course to live and grow apart from awareness of our divine home and health? That is a question I and many New Thinkers have struggled with, but I think I have an answer (or at least an explanation that sounds plausible). I think the origins of the perception of original separation stem from what we have learned in studying evolution and how organisms adapt. You'll need to use your imagination with me here. Even today, human beings are adapting and will have to continue adapting as the planet's climate and culture shifts. The key lies in the importance of struggle and dissatisfaction in sparking growth and evolution. Organisms evolve new biological features, and the ones that help them survive—the ones that best weather times of struggle—are passed on to future generations. In this way, life moves forward.

Now, think of God as consciousness before time, existing in oneness with all consciousness in a holistic completeness. No sense of separation, just holism. Everything is one; inextricably and inseparably one. The Creator, or Creation Itself, looks at this situation and surmises, "There is no growth here, there is just continued existence." It perceives that in order for consciousness to ascend to new levels of existence, it must grow and evolve. But how is this possible on a level of existence where there is no conflict or obstacle? So creation in its unexplainable intelligence conducts an experiment, crafting a cosmos and beings who are filled with the Spirit That Is Creation's Consciousness: humanity. Now the universe is inhabited by individual beings; endowed generally with free will, allowing them to act out of harmony with the whole, to do as they will both deliberately and instinctively. They are free to strive and fail and stumble and discover and learn and evolve, and in doing so they carry the Spirit of God—their divine selves—to new levels of development and evolution. Man's original purpose was to aid Creation in transcending Its timeless, limitless, spaceless existence!

Of course, the caveat here is that we stubborn, willful humans fell out of unity with God by forgetting our original selves. In doing so, we grew scales on our eyes that blinded us to divine light and caused us to believe we were physical beings eking out a fragile existence with no connection to God other than pleas to avoid damnation and annihilation, perceived as death. If this theory is true, then our efforts here are to return not only to our original state of being and consciousness but our original mission: to carry forth God's desire for evolving spirit on earth. That is why we experience the sense of separation: to grow, to learn, to become wiser, and to appreciate the magnificent Oneness once we return to IT in consciousness.

THE SINS OF DR. RELIGION

According to Christian theology, we were all regenerated by Christ through what we are taught was His sacrificial death and bodily resurrection from the dead. You recovered the lost and languishing self you were through the first Adam and redeemed the birthright of your bright, beautiful self—the one restored to you by the last Adam, whom Christians perceive to be Jesus. Other disciplines perceive redemption differently, but all are looking for something restorative and conciliatory.

Now, mind you, to some logical thinkers, this concept is nothing more than legend, speculation, imagination, and faith-fueled fantasy. So what? Proving or disproving our religious legends (or, to some, fairy tales) won't necessarily change the capacity and propensity of humankind to have and exercise faith in a transcendent being, ideology, or even science. Somehow we humans will always believe. It is our nature to do so.

All religions have their formulas for some type of redemption; I've just described the Christian one. The formulas may be different, but the end result seems always to be redemption and personal recovery. Either way, I am not here to promote, prove, or disprove any particular religious perceptions of truth as much as to remind you of an inner knowing we all have but seem to have forgotten, regardless of religious affiliation.

Inwardly, you already know the person you have always been. But somewhere along the line, someone (usually a religion or its leader), even for us Christians, presumed that your heart—which was supposedly already healed by Christ through His earthly life and sacrifice on the Cross—healed improperly and needed to be rebroken and reset. This is what doctors do when a bone has grown or mended improperly. Religion never fixes it right, though, because religion is incapable of doing what only the Creator can do through consciousness. Getting back to some interesting Christian theology that you already know by now, I believe this act of grace is already accomplished: restoring you to your direct inner connection with the Divine. That is not so much what the Christian religion seems to be about; it is what I, as a believer, perceive the Christ Principle to be. Religions are intermediaries, with self-appointed vicars to supposedly bridge you to God, as if you needed that sort of intervention. You don't.

Sickness, lack, poverty, and all other perceived maladies are artificial, created by the mind and brought into temporal manifestation. Institutional religion has convinced the people of the world that they are victimized by God and need further treatment by a false means in order to complete the healing process. The only real sickness is in our minds. Religion is a sugar pill, a placebo that, through the power of suggestion, makes you think it is addressing a problem that doesn't really exist. It promises you truth, but what it really delivers is its invented "truth" in the form of dogma, ritual, or prohibition.

Here's the truth: you were never "sin sick" in the first place; you just believed a religious presupposed lie and thought you were, and acted on the misinformation. You not only believed a lie but also have grown to rely on it and worship it. Think about that: allowing yourself to be deceived by Dr. Religion has given you the sense of shared pain that connects you with others, along with a self-reinforcing community that confirms and affirms your sick beliefs.

But is that connection worth the price of self-deception and self-deprecation? This has got to change; and it will, if we take the time to invest in the discovery of our selves.

Since I openly declared that I did not believe in the traditional concept of hell and that I believed the idea of Inclusion to be the true foundation of the Christian Church, I have suffered in body and soul. I have been betrayed and abandoned by those whom I trusted and who trusted me. I have suffered great financial loss at a time in my life when I should have been planning for a cozy retirement. I have felt the pain of being cast out of a community and culture that I love and helped build, like the founder of a company tossed off the board of directors. Again, I've adjusted my thinking about some things I was brought up to believe, but my love for the people who taught me and the culture in which that theology thrived remains strong. I am not as active or accepted within that community these days, and I admit that has been painful, but only by my physically and psychologically limited self. The infinite and begotten me does not acknowledge the illusion of pain, death, or so-called enemies. It doesn't recognize defeat, because in the end and in its essence, it is always victorious. However, I recognize this only when I am true to myself. All of us are exactly the same way, with the same godly ability to endure the trials and tests of life and follow the path that seems right to us—not necessarily our church.

The imperishable, immutable you is divine. It is genderless, nameless, skinless, sinless, and endless. It is without race and is not defined by or confined to some earthly ethnicity or nationality. This you is the Christ-principled you, the god that Jesus is recorded to have said we all are at the core of our nature.

WORDS OF HEALING

At the beginning of Jesus' three-and-a-half-year ministry, He spoke a sort of inaugural message in which He acknowledged that this truth can be difficult for some to face. Since this passage is so important to millions of followers of the Christian Bible, I'd like to walk through it from a metaphysical perspective:

> Luke 4:18–19: The Spirit of the Lord is upon me, because he hath anointed me to preach the gospel to the poor; he hath sent me to heal the brokenhearted, to preach deliverance to the captives, and recovering of sight to the blind, to set at liberty them that are bruised, to preach the acceptable [accepted, propitious, or appropriately received] year [cycle, season, or session] of the Lord. (KJV)

The English word *heal* appears in this passage, as the Greek word *iomai,* meaning "cure." The English etymology of *heal* is quite revealing. It is made up of *he* plus *al,* a root that refers to Allah, the Aramaic (not actually Arabic) word for God, or, in its English variables, *he* plus *all.* It is a prayer to the God of heaven and earth, or spirit and flesh. It is a request of all the forces of earth to restore health and wholeness to the sick one or thing. The powers of the universe are invoked to help cure the being prayed for—or to correct some sort of errancy, inaccuracy, or divergence from the path and place of awareness; a sickness of spirit or mind, so to speak.

I've spoken healing prayers over thousands of people during my more than forty years in Pentecostal ministry. The invocation has inspired faith for powerful and positive change in many lives. In prayers like that, we summon all the forces of the universe in God to ordain harmony and health in body, mind, and soul. But what are we really calling on? Are we calling on God the outsider to heal us? No, because no doctor can heal us without our consent. What we are really doing is invoking God as Consciousness, the consciousness to which we are all connected in spirit, to awaken the healing power (whole consciousness) that dwells within us. Essentially, we're saying, "Spirit, heal [declare anew or again] thyself."

Miraculously, it happens again and again. We are our own best medicine. Jesus implied this when He cited the proverb "Physician, heal thyself."

Jesus quotes the words of the prophet Isaiah 61:1–2, saying, "The Spirit of the Lord is on me, because he has anointed me to preach good news to the poor [*ptochos,* in Greek meaning "crouching, cringing, or cowering spiritual beggars"]. He has sent me to proclaim freedom for the prisoners and recovery of sight for the blind [*tuphlos,* "opaque, smoky"], to release the oppressed, to proclaim the year [the season or cycle] of the Lord's favor." (Though Jesus spoke Aramaic and Hebrew, the record comes to us in Greek, thus the repeated references.)

Your life began with death. Of the roughly 400 million microscopic sperm that chased the egg in your mother's body, all seeking to fertilize it and begin the biological process that resulted in you, all but one died. Life in this physical form is a terminal and incurable sexually transmitted disease. It is terminal because we all experience the transition we call death, but it is not untreatable. In a sense, people go to church for some worshipful group therapy, to treat our common disease of amnesia. The word *disease* itself is revealing: *dis-ease,* a lack of ease, an anxiety of the spirit and mind. We do many other things to salve and reduce the tensions that we feel in the face of fearing God, threats of hell, worries about money, loneliness, and feelings of powerlessness. Drinking, drugs, endless work, and retreat into material possessions are all escapes; manmade prescriptions intended to treat the perceived illnesses we create by allowing ourselves to be brainwashed into forgetting that we possess all the healing power we will ever need. There is no cause to be wounded or live in a religious infirmary.

METAPHYSICIAN, HEAL THYSELF

Worship and meditation can be some of the most powerful and effective steps toward recovering our lost selves. The English word *worship* was originally pronounced "worthship," and it had to do with valuing and evaluating God and the things He created, including you, the worshipper. Unfortunately, it is difficult to properly worship or value God when you perceive what *He* created—you—as broken, wrong, worthless, or evil. If you internalize the teachings of fundamentalist Christianity, which insist that you are an originally flawed being dangling by a thread above the pits of hell, you're more likely to resent God than value Him, even if only in the secret places of your heart or head.

In the secular world, if a manufacturer is judged to have produced a defective, hazardous, or fraudulent product, there is a massive recall. Automobile companies have done this for years. It is expensive and a logistical nightmare, but it is illegal not to do it when the manufactured product is harmful or intrinsically flawed. Jesus seems to have viewed that part of humanity that was entrenched in legalistic, dogmatic religion (which is to say, most of humanity) as broken at its core through its own misperception. He attempted to mend this break, beginning with His own Jewish race and religion by reawakening them—and all who would listen—to our true and more accurate spiritual nature.

The Greek translation of the word *brokenhearted* is *suntribos,* meaning "to crush completely or to shatter." Jesus saw people operating in their accidental selves rather than their essential selves. He saw them broken and fragmented by a spiritual accident that warped their self-perception and enslaved them to a dominating religious hierarchy that had everything to do with power and politics and little to do with self-discovery, love, or eternal awareness.

Suntribos is made up of two words in Greek: *sun,* which literally means "one with" or "inextricably tied to," and *tribos,* which means a rutted or worn track of being or thinking, which is an excellent way to describe dogmatic, bound-by-its-own-rules religion. It is also associated with words that refer to a gate's sound: creaking, worn, and squeaking. By this metaphysical reading, the broken-hearted being is the creaking, rutted, broken you who has fractured into any number of pieces and personalities created by painful memories and the lies embedded in those memories. It is you who has been wounded by life and told that you do not possess what it takes to recover—that you are *not strong enough*! But that is a lie—you *are* strong enough. (I use the rather incendiary word *lie* to jolt us into recognizing the fog we've been in for centuries.) You carry the strength of angels in your spirit if only you can recognize and recover that part of you. Jesus recognized this. Otherwise, He would not have been willing to be persecuted and executed for identifying it in all He met. No physician tends to a patient whose condition is hopeless; he or she says, "Make them comfortable, there's nothing more we can do."

You know your "worthship." The traditional church is afraid to allow you to discover it because you may lose your codependency on it. As you read this book, I hope you will begin a kind of fact-finding mission to discover not so much why you hurt but the source of the pain. Do some self-excavating and interrogating. Most of our pain is historical, coming out of our past, obscuring our present, and thus perverting our future. But we can stop this degrading and deteriorating process.

Jesus, called Christ, appeared in history claiming He was sent to heal the brokenhearted, and when He died, He said, "It is finished." In Christian idealism, this means that humanity is healed, but evidently someone has convinced us that we're not. Let me ask those of you who are Christian: is it possible that the intent of God, to send Christ to earth as a messenger and teacher to open our eyes to the healing power of our true selves, could have failed? No, it is not. Especially if the mission is supposed to have been sponsored by

God or by eternal purpose, something that most Christians claim to believe. Therefore, the message that we need to somehow placate an angry God in order to be saved *again* must be false! What has convinced you that you are not intrinsically healed? Is it an institutionalized lie that you have inadvertently adopted as truth and are now acting out as the delusionary suggestions of a false reality?

In my past theology, I would simply have said, "The devil deceived us, and we are now sick and sinful because of his deception." The problem with that is, once you put the blame on an invisible entity outside of or other than yourself, you have empowered the concept and put responsibility elsewhere, giving up your power to change things. It is a simplistic answer for a simplistic audience. When you accept it without question, you become a helpless victim of the unseen. This is an invalid and inaccurate picture of who and what you are. You are mighty in your own right, able to cure your own ills once you see what has caused them.

This false reality has crafted personalities with which we have become familiar and tolerant of, to the point that many are (as some would say) "stuck on stupid" and don't know how to get free. So let's dig deeper now that we're wading hip deep in the waters of what some would call blasphemy and religious rebellion. Let's identify some of these persons traveling with you in mind and memory.

DIVINE PERSONALITY DISORDERS?

You have two personalities today: the wounded, limited, and accidental personality that is bound by fear, and the infinite personality that comes from Divine Consciousness. The challenge is to unite your dual personalities as one: an earthly self that functions day to day under the sun, and the eternal self that cannot die and has the power to manifest anything in thought. This book is a ministry between two covers, but it is not just about training—it is about enlightenment! I am summoning you out of darkness and into the marvelous light of self and soul awareness.

In 1 Corinthians 13:8–12, the writer expresses a part of this hopeful view in language that demands precise interpretation:

> Love never fails. But where there are prophecies, they will cease; where there are tongues, they will be stilled; where there is knowledge, it will pass away. For we know in part and we prophesy in part, but when perfection comes, the imperfect disappears. When I was a child, I talked like a child, I thought like a child, I reasoned like a child. When I became a man, I put childish ways behind me. Now we see but a poor reflection as in a mirror; then we shall see face to face. Now I know in part; then I shall know fully, even as I am fully known.

Fail is the Greek word *ekpipto,* which translates "to be driven from one's course, to lose one's way." I interpret the meaning of the reference to prophecies in the context of these modern times: that one of these days, religious forecasts will stop and gleeful talk of the end of the world will cease. Such fearful, ignorant messages won't be needed any longer because we will have arrived in consciousness at that place where the Lord (as it were) really is our shepherd and we shall not want, lack, or need—and more important, we are our own shepherds joining with God in cocreating the next stage of evolving reality.

"Where there are tongues [the need to be excessively verbal], they will be stilled" indicates that in this future time, dependency on verbal communication will no longer be an issue, because we will all be in communion (common union) with God and one another. There will be no more verbal sparing or opposing views talking over each other and demanding each other's attention and creating additional tensions. "Where there is knowledge, it will pass away": we won't need to *know* anything because we will "be" everything.

"For we know in part and we prophesy in part, but when perfection [*teleios,* "the purpose or result of an act"] comes, the imperfect [imprecise and inaccurate] disappears." This passage means that when our knowing arrives and rises, our perfection or maturity of consciousness will make itself known. Paul continues: "When I was a child, I talked like a child, I thought like a child, I reasoned like a child. When I became a man [an adult], I put childish ways behind me." This could not be more obvious; we are living in a childish state of awareness in which we are told to believe in the fairy-tale imagery of God's bogeyman, the devil, and the Superman version of Jesus coming to save us. This is ironic because in the philosophy of Friedrich Nietzsche, Jesus actually *was* a superman. However, he didn't mean a superficial fairy-tale personage with a cape and an antipathy for kryptonite, but a fully realized man living at the peak of all His temporal and spiritual powers. If and when we, in our maturity, abandon childish or underdeveloped things and ways, we will awaken to the adult version of faith that reminds us: we are God, we are our own salvation, we require nothing else, and nothing else is required of us. I perceive this as the ultimate will of God for us on this plane of consciousness.

The passage concludes: "Now we see but a poor reflection as in a mirror; then we shall see face to face. Now I know in part; then I shall know fully, even as I shall be fully known." In our fragmented and fractured realities, we are not getting an accurate picture of who we are. Most people, Christians included, see through a glass darkly, dimly, or barely, if they see at all. We don't perceive clearly because we have been convinced that looking too closely is unsanctified and dangerous. Because of our obstructed, obscured, and prohibited vision, we impersonate people of faith, when we are really people of fear; we parade around as though we have it all figured out, when in reality we are nothing more than children reciting memorized rhymes from a book of poems and religious mantras. Fear-based spirituality is not salvation.

Who's Behind the Wheel?

We all travel along, but none of us travels alone. We've picked up hitchhikers along the way. We have become so used to this traveling pack that it has become a kind of false life support system that we depend on for our very breath. This pack of passengers is the various roles you play, the personas you adopt, as you try to fit into a false sense of self and community—as you try to fit into a life you know deep down is inaccurate. You can never be healed until you take the wheel and all the passengers gladly head for the same destination.

So . . . who's driving your car? Who are your passengers? Where are you all going, especially if you're not bound for the same place? Where are your passengers taking you or insisting you take them? How do you feel about these passengers that masquerade as you or that you impersonate (often unwittingly)? Do you like the person you so often pretend to be? Have you become accustomed to the crowd, or do you feel smothered?

It can seem impossible to get to know your true self when you are always badgered and bothered by this multitude you host inside your mind. But it is important to know these personalities that you fight with over who gets to sit behind the wheel. Because when you can name them, you can gain power over them. You may not be sure if you even know all their names. They've been there so long, these imaginative personalities or personifications have become lifelong playmates; or in some cases, cell mates. You have bonded with them and they with you. There's the questing you, who wants to ask questions but is thwarted by the fearful you, who dares not defy convention. There's the fleshly you, tempted by shallow pleasures, and the spiritual you who feels guilty and is always trying to transcend the need for earthly things. Doubtless there are many other sides to you, many other seats in what must surely be an SUV on your life road. I don't refer to these so much as personality disorders, just personalities out of order!

These fellow sojourners are not explorers of truth, but perhaps of lies. If you stop, clear, and settle your mind, you can name them, or give them names. You can identify them because you know them well, better than you may know your real self. They switch places in the car and sometimes drive recklessly. Some break the speed limit; others never do. But it seems that someone other than you (the real, divine you) is always fighting for the driver's seat—and when they're not, they make their presence known from the backseat. Some you can see in the rearview mirror of your past. Others you can't see until they sneak up from behind and surprise you!

Are you ready to name some of these passengers and drivers? They are fear, pain, hurt, abuse, abandonment, shame, helplessness, powerlessness, cowardice, confusion—is this a familiar list? All are great liars and impersonators. They have almost supernatural powers of persuasion. We've given them those powers over the years by abdicating our own responsibility for our development, our future, our healing, and our salvation. When you take back that power consciously, you not only take back the wheel, you take back yourself—your lofty and liberated self.

Knowing that you are in a state of perfection already, that Christ and others in different spaces, places, and paces, came to remind us of our ability to create our own redemption, enables you to begin to heal your wounds. These wounds exist in memories of failures, losses, and times that you did not act according to the direction of your spirit but the direction of your dogma-induced fear. My goal is to help you begin to dismantle and disempower these memories. Not to *erase* the memory—because that robs you of a part of yourself—but to remove the lie or deception from the memory and grant you power over it instead of it having power over you.

We are naturally and almost unavoidably affected by these memories, but we don't have to be infected by them any longer. We can and shall heal. Theophosic counseling (*theophosic* means "God light") says, "Change the original lie in the memory, and you change the present." When you heal the past, you redeem the present. If you seek to change the present and do not change the original lie, you have only developed a stopgap in your behavior. Genuine recovery and healing demand not just removing the memory but transforming you, the being who carries that memory. It is a reinterpretation of your past that reshapes your future. Everyone has the capacity for that kind of freedom, and freedom it is. In the next chapter, we will look at using this new awareness and strength to produce the things you want most in life.

CHAPTER ELEVEN

WHAT YOU WANT WANTS YOU

When your desires are strong enough, you will appear to possess superhuman powers to achieve.

—Napoleon Hill

In the documentary *What the Bleep Do We Know?,* a narrative that posits a spiritual connection between quantum physics and consciousness, the question is asked: "Have you ever seen yourself through the eyes of someone else that you have become?" I would add, "Have you ever seen yourself through the eyes of someone else that you have become and are still becoming and getting to know?" They say in the movie, "The brain doesn't know the difference between what it sees in its environment and what it remembers." Perhaps the real secret to life is not being in the know but being in the mystery (or the "missed story"). You are not what you do, but you do what you think or are convinced you are, positive or negative. Some are convinced they are poor, needy, lost, and lacking, born in sin, shaped in iniquity, without God, and so on. The same is true when you think love, peace, grace, ability, creativity, and so forth.

The fact is that you are a cocreator of this world along with God and are in some ways equally as powerful; this is your birthright. We *create,* which is to cause to be or bring into existence. We *procreate,* which is to produce offspring. We *re-create,* or cause to be again, renew (reknow ourselves), revive, or renovate. Finally, we *cocreate,* which means that we realign ourselves with the Original Idea or Intention that spawned our existence. You have the ability to bring anything you want into being. You don't need to ask anyone's permission, least of all God's. God wants you to have what you want! You are actually created that way. You *are* what you want! God wants you to have you. This is both self-recovery and self-fulfilling.

We all say we love someone, but what we're really saying is we love the part of ourselves that we experience when we are with that person, be it parent, sibling, spouse, partner, child, or best friend. Most don't dare mention it, but life is all about self-love, self-satisfaction, self-gratification, self-validation, and self-affirmation. It all starts and stops with what we believe about ourselves, and how we experience that.

ARE YOU ANOINTED?

People evaluate you based on their religious presuppositions, as they did Jesus. Their perceptions are jaded by entrenched notions about how God views humankind, even though billions who claim to be Christians profess to believe in the finished, redemptive work of the Cross of Christian theology. We somehow still insist on seeing man as alienated from God by the same sin that according to Christianity Jesus atoned for and redeemed us from through His life, teachings, and sacrifice. But what others think of you matters less than what you think of yourself and how deeply you believe in your ability to have abundance in your life. Witness this lesson from Mark 8:27–30:

> Jesus and his disciples went on to the villages around Caesarea Philippi. On the way he asked them, "Who do people say I am?"

They replied, "Some say John the Baptist; others say Elijah; and still others, one of the prophets."

"But what about you?" he asked. "Who do you say I am?"

Peter answered, "You are the Christ."

Jesus warned them not to tell anyone about him.

I will change the question slightly and ask it this way; "Who do people say you are?" Then ask yourself, "Who do I say I am?" Peter said to Jesus, "You are the Christ," meaning, "You are the anointed one." That is the meaning of the word *Christ*. It's a Jewish concept but not confined exclusively to Judaism. If you answered your own question, would you say, "I am an anointed one"? Do you feel that you have an anointed, appointed destiny or purpose in your life? Are you messianic? Unfortunately, many people seem confused about their appointed destiny. Most have been conditioned to feel that they are less than who they actually are, but that is a falsehood. To be anointed means to be in the relative presence of the essence or reality we call God and to be aware of it. We have already established that as cocreators with God, we are always in that presence. Indeed, you *are* God's presence, at least a small and unique part of it. You are anointed all the time! The problem is that many don't know it or can't admit it or have forgotten it. But once you do, you can achieve wonders and also enjoy being wonderful.

There is not a person reading this book who has not been hurt by what people think about him or by what he presumes people are thinking about him or her. Again, perception is the ultimate reality, but not necessarily the ultimate truth. There are, no doubt, many people who read my books secretly simply because they are afraid of what people will think about them if they see them investigating such so-called heretical ideas. But people who fear revolutionary ideas are not so much afraid of you for encouraging wayward sons like myself; they are afraid of themselves. They fear who they are and who they are not, even who they might become.

Mostly, they fear that what they do not know or understand will *interest* them, and they will be forced to challenge their current beliefs and ideas—and most people don't feel safe or comfortable doing that! Remember this very important truth: *most humans would rather remain ignorant and awkwardly comfortable than have their eyes opened and face difficult truths.* Your toughest critic is always yourself. So when you know who you are and can face that truth, you are set free to be what God intended and what you ultimately and infinitely want. What you want wants you, because what you want is you!

THOU SHALT NOT . . .

My maternal grandfather lived to be eighty-four years old. I loved him dearly. He could neither read nor write, though he always had a good job and worked hard to take care of his wife and only child, my mother. Never once did he call in sick in over fifty years of working. When he made his transition, in 1992, he still did not believe the world was round or that man had gone to the moon. There was nothing I could do to convince him otherwise.

It is the comfort we have with outmoded knowledge that limits us and denies us. Some people are more comfortable with the idea that the earth is flat, even though it was proven centuries ago that it is round. It takes great courage to challenge illusions, especially when you are forced to look in the mirror and challenge that which you believed to be true about yourself.

Jesus was constantly confronted with and constantly confronted old and entrenched mentalities of religious superstition and stagnation. In Matthew 5:21, He is recorded to have said: "You have heard that it was said to the people long ago, 'Do not murder, and anyone who murders will be subject to judgment.' But I tell you that anyone who is angry with his brother will be subject to judgment. Again, anyone who says to his brother, *'raca'* [an Aramaic term of contempt], is answerable to the Sanhedrin. But anyone who says, 'You fool!' will be in danger of the fire of hell."

Jesus drew attention to the fact that for centuries people had relied on—and even deified—what they'd heard only through oral tradition, without questioning its accuracy. You can't even prove *that* it was said, let alone *what* they said. Neither do most of us try. Jesus is presenting all Bible-thumpers and those who love to shoot Bible bullets with a problem that almost sounds sacrilegious. He is outright *challenging* the Ten Commandments, the life and breath of the Jewish people to whom He was speaking.

Why was this something Jesus felt He needed to do? The people were living according to a strict religious code that dictated what they could and could not do—what they could or could not want—based on old rigid religious constraints that were literally choking out their lives. They were living around religious negatives: what they were told "thou shalt *not*" do, be, or become. When your focus is on what you cannot do or have, the power of your mind, which is a microcosm of God's mind, will bring into your life the same wanting and lack that you project.

It was to these same people that Jesus said, "Come to me, all you who are weary and burdened, and I will give you rest. Take my yoke upon you and learn from me, for I am gentle and humble in heart, and you will find rest for your souls. For my yoke [the spirit to which I am coupled with you] is easy and my burden [excise tax or invoice] is light." Jesus was saying, "I am not harsh, intolerant, cold, distant, stoic, and hard to get to know, as you have perceived God to be. I am come to show you what God is really like apart from your preconceived, traditional religious notions." He was trying to show them a self-identity greater than the "thou shalt not" habitual thinking of the time. He was trying to give them a sense of "thou art," not "thou aren't" or "thou shan't."

Christ was constantly trying to free the people from the past and make them conscious of the "now"—to be present. Eckhart Tolle writes, "Presence is the key to freedom, so you can only be free 'Now.' What we refer to as our life should probably be referred to as our 'life situation.' It is psychological time: past and future. Certain things in the past didn't go the way you wanted them to go. You are still resisting what happened in the past and, simultaneously, resisting what is. Hope is what keeps you going, but hope keeps you focused on the future . . . and this continued focus perpetuates your denial of the Now and therefore your unhappiness."

Tolle goes on to give some sound advice: "Forget your life situation for a while and pay attention to your Life. Your life situation exists in time. Your Life is Now. Your life situation is mind. Your life is real. Find the narrow gate that leads to life." It is called Now. It is not something that someone else labels you. Know who you are in reality, not the often-ambiguous impressions you get from your religion or politics or community. Who are you, alone and nameless? When you know that answer, vistas of possibility open before you.

THE POWER OF NOW

When Jesus asked His disciples, "Who do people say I am?" they all gave answers associating Jesus with their past. He was always someone dead and presumed reincarnated: John the Baptist, Isaiah, Jeremiah, and so forth. They simply could not see Him as He was at the present. Don't we all have this problem? We don't or can't or perhaps refuse to see ourselves as anybody but someone we used to know or heard about. The comparisons are infinite. We see ourselves in terms of someone else, some other ideal, some brand or profile of what we're supposed to be. But what if you are something new and fresh? What if there has never been a single soul on this earth who is just like you at this very moment, this very Now?

We all seem to be traveling from our past to our future while bypassing our now, like a highway exit we drive by without thinking about it. What's so intimidating about now? It seems to pass so quickly, and yet it never goes away. Tomorrow seems to be almost illusionary because when it finally arrives, it's only today. Writer Ambrose Bierce, author of the bitingly satirical *The Devil's Dictionary*, once said that all pleasure was experienced either in remembrance of some past event or in anticipation of some future event; no one ever was able to take pleasure in the moment. I have no doubt that he was accurately describing the majority of humanity. It requires introspection and deliberation to stop the flow of the day and allow your mind to be in the now. Yet now is everything; it is the stage on which the drama of life is playing out!

We believe in tomorrow because we were here yesterday. But tomorrow has its roots in today. The things we wish to manifest in our lives—health, prosperity, love, opportunity, dear friends—cannot come about in our futures unless we can visualize them and bring them into being with our minds today, in the now. So becoming fully aware and alive in the present moment, rather than living according to some hazy past, is essential to our realizing our full destinies and selves.

Jesus asked His disciples, "Who do people say I am?" Not because He was unaware of what people thought about Him or because He necessarily cared what people thought about Him—at least not in a way that was of any significant consequence to His self-worth. He wanted to help His disciples avoid perceiving Him as others did: through the eyes of their jaded religious presuppositions. The religious church of His Jewish heritage could only see Jesus as something or someone out of its past. It had no concept of the Now. All its tomorrows were repetitions of the past. The church members had nothing to look forward to but their past: who they used to be, what they used to think, and how they used or were supposed to live!

Also, look at the revealing wording. Jesus asked, "Who do they say I am?" God is recorded to have spoken to Moses, saying, "I Am That I Am." Not "I Am That I Was," or "I Am That I Will Be." The narrative suggests that both God and Jesus were indicating they were complete in the moment. They did not need the validation of the past or the promise of the future to complete their beings. They were complete and universal and whole in the now. As siblings with Christ and begotten children of God, we are the same as they are. We are perfect in the now, capable of the miraculous. This is why Jesus prayed, that we—His disciples in particular and all of humankind in general—would be one in consciousness as He was one with God.

SEIZE THE MOMENT

I've come to the conclusion that our primary objective in life is to seize not just *the* moment, but *this* moment and its momentum. Too many of us are busy waiting for *the* moment at some later time while we allow this one to pass us by. It's precisely like the apocalyptic thinking about the Second Coming, with happiness and fulfillment always deferred, a blank check never cashed. Both Jews and Muslims are still waiting for a Messiah, along with us Christians. *Every* moment is indeed a messianic moment, and all human beings are messianic missions and missionaries.

However, in some ways, we're all victims of what Tolle calls "psychological time." The crime scene is still intact, and we're held there in suspension by religious presupposition and ritualistic idolatry. As the detectives dust the room for clues, they find fingerprints all over everything, especially us, the victims. They are the fingerprints of time, memorialized by history.

We often use the term *buying time.* What has time bought or brought you? Has it brought you pain or joy, fear or courage? Time has brought and taught us stuff we don't need. There have been good things, but those things often are overshadowed by the pain and misery of memorialized anger and fear. This causes us to create conditions of apprehension and want in our present, and this suppresses and deadens the now. We do not lift up our heads to see what we want and envision the future, and because today is the planter's field for tomorrow, this gives us nothing to harvest in our futures. So it is no wonder that we are often unable to create what we want in life: we cannot allow ourselves to feel that we deserve it in our present.

We must learn to manage and master time—to turn Now into fertile ground for having the lives we want today, tomorrow, and infinitely. This is the primary life function of enlightened souls. Once we have made time our ally and mastered it through the power of the divine mind, harmonizing with it like music, we ultimately (through resurrection consciousness) escape or process into infinity.

Tolle says, "Look around—just look, don't interpret. See the light, shapes, colors, and textures. Be aware of the silent presence in everything and of it. Be aware of the space that allows everything to be. God is that mystical Space that allows everything, including Time, to exist." You are that presence, the God factor functioning in and through us by faith.

BE RIGHT FOR YOURSELF

It has been said that we see things not as they are but as we are. We all suffer from "truth decay," and our cure is not orthodontia but orthodoxy, "truth straightening." I don't mean religious orthodoxy, I mean spiritual accuracy. In the May 23, 2005, issue of *Newsweek,* columnist George Will wrote, "the greatest threat to civility—and ultimately to civilization—is an excess of certitude. The world is much menaced just now by people who think that the world and their duties in it are clear and simple. They are certain that they know what and/or who created the universe and what this creator wants them to do to make our little speck in the universe perfect, even if extreme measures, even violence, are required."

America, he goes on to say, is currently awash in an unpleasant surplus of clanging, clashing certitudes, and that is why there is such a level of a rhetorical bitterness disproportionate to our real differences. Some people think they have both the right to be right and the *responsibility* to be right. But why can we not be *both*? Why cannot God bless both streams of thought, Ishmael and Isaac, Pentecostal and non-Pentecostal, Protestant and Roman Catholic? Instead we have a tribal mentality, saying, "Look how many people agree with us. Look at the crowds that follow us. We must be in the right!"

The thing is, you are right—for yourself. You are always right about what is right for you when you approach living from the perspective of your true self, your eternal self. You may not be right for other people; indeed, no one can determine the right course *for* another spirit, which is why religion is wrongheaded when it tries to direct the lives of its congregants rather than inspiring them to choose wisely for themselves. Many churches would rather fish for their members than teach them to fish. The ultimate role of religion should be as a kind of spiritual self-help community that enlightens or reminds its members as to their true nature and helps them understand how they can use their new awareness to create the lives they want—and the world that God wants.

Let's look again at a passage from 1 Samuel 30 that illustrates this self-help principle, with some interpretive comments from me. (Remember, I'm a fourth-generation preacher.)

> David and his men reached Ziklag on the third day. Now the Amalekites had raided the Negev and Ziklag. They had attacked Ziklag and burned it, and had taken captive the women and all who were in it, both young and old. They killed none of them, but carried them off as they went on their way.

The fortunes you think have been robbed from your future are not dead, they are just in captivity to your own self-doubt and ignorance of your true power. But you can recover them.

> When David and his men came to Ziklag, they found it destroyed by fire and their wives and sons and daughters taken captive. So David and his men wept aloud until they had no strength left to weep. David's two wives had been captured— Ahinoam of Jezreel and Abigail, the widow of Nabal of Carmel. David was greatly distressed because the men were talking of stoning him; each one was bitter in spirit because of his sons and daughters. But David found strength in the Lord his God.

Self-actualization becomes part of your healing and recovery process. We must all learn to apprehend our self and soul to God. How did David do this? More than likely he recalled his past victories and successes in God. He recalled the lion he killed with his bare hands, and he could never forget his victorious confrontation with Goliath the giant. While to some these stories may simply be legends and illustrations, they still make for good conversation with powerful morals.

Part of healing one's wounds is remembering your good (God) works and inspiring yourself with the knowledge that you have more miracles inside you.

I've seen my church packed and the parking lot full. I remember a time when the neighbors came running across the street to complain on a Sunday morning that our congregants were parking on their street because there was no room left in the parking lot. I remember the nationwide television broadcasts, the great Azusa conferences I hosted for fifteen years, attracting tens of thousands a week, and all the blessings and bounty we felt was from God. Well, nothing has changed. Some of my views and perceptions have changed, but I have not changed. My spirit is eternal and immutable; its essence is the same. God is still with me and in me and, I like to say, as me. I am available to God, as God is to me. Scripture says God will never leave or forsake us but will be with us always, even to the end of the age, of the life and level you are in and on now. David is at that point in this story, the point of vital transition.

> Then David said to Abiathar the priest, the son of Ahimelech, "Bring me the ephod [an official prayer garment, covering, or cloth]." Abiathar brought it to him, and David inquired of the Lord, "Shall I pursue this raiding party? Will I overtake them?"
>
> "Pursue them," he answered. "You will certainly overtake them and succeed in the rescue." David and the six hundred men with him came to the Besor Ravine, where some stayed behind, for two hundred men were too exhausted to cross the ravine. But David and four hundred men continued the pursuit.

At this stage, David has made the decision to give up passivity and pursue his inner demons, which are little less than distortions of inner dreams. When your mental passengers—fear, confusion, isolation, humiliation, and paranoia—have nothing to feed, sustain, or support them, they vanish. They are created and motivated by lies, things you believe about yourself and God that are not true. We are made in God's image and likeness. Anything else is an impersonation. The priest told David to pursue these enemies. The goal was not just to capture them but also to conquer and eliminate them, to change the conditions that made them possible. True self-transformation means changing your inner ecosystem to support a different kind of life and energy.

> They found an Egyptian in a field and brought him to David. They gave him water to drink and food to eat—part of a cake of pressed figs and two cakes of raisins. He ate and was revived, for

he had not eaten any food or drunk any water for three days and three nights.

Don't look for or expect help from normal means or people. Help often comes from marginalized people who live outside the norms of dogma and conventional wisdom inflicted upon people by others. They are often called madmen or saints because they live based on their own wisdom, going against the grain of society. You will rescue them, pick them up, feed and revive them, and they will help you recover yourself, to discover who you are and what you want.

> David asked him, "To whom do you belong, and where do you come from?" He said, "I am an Egyptian, the slave of an Amalekite. My master abandoned me when I became ill three days ago. We raided the Negev of the Kerethites and the territory belonging to Judah and the Negev of Caleb. And we burned Ziklag."
>
> David asked him, "Can you lead me down to this raiding party?" He answered, "Swear to me before God that you will not kill me or hand me over to my master, and I will take you down to them."

This will not be a violent, hostile takeover. What we need to recover is not dead or dying. It is in active service to another master: the you that lives, based on fear. You can get it all back: your self-respect, self-worth, grace, and purpose. You don't have to be angry, hurt, frustrated, and insecure. You don't have to be a paranoid, addictive, compulsive, codependent religious junkie. At this point, David has begun to see that what he wants has never been separated from him by anything more than his mind-set.

> He led David down, and there they were, scattered over the countryside, eating, drinking and reveling because of the great

amount of plunder they had taken from the land of the Philistines and from Judah. David fought them from dusk until the evening of the next day, and none of them got away, except four hundred young men who rode off on camels and fled. David recovered everything the Amalekites had taken, including his two wives. Nothing was missing: young or old, boy or girl, plunder or anything else they had taken. David brought everything back. He took all the flocks and herds, and his men drove them ahead of the other livestock, saying, "This is David's plunder."

No conquest was needed, nothing had been lost. David found what he wanted because he was willing to search, and it came to him in his mind before it came to him in his material reality. Because he quested, because he was at the time merciful and just, because he sought what he wanted from a spirit of justice and self-knowledge, his mind made it possible to find that great goal. He manifested what he wanted through the power of both thought and action.

WHAT YOU WANT WANTS YOU

The loneliest moment in life is not when you lose friends, family, or things. You are loneliest when you are away from or unaware of your true self. Each of us has an ideal in our minds of what life can be and what we deserve. It's like a taste that we can't shake, a scent that arouses vivid memories that haunt us. But it's very real. Most of our values, responses, and actions are based primarily on what we believe about ourselves. In this way, belief does become reality. You will only bring into your life what you believe is possible; everything else will be an accident.

As stated earlier, what you want wants you—and what you want *is* you. What do both those ideas mean? "What you want wants you" means that the universe is designed to channel abundance and joy your way, because that is how Creation is designed.

Remember, God is not a God of hell and horror but of love. However, because you have free will, you can block that natural flow of richness by harboring fear, resentment, or feelings of low self-worth. Sometimes all you need to realize your dreams is to wake up, get out of your bed, and let good come to you. No matter how intensely you *want*, nothing will come to you if you don't know and believe in your self that you *deserve* it. One of the greatest misunderstandings in the religious disciplines is that poverty is a virtue of piety. It is not. Even Jesus wore a seamless garment, which was the equivalent of a Versace in His day. Why else would the soldiers around the Cross upon which He was crucified gamble for it?

As for "what you want is you," that is a central principle of New Thought. Since we are part of the wholeness of God's being and consciousness, and God is all things in mind, we must therefore be all things as well. So you have in your mind the mental existence of all that you need: money, shelter, relationships, health. There is nothing you can achieve or create for yourself that does not already exist in your vision. What you must do is accept that this is true, visualize what you want to manifest in your life, and hold that powerful and transcendent thought in the face of all the storms of life—all the religious presuppositions telling you that you are *not* sufficient, that you're not good enough.

So you can see that you *are* what you want and it *wants* to flow to you! You must *become* in mind the financial security that you wish to see, the reconciliation with a loved one that you wish to achieve, the place, space, and pace you desire. Once you become those things in mind, they will manifest for you in material experience. That is the essence of your nature as divine and the destiny that God wants you to reach. You cocreate your world and experience self-actualization by using the principles—the spiritual ecosystem—that the universe already has in place.

Sounds wonderful, doesn't it? But to achieve that state of being, we must get rid of all those beliefs that are pulling at the back of our mind, the ones we find hard to ignore when assaulted by religious doctrine or beliefs that tells us we are worthless, meager, and miserable. Remember, we become what we think about. When you think it, you experience it. The images in your mind literally pull you toward those outcomes like magnets. Thoughts have inventive and creative might, so if you unconsciously feel that you are good enough only for a minimum wage job, guess what kind of job will be offered to you all your life? The universe doesn't discriminate or excuse; it returns to you precisely what you give to it. Your thoughts are the raw material of your reality; the cosmos is the manufacturing plant. I read somewhere that you can have your dreams and you can have your excuses, but you can't have both!

Tolle writes, "Your sense of who you are determines what you perceive as your needs and what matters to you in life—and whatever matters to you will have the power to upset and disturb you. You can use this as a criterion for how deeply you know yourself. What matters to you is not necessarily what you say or believe but what your actions and reactions reveal as important and serious to you. So you may ask yourself the question: what are the things that upset and disturb me? If small things have the power to disturb you, then who you think you are is exactly that: small. That will be your unconscious belief."

The Infinite Ego

Many of us like to call ourselves agents of change, peace, and freedom. But have we changed? Do we have peace? Are we free? You can't teach what you don't know, and you can't lead where you don't go. No one wants to be a public success and a private failure. Anger is a signal emotion indicating unresolved issues of fear and anxiety.

There's a phrase that says, "Don't sweat the small stuff." I like to rephrase it as "Don't sweat the small you." Instead find the larger-than-life you, the divine being who is capable of miracles, and begin living every day with that in mind. Recover the best you, the one that God has been waiting to raise up among the enlightened of the world.

Over the last several years, I've had out-of-body experiences, so to speak. I've been kicked out of the institutionalized so-called Body of Christ, the traditional evangelical Pentecostal/charismatic world, and through my "excommunication," I've had to look back at the body that I left behind—the one that some people are still trying to resuscitate. It's as if I'm hovering above in a higher consciousness of self while looking down on the lower consciousness in which I used to dwell. This is not to say I have become superior to the people in that community, whom I loved and still love, only that I have elevated myself above what I used to be in consciousness. Jesus, in Luke 15, shared the parable of lost things. It reminded me of the lyrics of a song I used to sing: "I lost it all, but I found everything, I died a pauper, to be born a king, for when I learned how to lose, I found out how to win, I lost it all . . . to find everything."

Jesus' reference to the prodigal son was a reference to the extravagant, exaggerated self: the ego. The ego is the false centeredness of the human self rather than the transcendent self. The ego is a delicate balancing act. When I speak of the typical human ego, I'm speaking of the earth-centered self that cannot look past its own physique or physical nature and therefore its earthbound problems. But when the mind awakens, the ego comes into balance: the infinite self that truly *is* the center of the universe but is not bound to any limitations. The difference? The human ego, in contrast to the divine ego, is self-centered, boastful, and focused only on self-gratification. The divine ego is about profound gratitude, knowledge of self as eternal, and the desire to manifest God's creative glory for all. It is a generous spirit of creation, not hoarding or self-aggrandizing.

Our friend Eckhart Tolle calls the small ego "role-playing." He writes, "To do whatever is required of you in any situation without it becoming a role that you identify with is an essential lesson in the art of living that each of us is here to learn. When you don't play roles, it means there is no ego in what you do . . . There is no secondary agenda . . . as a result, your actions have far greater power."

The ego hides the better and more beautiful self and mutes the voice of our deep inner priests of soul—the lost voice and vision that show us what and who we really are. When we can see that truth, we become like Zacchaeus, the biblical tax collector (really, almost an organized crime boss) who climbed a tree so that he could see who Jesus was. We referred to him earlier.

I see us all as climbing trees (truths) because we know that the Christ Principle is coming our way. In the Gospel of Luke, Jesus admonishes His disciples to "seek first the Kingdom of God" and all material necessities and desires will come to them automatically. Self-actualization is the Kingdom of God (divine reality) that causes everything else you think you need to fall into place as the recipe calls for it. We were created with the ingredients, but we must learn or remember the recipe.

You think you want stuff (things), but perhaps what you really want (and perhaps all you need) is your authentic self. Recovering and reconnecting with "you" is the only salvation you'll ever really need. Everything you want can be found there. Now let us take on one last "spiritual reengineering" task and look at how you can make the most of the changes this transformation will bring about.

CHAPTER TWELVE

THE ART AND ARCHITECTURE OF CHANGE

Keep changing. When you're through changing, you're through.

—Bruce Fairchild Barton

Charles Darwin wrote: "It is not the strongest of our species that survive, nor the most intelligent, but those most responsive to change." I so agree that our very survival as humans and individuals depends on our ability and willingness to change.

At the root of all growth, we find change. Occasionally, change and the circumstances leading up to it are a source of extraordinary joy, but more often than not they provoke awkward feelings of discomfort, fear, or pain. Though many changes are unavoidable, we should not believe that we are subject to the whims of an unpredictable universe. It is our response to those circumstances that will dictate the nature of our experiences. At the heart of every transformation, no matter how chaotic, there is substance. When we no longer resist change and instead regard it as an opportunity to grow, we find that we are far from helpless in the face of it.

I can speak personally to the truth of this. My transformation, in case you don't know the story of how I became "God's heretic," stemmed from an encounter in consciousness that came upon me like a bolt of lightning. The shocking truth about the unreality of hell (the way I'd been taught it) that I encountered left me with two choices: keep things the same as they were and ignore this epiphany, knowing that I would be betraying the spirit of God that chose to enlighten me and betraying my own moral sense; or change everything I had known. I did not see that choosing to condemn the idea of hell and to preach Inclusion—the concept that the whole world is saved but just doesn't know it—would cost me so dearly, but once it became clear how toxic the fallout would be, I still chose to accept the change and my own evolution consciously, both to honor and own it and its results. It was actually something that chose *me*, rather than me choosing it.

I lost my church, my income, my standing and position, and many relationships. But once I saw this not as disaster but as radical change leading me to a new and more radical destiny, I was able to embrace it; to ride the wave instead of being swept under it and drowning.

Our role as masters of our own destinies is cemented when we choose to make change work in our favor. Yet before we can internalize this power, we must accept that we cannot hide from the changes taking place all around us. Existence as we know it will come to an end at some point, making way for some new mode and possibly mood of being. Some call this death, but I call it transformation or transition. Death as we tend to perceive it is an opulent, extravagant, and arrogant illusion. We are eternal, so we do not cease; we change or transition infinitely and into infinity.

Change and transformation will take place whether we want them to or not, so it is up to us to decide whether we will open our eyes to the blessings hidden amid disorder or close ourselves off from opportunities hidden behind obstacles and the mysterious. The Apostle Paul wrote, "I die daily," meaning that he was subject to the buffeting forces of change daily, making him into a new and evolving man. By embracing his purpose, he, like Jesus, was able to ride those waves and even create some himself.

Making Change Work for You

To make change work for you, look constructively at your situation and ask yourself how you can benefit from the transformation that is taking place. As threatening as change can seem, it is often a sign that a new era of your life has begun—a gateway to a new mode and model of being, thinking, or feeling. If you reevaluate your plans and goals in the days or weeks following a major change, you will discover that you can adapt your ambition to the circumstances before you and even *capitalize* on these changes. Optimism, enthusiasm, and flexibility will aid you greatly, as there is nothing to gain by dwelling on what might have been. Change can seem painful in the short term, but, if you are willing to embrace it proactively, its lasting impact will nearly always be physically, spiritually, intellectually, and circumstantially transformative.

Romans 12:1–2 weighs in on this reality:

> Do not conform any longer to the pattern of this world, but be transformed by the renewing of your mind. Then you will be able to test and approve what God's will is—his good, pleasing, and perfect will.

What is the difference between what is holy and pleasing to God and what is holy and pleasing to us as gods who frequently don't know we are divine? What if pleasing God, the Ultimate Reality, in holiness is also pleasing ourselves? This would certainly derail the very puritan thought that pleasure is fundamentally sinful, which is a ridiculous idea on its face, as God would not have created us were there not pleasure taken in us. We can't see God; all we have is a book of rules—most of them man-made—that we revere as sacred and nearly idolize as the embodiment of God. But what if the closest personal experience to God's holy will is that which fulfills us most inwardly as holy, pure, and pleasing? Think about this: since we are made in the image and likeness of God and possess divine genetic code, would not what pleases us in spirit please God? I'm not talking about the pleasures of the flesh or food, but pleasure in creating, envisioning, and bringing joy through love and self-discovery.

You are an element of God placed in this world in order to evolve and grow, and that means being unafraid of change. When you have achieved the healing and recovery that awareness brings and discovered what you want, the next stage in your evolution in God is to embrace change in your life—to lose your fear of it and understand that change means you are alive in divine awareness. Static individuals, fearful of living and trapped in the words and ideas of others, die long before their deaths. So how do you become an agent and artist of change, creating a new self, like a painter crafts canvases?

When I use the word *change,* I use it in the sense of the more accurate functions of the self and soul. Change in this realm means ascension to higher consciousness and broader hope, not hype or hypocrisy. This is about owning and honoring who you are in essence, the *person.* You are making a transformation to Original Thought—the Idea or Logos (logic) that birthed you—and from that transformation comes the change in your own thinking that moves mountains or re-creates them and changes your world. Transition is a universal progression; nothing is standing still. Even your eternal self, which goes on existing and growing after your physical body dissolves, undergoes its own continual evolution. That is the purpose of physical existence. We prepare and repair here, then we move on.

We are all agents, artists, and architects of change. Change happens not only *to* you, it happens *through* you and extends its transformative dynamic to others. We are learning first to make change, mark change, manage change, and ultimately master change! Change is the beautiful and bountiful evolution of the soul, the powerful expansion of the self.

LIFE IS AN EXPERIMENT

Harry Emerson Fosdick, first pastor of the historic interdenominational Riverside Church in New York City, who lived from 1878 to 1969, said, "Christians are supposed not merely to endure change, nor even to profit by it, but to cause it." Of course, we actually do profit from change, but we also act as *prophets* of it—at least, we do when we act in the true spirit of Christ. Christ's very nature was one of creating upheaval: He arrived into a hidebound, stratified religious bureaucracy and set about turning it upside down. He faced fierce opposition in this mission from people who had a vested interest in seeing that change did not occur in the society they controlled, but He knew a vital principle: once spiritual change is set in motion, it does not matter what temporal obstacles are placed in its path. It will come to pass in the physical world as surely as it did in the spiritual. This is a law of change.

Hannah Hurnard, the author of *Hinds' Feet on High Places*, wrote, "If we try to resist loss and change or to hold on to blessings and joy belonging to a past which must drop away from us, we postpone all the new blessings awaiting us on a higher level and find ourselves left in a barren, bleak winter of sorrow and loneliness." This can be the hardest aspect of bringing about change in our lives. It is tempting to hold on to a past that no longer wants us or no longer exists because it has a sense of certainty to it, whereas the future, no matter how promising, is filled with uncertainty. Uncertainty is the basis or beauty of mystery and the entrance into renewal and reknowing; indeed, remembering.

At times, I still wrestle with letting go of that aspect of my past life that was taken from me (or perhaps something given back) due to my journey into Inclusion Consciousness and New Thought. I find myself at times inadvertently mourning for what I have lost—not in my conscious, but in my subconscious reality. I don't do it willingly or deliberately, or even knowingly at times, I just sometimes do it habitually. We have all developed a habit of protesting change in some way rather than embracing its potential for creating "fresh good" and blessings in our lives and the lives of others. We mourn and grieve what we perceive ourselves as losing. We put on our own going-away parties that are nothing more than pity parties over the fact that we don't have complete control over what happens.

But while we do not have control over what happens, we have total control over how we respond, and we have the godlike power to look into the future and make plans for it based on our insight and vision. Experience is not only what happens to us but also what we do with what happens to us. Ironically, while we can live only in the present, the past can teach us much about how to respond to the present and create our own future through the decisions we make and the changes in our spiritual selves that we consciously bring about. So we must be beings in balance, living simultaneously in the lessons of the past, the experiences of the present, and the promise of the future, without dwelling too much in any one state.

Life is both an experience and an experiment. I say experiment because though I don't necessarily think we've been *here* before, we have *been* before and always were—indeed, are! This human encounter then becomes a kind of experiment in the time continuum. An experiment is a tentative procedure that uses the scientific method: it observes a phenomenon; forms a hypothesis about why and how the phenomenon might occur; performs an experiment to determine if the hypothesis is accurate or not; and, based on that evidence, develops a theory that explains and predicts how and why the phenomenon occurs. Our sojourn here in this earth realm is a temporary experiment in the power of thought to cause reality to evolve. It is impermanent and an illusion, bounded by birth and death but not limited to them, as our eternal selves continue into the next level of existence.

CHANGE AND CHANCE

One of the aspects of the New Theology that many die-hard fundamentalists (as I once was, so I know whereof I speak) have a hard time dealing with is the idea of chance. They are used to giving up the wheel of their religious automobile and assuming that everything that transpires is the direct plan of God, that there are no surprises. I will say this: there *are* surprises, but there are no accidents. An accident is something that occurs without intent, and God's intent is completely fulfilled in us when and as we exist according to our divine nature. So nothing can be accidental. However, because we are not automated robots and have free expression to choose how we live our earthly lives, we can, superficially, create the illusion of surprising God and ourselves by thinking ourselves onto twisted life paths and patterns that bring results we did not intend.

Does this mean that God is not overseeing every single detail of our lives by virtue of omniscient will? More than likely. We are predetermined generally but not specifically—why would we want to be? The new science of time, combined with new experimental work that shows that humans can naturally react to and predict future events (precognition), shows that time flows in all directions at once, and that our intention can not only influence our future but reach back and influence our past. If God determined everything that happens to us, what role would we play? How could any intention or act have meaning? The universe operates under a divine incentive but leaves room and relevance to individualized intelligence, will, logic, and creation.

The idea that God may not act as a cosmic safety net to catch us when we make foolish choices disconcerts many who have grown up with the tradition that God determines the fall of each sparrow. Scripture says that God *knows* the fall of every sparrow, which is a metaphorical reference to divine omniscience, but that does not mean the Cosmic Mind necessarily intervenes in events. The juvenile father-God concept falls to the wayside when we take full responsibility for ourselves. Accordingly, the idea of being accountable for your choices and thoughts can paralyze and terrorize people who have not learned "ultimate trust." I personally find the freedom of choice exhilarating, but that comes from the sense of self-trust that can be enjoyed only when we get past the self-hatred that suspicion of self tends to instill in us. Freedom is not for cowards. Being "unsupervised" by God becomes a world of thrilling possibility. Nothing limits us. We are either free-flying or free-falling, but either way, we ultimately land safely and remain free.

Opportunities for genuine change, the kind that sends your life vectoring in a fresh direction and alters the fate of communities and nations, come in intervals that disrupt the normal flow of things. This is why change is disruptive and many people fear it. Those operating in sin consciousness see change as upheaval, a challenge to their false belief that they are in control, albeit superficially. But those who are enlightened and liberated see the wave of change as something to ride and savor, to build upon and discover new aspects of their divine selves. Don't treat this earthly interval as something unholy. Perceive the negative as attracting a positive. In quantum mechanics, the physics of the very small energy exists only as possibility until thought makes it actuality. If you can see each wave of change as a new possibility for shaping a new future, change will lose its fearsome visage and become truly transformative.

We are all circling and recycling souls. We are constantly coming and going. The energy from which we are ultimately formed cannot be separated from the rest of creation. Electrons, protons, and neutrons are all particles of the atom, which is Greek for "indivisible." Even these parts are made of still smaller bits of matter called quarks, but in the end, the atom is the fundamental base state of matter. These elementary particles cannot exist unless they are joined together as an atom. We cannot exist without being joined together as one with God. That is our subtle, more than supernatural state.

Indivisible is surely one of the more accurate descriptions of God, along with "unconditional love." This is why I say that we are all inextricably connected with and to each other and the Divine. The Ultimate Reality we call God doesn't need or have to change or alter being for anyone's rule or reason. God can be perceived or experienced in many ways and environments but is not in essence changeable or alterable. God is beyond change, which is why *we* in our humanness must learn to change and evolve. We are God's ability to experience struggle and transformation! This is part of divine process and progress.

You, the Quick-Change Artist

Art is defined as skill acquired by experience, study, or observation. It is a branch of learning. It is the conscious use of skill and creative imagination, the faculty of carrying out expertly what is planned or devised. The art of change is the skill to create a transcendent new reality of you—not just your situation, but yourself. We all seem to want more, but we don't always want to *be* more. Behavior has to do with *being,* that's why it starts with *be.* Part of being is having all you need, want, or require. Some folks know the recipe but, obviously, don't have the ingredients. Others have the ingredients but not the recipe. You have both in your new awareness of self. You have the skill and artistry to capture the energy of change and create a masterpiece.

Angle means the precise viewpoint or perspective from which a thing is observed or considered. When the opportunity for change comes, how we see it depends on our angle. We may see it as a chance for greatness or something to hide from, to shun. But resenting or resisting change is what causes negative friction in our soul. It is crucial to concede to the imminence of change, to say yes (or, for some, "Yes, Lord") to all that concerns you in consciousness. Change is a culture, course, and a cause in life.

Architecture is the art or science of designing and building structures, especially habitable ones. The metaphor is quite apt for us: architecture is part art form, with its creative applications to design, form, location, and texture, but it is also a science, as one must know the physics and engineering of structures. In the same way, we blend both disciplines of art and science. We must learn to both *build* and *be* change as a lifestyle. Change should bring resolution to life. We must be architects of the change that comes into our lives—shaping it, crafting it, lending line and form to it as an artist does, taking the inspiration that flows through us from divine vision and giving it reality in our minds, and then in our material experiences.

Around my house, we now have high-definition television. According to the brochure, we are supposed to see things more clearly thanks to this technology. The architecture of change requires clarity, the ability to see not just the steps and methods of change but also the significance of each decision you make. This is prophecy, the power to examine all possible forks in the road and know what the outcome of taking each should be. That's deep awareness, but it is possible. It is available to you.

I love this idea of *intentional* living, living both in purpose and on purpose—deliberate existence. It is life lived out loud, without fear, without apology to anyone, not even God. This makes us co-creators of our lives and procreators of same.

BRINGING IT ALL TOGETHER

Art, the angle of perspective or seeing, and architecture carry an implication with them: that you are the master of the material, whether that is paint and canvas, light and a camera, wood and stone and metal, or life and divine energy. In any case, personal transformation puts you in the captain's chair, in control of titanic, tectonic forces that can send not only your life but a business, a family, or a community on a completely new course. That sounds and feels like a role best played by God—and it is. You are God, remember? If you have not been able to shed bitter memories and recall your true self to this point, do it now. Understand that if you have the vision to leave behind the limiting teachings of dogmatic religion and approach God on your own terms, unfiltered, change will become your tool to create an authentic life and love both the creation and the creator: you.

Authentic life is not something you learn so much as *remember.* This is what Scripture calls *reconciliation,* but it has nothing to do with Christ saving you from damnation. According to Inclusion theology, that was done already long ago, including before the foundation of the world. In any case, damnation does not exist unless you create it—if you refuse to evolve and spiral down into the darkness of numbness, stagnation, and an unfulfilled life—an un-full-*feeling* existence.

Reconciliation means returning to God by rediscovering, re-covering, and reclaiming who you are—who you have always been. It is not business as usual but an extraordinary act of creative fire, force, and genius. When you change who and what you are, you are creating a new genesis every day, creating a new world in consciousness. Leverage all three aspects of change: be the artist in your inspiration and passion, the prophet in the wide angle of your seeing, and the architect in your planning and execution.

It has been said that life is but a series of footnotes to a vast, obscure, and unfinished masterpiece! Tragedy is not that people die but that far too many people never really live. Realizing, finally, that you are far more than a nameless soldier to carry out the demands of a legalistic religious system and instead are a divine being whose acts of courageous change can also change and recharge the world makes true living inevitable. You cannot turn back from that path once you go down it. Once you have the eyes of an artist, you will never see the same way again.

REDISCOVERING THE MYSTICAL YOU

> All changes, even the most longed for, have their melancholy, for what we leave behind us is a part of ourselves; we must die to one life before we can enter another.
>
> —Anatole France

We often refer to God as Father. Why do we do that? I am not necessarily suggesting that the Divinity is male or female (as I have said, gender is irrelevant), but we use the word *father* to suggest the concept of divine sponsorship of our authentic selves in the time/space continuum we call life. We all came from a source of love and well-being that we call the "Fathering Spirit," the spirit or energy that spawned our existence on this planet and in this plane of reality. In effect, this is God, what Dr. Michael Beckwith calls "the timeless dimension of reality."

On my last Father's Day (at the time of this writing), I had spent fifty-five years as a son and fifteen as a father, if you count the nine months that Gina carried our firstborn, Julian. (I should, because *she* does, having borne every ounce of his weight.) Because of this, I am unusually reflective of where I came from and why I am here. My father is eighty-three years old. We don't know how many more Father's Days we will celebrate with him, but certainly far fewer than we have up to now. Naturally, Father's Day for us means much more than a new tie, a pair of socks, a new lawn mower, or even a trip around the world. Father's Day now shouts at me to know who I am and why I am here. I imagine asking my dad questions I don't expect him to answer, knowing that they will ultimately answer themselves. Questions like:

> How and why did you love yourself and your life? Why did you love it enough to engage in it for so long?
>
> Why did you love our mother enough to marry her, have seven children with her, and stay with her for over sixty years? What on earth could you have been thinking? It couldn't have been easy to submit yourself to such prodigious responsibilities and obligations. Did you do this deliberately, or was it some kind of supernatural instinct?

My father has played such a huge part in who, how, and what I am that I can scarcely avoid an almost worshipful reverence of him. He and my mother were my first god and goddess. Without them, I would surely never have developed the courage to take the difficult steps toward Inclusion and away from my ministry. I am aware that everybody doesn't share this same sentiment with regard to their parents—I am very lucky—but we all share the same inquiries as to why we're here. Somehow we all have an image of God based on our image of our fathers. I bring this up in the final part of our journey together because I want to draw a comparison between earthly fathers and God the Heavenly Father (as most Christians like to title him), and to help you understand what the mystery we call God may really be.

DAD

My dad was talkative, but not always about himself—unless he was teaching us a lesson. He talked only when he wanted to and about what he wanted to. He usually talked to us about ourselves, and when talking about himself seemed relevant, he would do so. I often think he spoke to us about us because all of us represented another chance for him to be resurrected, to evolve into more of who he wanted to be or perhaps who he is. I get to do that now with my two children; before they came along, I sought to do that with the people who came to my church, who read my books, who listened to my music, who lent their precious and rare attention to what I had to say, even at a time when I was being called an outcast. In a sense, everybody you meet is a version of yourself. I heard my friend Bishop E. Bernard Jordan say that we meet no one but ourselves through every experience and encounter. I believe that life itself becomes an echo of you. My siblings and I are echoes of our parents, their beliefs, love, and faith. My parents, of course, are echoes of their parents, and the cycle goes on. We are also all echoes of God the Ultimate Parent.

We are God's children, each of us. So just as each of my father's seven children has presented an opportunity for him to be "born again" in a new way, shaped by each child's free will and proclivities, each of the more than six billion beings in this world represents a new and different way for God, the Ultimate Reality, to be reborn—for God to evolve and grow. God is beyond time and space and knowledge; God is all those things, as are you in your most accurate essence. But through us, a creator God can experience what it's like to learn and grow and change and struggle and overcome. A life well and boldly lived is a gift to God and a God to gift!

But I told you I would talk about what I perceive God to be, didn't I? And I will. The nature of the Father—and your role as His proxy in this physical world—stems from your ability to transcend the limits of your religious conditioning and claim your true self. To cast off the bonds of blinkered thinking and become the divine mind you were meant to be, you must do more than speak affirmations or meditate. *You must rediscover the mystic in you.* God is nothing less than the mystical energy of the universe.

MYSTICAL MEMORY

When do you remember first being consciously aware of your being? Can you recall your first realization of being alive? Usually alarm is your first and most poignant memory of being alive; it doesn't have to be, but it is at least the memory that sticks the longest.

When did you first realize that you were alive and that you were human or a higher order of earthly intelligence? That you were male or female? When did you first recognize that you were black or white or different or unique from others? How did that make you feel? Was it a difficult revelation? If so, why, and is it so today? If not, why not?

I ask these questions because your future or journey is affected by your answers. How you respond to these queries determines or at least affects how you cocreate your life. We are assigned and designed to create our own life experience. Notice I didn't say "life experiences," plural. Life is one unified experience and experiment; only in our awareness of separation does it appear to be a series of connected and sometimes disconnected experiences separated by periods of sameness or boredom.

We are all eternal beings in physical form who have chosen to participate in this life experience. And formless, vague, and fleeting as it is, the mystical experience is the bedrock of spiritual life. In it, the soul, acting in unity with the brain and the senses, rises above the mundane and becomes the center of being. When we exit the caves of the paranoid human construct we call religion and enter the realm of unmediated and unmitigated mystical reality, we discover the way out of the bondage.

This seems to have been the original objective of the modern Pentecostal experience and apparently much of ancient first century Christianity. How else can we explain such things as speaking in tongues and laying on of hands to cast out devils or to control our petty demons? Clearly, the faith was originally something more primal, akin to native, animistic spiritual traditions like Santeria or voodoo. And, in fact, twentieth-century Pentecostalism stems from certain elements of African spiritualism and the ancient mystery religions. It presupposes the efficacy of transcendence, which is hinted at in all of the world's religions. It embraces "spirit" possession or being possessed by spirit or a spirit, albeit Holy Spirit. However, Pentecostalism (along with most other aspects of Christianity) was hijacked by fundamentalist ideologies of stagnation and spiritual ineptitude.

We seek the road back to that sort of pure, passionate spiritual experience untainted by rules and regulations and intimations of damnation. A soul-deep mystical experience. To truly recapture your original essence, you must become a practicing mystic!

MYSTICISM REVEALED

Today mysticism is out of fashion, but it is slowly reappearing as spiritually in vogue. To a world steeped in *scientism*—the belief that only empirical investigation can reveal any fundamental truth about existence—mysticism is valueless. But to those who know that subjective reality, contemplation, and consciousness itself are fundamental to existence, mystical awareness and experience are key paths to knowledge. Valueless? To the contrary, they are invaluable.

I would define mysticism as the act of union with the broader and more ultimate reality. It is what Pope Gregory I described as arriving at "absolute being." Faith is the mystery of religion. Having faith in a particular line of spiritual activity—a religion—is one thing. Having faith in the Ultimate Reality is totally different. The word *ultimate* comes from the Latin term *latimatus* and means "last," "final," or "farthest." The idea of "the ultimate" may seem a bit elusive, even remote, but that's only when it is pursued by fleshly or carnal means rather than on a spiritual level. Both have stimuli, but one is mythical, because it is impossible to achieve any definitive or ultimately transcendent experience in the physical world. The other is mystical, transcends common reality, and is neither apparent to the senses nor obvious to normal, everyday awareness.

There is much about Christianity that is considered sacred, but what interests me most are certain aspects of Christianity that are mysterious, or that retain their mystical feel and timbre. I remain fascinated with the unknown. There is a creative energy in all religions to which most religious people remain oblivious. This is also true of the sacred writings of most of the world's religions. The monks, mystics, and masters of the world faiths were rarely understood by their peers; thus their sayings and writings are usually misinterpreted and misunderstood by the masses, who may follow some aspect of their traditions but completely misconstrue others. The confusion over the idea of Jesus only saving a small elect of humanity is an example. That is the legalistic letter of the Bible, not the reality of God.

ANCIENT TRADITIONS, ANCIENT OCCUPATIONS

The fact is, the holy men and women of the ancient world wove spirituality into their daily lives and with few exceptions had to make a living as well as cultivate their mystical traditions and craft. The Greek version of the word *witchcraft* is connected to the practice of *pharmakeia,* from which we get our English word *pharmacy.* It is translated as "medication," which is a reference to magic or sorcery—a reference to Old Testament magi (magicians) or to mysticism. If you recall, it was the Magi, or "wise men" (spiritually enlightened men), who saw the star above the place where Jesus is said to have been born. They were obviously astrologers as well. Many of the ancient mystics were both pharmacists as well as stargazers. Even our modern word *pastor* (*p-astor, astor* being derived from the Latin *aster,* meaning "star," as in *dis-aster*) is a hint of religion's tendency to stargaze. Practical mysticism is everywhere we look under the cloak of our oh-so-proper modern faiths.

Faith, fertility, and sun worship are inextricably tied to most ancient spiritual traditions. *Anthropos* is the Greek word for man and can be defined as the "upward-looking one." That speaks clearly of religiously inclined humankind, looking to the skies and at the stars and wondering what those great entities or presumed beings could be. There is nobility in that seeking, however primitive. We look upward to God and outward to each other through fertility. Our constructed religions connect us to the infinite even as we labor with the ordinary.

In Native American culture, holy men were called medicine men and were considered the most spiritual or mystical people in the tribe. In other cultures, they are called shamans, but the idea is the same. The original function of a shaman was to understand the use of various types of plants and herbs (especially mushrooms) to cure disease, banish evil spirits, and induce mystical states of consciousness. These were made into medicines to treat sickness or induce hallucinations. This led to fortune-telling, veridical (verifiable) visions, conversations with the dead, and other paranormal phenomena.

It is said that our alphabet was the result of hallucinations by scientists who were seeking arcane knowledge through the use of mushrooms and other natural mind-altering substances. Scientists and spiritualists should be the best of friends—and they can be. It is the theologians who tend to cause friction. Letters, numbers, religion, and science are all of similar source—that is, knowledge derived from mystical experience in some way. Some of the early mathematicians were accused by the church of using witchcraft or divination. Science and spirituality are essentially friendly cousins, but, in recent millennia, they have been perceived as opposites, competing with rather than completing or complementing each other. This can change, and indeed it should.

People are seeking otherness. They are interested in their transcendent selves but often don't know how to access that aspect of the self. Here again, where religion should awaken people spiritually, it often lulls them to sleep. This is the reason there is so much substance abuse. People are hungry for a higher consciousness—or just different consciousness—and the awareness of spirit. They seek the easiest and most accessible means they can find to alter their consciousness, and drugs and alcohol are a quick but often costly shortcut. The abuse of drugs in today's culture may be, in part, the fault of plastic religion that doesn't satiate spiritual hunger.

AN END TO IGNORANCE?

In some ways, mystics, medicine men, shamen, psychics, and other seers or prophets are much more spiritually relevant than some of the more authoritative and decorated religious leaders. A careful study of the mystics, masters, and so-called magicians of the various cultures will show them to be the ones who seemed to be most in tune and in touch with God or spirit or their spiritual selves. They often lived transcendent lives of simplicity, humility, and meditation. In altered states of consciousness, they saw, heard, felt, and experienced things most of us never do, simply because we are jaded by religion and bypass our own transcendent possibilities.

There is a unique and—to me, inextricable—connection between science and spirituality though it is often disregarded. Both revolve around knowing or gaining knowledge deliberately. However, until recently, science has disregarded spirituality as a relic of a primitive religious instinct—a vestige of humanity better done away with, like the appendix. Inner life has been regarded reductively as a side effect of brain activity, with the conclusion being that there is no soul, purpose, or consciousness to life. But finally science is beginning to recognize that such a position is erroneous and that spirituality and mysticism have a place in the pursuit of truth. Would that religion came to the same conclusion!

Again, the use of letters, figures, and numbers or arithmetic (all vital to science) was considered witchcraft in earlier millennia, and sometimes those who used them were executed by the church. During the Dark Ages, it was illegal for millions of people to read or write. The church not only banned books, it literally destroyed them in huge bonfires. Many of the world's most renowned artists, scientists, and inventors were aware of the mystical presence of higher consciousness. They worked in, walked in, and wrote about the miraculous. We owe them much, though many were tortured and executed in the name of religion, especially Christianity.

Keeping people in ignorance has always been one of the manipulative moves of the church. Growth and self-expansion were always a threat to those who sought to maintain control of the people. Karl Marx called religion the opiate of the masses. This social numbness is what opened the door for pernicious, atheistic philosophies such as Communism.

The hope of humankind lies in the undiscovered depths of the mystical knowledge we carry within us. The time has come for people everywhere to disengage with the fruitless search of the temporal world and undertake a courageous quest into inner space. All else is artificial and delusional. It is in this more real world that the great spirits of transcendent consciousness realized their being.

SAVING PENTECOSTALISM

The Reverend Willie Wilson, in his book *How African Religion Changed the American Church,* calls the Pentecostal movement of the twentieth century a kind of African religion in America. As a fourth-generation Pentecostal, I fasted, prayed, danced, wept, spoke in tongues, and enjoyed numerous transcendent experiences. To this day, my ethereal consciousness is piqued by my fifty-five years of exposure to this modern-day mode of African spirituality.

My years in Pentecostalism exposed me to the mysteries of transcendent consciousness and prepared me for the transition I made into Inclusion Consciousness. Pentecostalism (a form of African spirituality) enabled African-Americans already converted to Christianity to endure the racism and discrimination they experienced living in exile from the motherland in a brutal new world of Western thought, where their traditions were demonized and expunged. They survived through their cultural, spiritual tradition, which they considered sanctified by religion or Christianity.

Voodoo is one word we have already examined, a native word referring to Spirit. But the Europeans, in their insatiable desire to colonize even the soul, demonized the term, perverting its meaning to suggest evil. Slaves, including some converted to Christianity, fell back on the practice as the only recourse they had to manage the agony of slavery.

Slaves and indentured servants saw the Christians who taught them the Gospels also demean and attempt to destroy their cultural and spiritual uniqueness, using Scriptures like "slaves, obey your masters" (Ephesians 6:5 NIV) to justify their abusive treatment. Our ancestors' only recourse was to go within. Their Christian moral consciousness taught them that they must not hate or retaliate and to overcome evil with good, which they interpreted to mean God. So they sought God based on their African and identifiable cultural spiritualism and its roots in transcendence. Our testimony has been for centuries that God and God alone brought us through. But in reality, our own spiritual passion and awareness of our deep connection to divinity got us through. Our mystical enhancement kept us from despair. Spirit has no moral connotations. It is a transcendent term that cannot be associated directly with any particular religion. To the early African slaves, "Spirit" was the sacred germination, not a religion that emphasized the dogmas of right and wrong.

The organizers of modern American Pentecostalism—William Seymour and Charles Harrison Mason—loved God and followed Christ but wrestled with resentment, disappointment, and their own anger in dealing with the double standards they saw within Christianity. They longed for the purity and naked spiritualism of their African ancestry. Creating a hybrid of the two traditions was the only way they could escape the cultural and societal racism of their era. They had to create a different reality, and they helped millions of us do likewise.

Through the pain of my own shift out of the old "wineskins" (Matthew 9:17) into my new wardrobe of spiritual clothing, I leaned heavily on my own Pentecostal mysticism to transcend a reality that was treating me harshly. In this way, I found peaceful harbor within myself. I remembered both who I was and who I wasn't. The contrast was transformational to me. My life will never be the same.

My faith tells me I can re-create my life—and that you can re-create yours. The Bible tells us that faith comes by hearing the word (Logos/Logic) of God, but it takes time and stillness to hear and heed your inner priests and maintain your inner peace. Some people never do it until trauma or tragedy causes them to reflect more deeply on their truer, more accurate selves. An ancient proverb says: "Learn to pause, or nothing worthwhile will catch up with you." But why wait for tragedy when brave mystical transformation will get you to that place of great awareness before and without it?

When everything that I was engaged in as part of my religious life slowed down and stopped, I was forced to reflect—not on what I had lost but on what I had found, what I had gained or recovered. I began to realize for the first time both who I was and who I wasn't. I was not a slave to a mindless doctrine that took me in a direction that my spirit rebelled against. I was a leader and a scout into new territory; a mystic reclaiming my ancient tradition and exclaiming, "Yes! This is real and good." In my former days, I'd have said, "This is God!" In many ways I still do.

LIVING IN THE LIGHT

Transition leads to transformation, transcendence, and ultimately translucence, meaning that God's light of truth shines through you so that others can see clearly. Light is an expression of eternity. It passes through the pollution of time but is not limited by it. It is mystical, mysterious, and powerful, traveling so fast that light knows no time. It is eternal.

Ask yourself what might you be doing that constricts or blocks your mystical light? Religion presumes that only it has the right to carry the torch for you and millions of others. Often the opposite is true. Religion often obscures and obstructs light—sometimes inadvertently, sometimes deliberately. True mysticism is a combination of *luminescence,* the presence of light, and *illumination,* the emission of light. Your mystical self has the ability to perceive and create both. You are that light.

In the Gospel of Luke 13:6–9, Jesus shares a parable:

"A man had a fig tree planted in his vineyard, and he went to look for fruit on it, but did not find any. So he said to the man who took care of the vineyard, 'For three years now I've been coming to look for fruit on this fig tree and haven't found any. Cut it down! Why should it use up the soil?'

" 'Sir,' the man replied, 'leave it alone for one more year, and I'll dig around it and fertilize it. If it bears fruit next year, fine! If not, then cut it down.' "

I don't remember when I have been more excited about entering a new year than I am about this year and the years to come. This may be because recent years have been filled with pain and upheaval, but it may also be because the future is beginning to unfold before me, and its possibilities are thrilling. I still feel pain from my past, but it is not punitive, just corrective and remedial. I feel improved rather than impoverished by it. In Jesus' parable above, He speaks of striving for excellence for one more year. Just like we revolve around the sun every 365 days, we evolve around the Son or Christ Principle, Person or Purpose, and, indeed, Consciousness as well. Both are effortless on our part. Were it not for the various New Year's celebrations, many of us wouldn't even realize we'd made the revolution again. That's how automatic it is. Personal evolution is just as automatic, and we can miss it if we don't deliberately anticipate, participate in, and celebrate it.

How do we do that? By engaging our minds to embrace and coordinate the process. Whatever is going on in your mind, you are attracting into your life. In the book *The Secret,* one of the authors writes, "Everything that is coming into your life, you are attracting into your life . . . every thought of yours is a real thing. It is a force, a power or energy in your life." You change everything by embracing your mystic self and claiming your birthright as a creator.

YOUR MYSTICAL FUTURE

As human beings, we're always trying to locate the place within ourselves where we are most at peace; the part of ourselves we love unconditionally. I think we can find this place by asking and honestly answering four questions:

1. What do you believe most about yourself?
2. Why do you believe it?
3. What do you love most about yourself?
4. Why do you love it?

The mystery of your future is *you*. Not the mythical you, but the mystical you. The myth is the illusion that society, influenced by religion, has sold to you and which you put on like an actor donning a costume. The mythical you is legend and folklore, gossip and rumor. The *mystical* you is the essential, precise, exact, uncensored, and unedited you! It is the you that is as Adam and Eve were: naked but with no shame, because they were utterly at one with God the Creator and with creation itself. It was not a matter of effort or asking; they just were their shamless, shameless, and authentic selves.

As we look to and anticipate the future, know that your future is your own personal resolution, of who you are and why you are! You do not just create your future; you *are* your future. It will materialize based on the thoughts you harbor and the spirit you express.

You want to know where we're all headed and where this all ends? We're going back to our future: to who and where we were before we got here, back to our pre-incarnate selves. The most reliable way to predict the future is to cocreate it. When you take an active role in your own life, things are far more likely to go well for you. You are much more in control when you are at the wheel of your life in all areas: body, mind, and spirit. It's easy to blame your troubles on the government, the economy, the church, or even God. Instead accept responsibility for it all. There is no one else to blame, but there is also no one else who deserves the credit when you make an extraordinary leap into transcendence.

Even if the challenges you face are not your fault, begin to treat them as your responsibility (which can also be read as "*response ability*"), and you will begin to have control over them, or at least your response to them. See your future not as the inevitable result of your past but as the evolving result of your present. Visualize your future as the best, most positive, most valuable, and most creative response to your present possibilities. Your future can be so much more than an extension of your past. You are bound by nothing, limited by nothing, and defined by nothing but you, your mystical self.

Epilogue

In closing, I am continuing the process of evolving and growing in the mysteries of self-awareness—and loving it. I continue to develop the courage to be myself while facing and fixing my fears. I'm not sure how to arrive, but I am determined to keep on going and growing through it all. I will be myself, owning and honoring my Truth as I perceive it. We all have emotional, practical, and promising rights; we should both claim and cuddle them. Being fond of myself is a choice of natural selection, not contrived or deprived. I will no longer feel apologetic for believing not only in fulfillment but in feel-fulment as well. I accept that the universe does not judge me by what I feel but by what I think about what I feel. I will eagerly do both.

I will give myself permission to allow my primary motivation to be fun rather than fear. I've come to recognize and believe that discouragement is a serious waste of time. I accept as laws of physics that anything in motion causes friction, and that friction provides the traction for forward thrust.

In the deeper recesses of consciousness, there are no such things as mistakes, just misinterpretations of certain realities. All things really do work for and toward the ultimate good but are realized only by those who are true believers in Divine realities. And finally, I will develop and cherish healthy, supportive, and constructive relationships, remembering to make forgiveness a priority, beginning with myself, which makes it all the more easy to forgive others when it seems necessary. I will laugh often as an article of faith, and love strongly as its act and sacred discipline.

Welcome, my dear friends, to one more season! One more season, cycle, and session of Self. Let this be the year or season when you discover, uncover, and recover the God within.

No, God is not a Christian, nor a Jew, Muslim, or Hindu, but you can be one, or anything else you are so inclined to be, as long as you don't let whatever that is obscure the magnificent, mystical, and transcendent spirit you are and will always be!

Peace is possible. Blessings,

CDP

ACKNOWLEDGMENTS

Always, to my dear wife, Gina, and our two children, Julian and Majeste, who share me with my imagination and revelations of soul when I write. Thanks for snuggling with me; it is my favorite comfort.

To all my New Dimensions members who released me to the larger focus of thought and reach of consciousness to help build a brave new world, I'll love and serve you always.

Benjamin Shell, you were there for me through one of the most tenuous times in my ongoing process and evolution. Your encouragement and assistance in getting my books published were unparalleled. I couldn't have done it without you.

Special thanks to Mark Victor Hansen, who helped guide me into my greater sense of journalism and writing and through whom I met Jillian Manus, whom I affectionately call my Angel Agent. Watching her do her magic is a high and fascinating privilege. What a huge dynamo in such a tender and delicate package! A true professional.

Thanks to John and Sara Powell for your friendship and encouragement, and for staying and standing with me and my family while reminiscing with me about the precious memories of our COGIC roots sentimentalities. I know it cost you to stay connected to us. You are wonderful listeners.

Dr. John Destito (Johnson), my ever-present friend, brother, and confidant through all these years. I love you dearly.

D. E. Paulk, Brandi, and the New Cathedral of the Holy Spirit family in Atlanta, Georgia, including Don and Clariece and my beloved Kirby Clements, I love you all, and particularly our bittersweet journey together these last few years. The best is yet to come.

Thanks to Harold Lovelace, our Universalist godfather and friend.

Thanks to my dear friends Marlin Lavinhar and the All Souls UU Church in Tulsa, Oklahoma, for allowing we New Dimensions pilgrim wanderers to find a final resting place among your warm and hospitable congregation and community. My family and I will always feel like members there.

Special thanks to Tim Vandehay, my "book doctor," whose brilliance and literary genius fits my thought and spirit like hand in glove. You're the best!

And finally, to my new church family and friends at the Christ Universal Temple in Chicago, Illinois, founded by the great Johnnie Coleman. You have received me and my family into your hearts and spiritual home to serve as Interim Sr. Servant/Minister. We have come together in love, attracting and manifesting each other in consciousness around the universal Truth principles we teach, preach, reach, and live. What a delight. It'll work if and when and we work it!

BIBLIOGRAPHY

A Course in Miracles. New York: Foundation for Inner Peace, 1992.

Acharya, S. *The Christ Conspiracy: The Greatest Story Ever Sold.* Kempton, Ill.: Adventures Unlimited Press, 1999.

Allender, Dan B. *The Healing Path: How the Hurts in Your Past Can Lead You to a More Abundant Life.* Colorado Springs, Co.: WaterBrook Press, 2000.

Brooks, David. "The Neural Buddhists." *The New York Times,* May 13, 2008.

Byrne, Rhonda. *The Secret.* New York: Atria Books, 2006.

Chopra, Deepak. *How to Know God: The Soul's Journey into the Mystery of Mysteries.* New York: Three Rivers Press, 2000.

Ellul, Jacques. *Anarchy and Christianity.* Translated by Geoffrey W. Bromiley. Grand Rapids, Mich.: Wm. B. Eerdmans Publishing Co., 1991.

Grierson, Bruce. "An Atheist in the Pulpit." *Psychology Today,* February 2008.

Heinlein, Robert A. *Time Enough for Love.* New York: Ace Books, 1988.

Holmes, Ernest. *Can We Talk to God?* Deerfield Beach, Fla.: HCI, 1999.

Jordan, Bishop E. Bernard. *The Laws of Thinking: 20 Secrets to Using the Divine Power of Your Mind to Manifest Prosperity.* Carlsbad, Calif.: Hay House, Inc, 2007.

Kauffman, Stuart. "Perspectives: Why humanity needs a God of creativity." *New Scientist,* May 2008.

Lewis, C. S. *The Great Divorce.* San Francisco: HarperSanFrancisco, 2001.